The Mermaid Chronicles

A Midlife Mer-moir

Megan Dunn

PENGUIN BOOKS

PENGUIN

UK | USA | Canada | Ireland | Australia
India | New Zealand | South Africa | China

Penguin is an imprint of the Penguin Random House group of companies, whose addresses can be found at global.penguinrandomhouse.com.

First published by Penguin Random House New Zealand, 2024

10 9 8 7 6 5 4 3 2 1

Cover design by Carla Sy © Penguin Random House New Zealand
Text design by Katrina Duncan © Penguin Random House New Zealand
Front cover photograph: Hannah Mermaid by Pa Dao Vang (Enchanted Photography)
Back cover photograph © Hannah Mermaid and Brett Stanley, 2024
Author photograph by Robert Cross
Prepress by Soar Communications Group
Printed and bound in Australia by Griffin Press, an Accredited ISO AS/NZS 14001 Environmental Management Systems Printer

A catalogue record for this book is available from the National Library of New Zealand.

ISBN 978-1-77695-086-7
eISBN 978-1-77695-393-6

The assistance of Creative New Zealand towards the production of this book is gratefully acknowledged by the publisher.

penguin.co.nz

Discontents

Oh, was enlightenment found?
No, but I'm trying, taking it one year at a time.
— LORDE, 'OCEANIC FEELING'

If you put on a cape and pretend you're a superhero, you won't really fly. But if you put on a tail and swim in it, you really will feel like a mermaid.
— RAINA MERMAID

1.

No One Forgets Their First Mermaid

I was a woman with a geriatric womb waiting for an upcoming appointment with the Fertility Associates when I discovered a slogan from the mermaid community on a coffee cup online: 'I'm done adulting, let's be mermaids!'

I analysed the mug's design and fonts — quickly, intuitively — using my skills as an art writer and the dregs of my old art school degree. Those cursive, blue-and-turquoise letters reeked of feminine frippery, of beach days lolling on the sand by the sea. The mermaid's face was concealed beneath her art nouveau locks, like a blank screen you could project yourself on to.

What do mermaids do? I asked Google. I had been trying to write a novel about a mermaid who grew legs and arrived in a small seaside town on the Norfolk coast. What next? She met a dark-haired waif who closely resembled my partner, Richard. In the book, I called him Rupert and he worked in a little second-hand bookstore called The Rack and Ruin. Books *are* ruinous items — I knew that because I was working in a bookshop when I met Rich. Books hadn't done me much good, but he had.

The mermaid opened the door to the shop and came inside wearing a black bikini. She had webbed feet; her nipples nosed through the nylon; she was dripping wet. In a thick Russian accent (where did that come from?), she barked, 'I need a book on mermaids.' Rupert jumped up from behind the empty till, rushed over to the children's section and handed her a copy of Hans Christian Andersen's *The Little Mermaid*.

What happened next? Shy, frighteningly intimate sex in a B&B overlooking the sea, the waves thick as mushroom soup, sloshing around the long legs of the Victorian pier. Later, zombie games in an arcade, then eating fat, greasy chips pierced by vinegar and the two unlikely prongs of a chip fork. Chip forks are so bloody British, as strange as mushy peas.

They say fact is stranger than fiction, but in my case it wasn't. What happened in my Word document was exactly what happened to me the weekend I went to Norfolk with Richard, bar the black bikini.

'If you were a mermaid, what would you do?' I asked Anna, the web editor. We sat back-to-back in our open-place office, partitioned into a corner. Anna spun around. She was a woman with a savage wit and the merciless button eyes of a teddy bear. Anna was my coffee and scone buddy. We worked at a charitable trust that promoted the arts as good for society — we were preaching to the choir.

Anna squinted in the bright sunlight flooding the office. 'It would probably only be fun for a day. Then it would be boring.'

'Boring?' I asked.

'Well, you'd just be swimming around in the sea all the time fighting off predators. There'd be no TV, no magazines, no internet,' she said.

Anna swung back round to her screen. She was probably on Facebook again, promoting the arts to the hordes who hung off her every status update, presumably because they were mums trapped at home with nothing better to do.

A photo of a woman in a gold fishtail landed on my screen like the catch of the day. The woman was parked on a generic-looking beach, the tide frothing like a cappuccino behind her. I read the Wikipedia entry in one thirsty gulp.

'Did you know there are professional mermaids?'

Anna snorted but didn't spin around.

'They work in bars and aquariums and do live events. I'm here trapped in this office while other women my age are working as professional mermaids, navigating the oceans, saving the world, getting selfies with sharks and looking fucking great doing it.'

'Do you actually want to be a mermaid?' Anna asked.

'Well, I'm not a good swimmer.' An understatement, my white legs hadn't been poolside in years. 'But I'd rather be a mermaid than a project manager.'

In the eighties, as a little girl with buck teeth and red pigtails, I didn't dream of growing up to be an arts project manager. For fuck's sake! I wanted to be like Madison, the mermaid played by Daryl Hannah in *Splash*. Instead, I worked on the thirteenth floor of an industrial office block in central Wellington, New Zealand. I swivelled round in my chair and looked out the window at a square of the harbour, the blue waves glinting, behind a black-mirrored skyscraper. I didn't believe there were any mermaids in Wellington Harbour.

Our open-plan office was library-quiet, as per usual.

Clive, our captain, was an old newspaper man now in his early seventies, with bright pink cheeks. His house was mortgaged to the hilt, but his blue eyes still sparkled with unrestrained optimism. He wasn't often at his desk.

'Isn't Clive supposed to be in this morning?' I said. 'We have a board meeting next week. I haven't been able to raise any sponsorship money yet.'

'He's not coming in today,' Anna said. 'He's not feeling well.'

'I'm not feeling well either. If I never have to think about extolling the virtues of the arts again it will be too soon.'

Anna laughed. 'It's not that bad,' she said.

Easy for her to say. She had the website to update and an online newsletter to rotate. Her life had a rhythm and a logic, plus she got all the likes.

I sighed, smoothed down my op-shop dress with seagulls on it, and swivelled back and forth in my Mary Janes, looking at image after image of real, grown-up women dressed as mermaids. Each rubbery tail a giant exclamation mark, *Look at me! Look at me!*

'Do you want a coffee?' Anna finally asked.

'Yes! And a scone,' I said.

~

In the lift to the ground floor, I bitched about our boss again. 'I don't think he knows what he is doing,' I said.

'If you're looking for a job with structure, this isn't it. Clive is not going to change. You have to learn how to manage up,' she advised.

But the lift was going down. And we were trapped in it like the last two sardines in a shiny aluminium can. I was worried the whole place was going down. Nothing about working here gave me a feeling of solvency. I was staring down the barrel of middle age, and my pockets were empty.

'I don't need structure,' I said. 'I just need a plan.'

Anna made me sound like a child. I wanted a job with pizzazz, I wanted cash and clout, I wanted a gigantic mermaid tail to slap across the board table. A tail — now that has structure. Instead, I queued for a flat white and a cheese scone, 'without butter', I said to the barista.

'What do you think I should write about next?' I said, as we rode back up to the thirteenth floor. 'A disgruntled bookseller, or a mermaid who arrives in a small seaside town and changes everything?'

'The one about the mermaid,' Anna replied. Did she find me annoying? Was I annoying? I was constantly irritable. Maybe it was my personality. Maybe it was the role. My job as project manager was a made-up position — I was the first person in it. I had to invent projects, but had hardly any budget to make things happen.

At home, I did some art writing on the side, but it paid next to nothing either.

The lift doors opened and we returned to our light, bright office. Back at my desk, I decanted the remains of my scone into my mouth, threw my empty takeaway cup in the bin and fell down the Google rabbit hole again. *Mer* is a surprisingly elastic prefix. Add amazing and you have *mer*mazing. Mer plus pervert equals *mer*vert, the natural enemy of the professional mermaid. I turned back and forth, lapping up the fin-tastic puns of the mermaid community.

'Listen to this: *Be a mermaid in a sea of fish*,' I said to Anna. '*Mermaid hair, don't care*!'

Anna groaned, but then she had a short blunt bob. I had long flowing hair that cascaded over my shoulders, with a weird little kink in the back, like a wave.

'*Seas the day*. Get it?'

'That's terrible.'

'Shell yeah!' I said. 'Did I ever tell you I made a video about Daryl Hannah when I was at art school?'

'No!'

'Yes,' I said. 'I made a video using the bath scene from *Splash*. That was always my favourite scene. I remember watching it at the movies when I was little. I came home, ran a bath and pretended that I had turned into Daryl Hannah.'

Anna didn't miss a beat. 'Everyone our age who watched *Splash* wanted to be Daryl Hannah.' She spun round again.

'Yeah. No one forgets their first mermaid,' I said. 'Especially if she's Daryl Hannah.' I gestured towards my computer screen as though I was a magician pulling a rabbit out of a top hat. 'Look at her. This is clearly a *Splash* reference!'

On my PC was an image of a buxom, tanned blonde in a strident orange fishtail, seated in a decadent bubble bath. The photograph had been taken from above, so the white oblong bath was fully captured. A golden faucet jutted out, as did the mermaid's epic tailfin, overhanging the end of the tub. The fin was huge, like an upended anchor, and shaded black to orange to yellowy gold. That tail had bloody structure.

A tap had turned on inside me, psychic and hot. That mermaid and I were cut from the same cloth. Her tail was a dead ringer for the one Daryl Hannah wore in the movie — fiercely, unapologetically orange. Everything about it screamed professional.

'What do you think her KPIs are?' I asked.

'I don't know, but I bet she's had a boob job.'

That wasn't the point.

'My tutor hated my video about *Splash.*'

At the ill-fated art-school critique, I sat in my feminist tutor's office and inserted my grainy *Splash* bootleg footage into her video recorder. She watched my new bath scene unspool. I had changed the footage from colour to black and white. This had no artistic merit; I was just trying to distinguish my work from the original. The entire video consisted of Daryl in character as Madison, running a bath, pouring sea salt into it, then sliding down into the water, with a roll of her head. Her legs disappeared, and the shot cut to her orange fluke unfurling over the edge of the tub. Daryl submerged and smiled underwater, a bubble forming on her lips.

It was a magical scene — that cosmic unfolding which thrilled me so much when I first saw it as a little buck-toothed redhead. Then I bought a goldfish and named it Madison, though it didn't live long. Maybe I overfed it? It was the start of a short run of dead goldfish. My grandmother bought me my second one, Pearl — it was so white you could see its blue intestines. I didn't like the white fish, didn't want to think about its physiology as it glided around Madison's tank, a coil of poo hanging from its bum. I can't remember Pearl's death. I gleaned no wisdom from it.

None of this featured in my short, appropriated video artwork because anything confessional was shameful. I thought I was being clever — cleverness was the one thing I had. I had been exposed to great feminist artists who made work about vaginas and doing the dishes and a place for women at the table of art. My *Splash* reboot was a stab at greatness too.

In *Splash*, Tom Hanks is outside the bathroom knocking to be let in. He doesn't know that Madison is a mermaid and can't answer the door. When he finally breaks into the bathroom, Daryl is on the floor, blasting a hair dryer over her legs. She's turned back into a human, just in the nick of time.

But in my bootleg, Tom never gets into the bathroom; he has no relevance. Instead, Daryl stays a mermaid. I ended the video on a two-second clip of her diving into the sea at sunset, her fluke cascading over the horizon. Fin. I replaced the film's soundtrack with affirmations from a Louise Hay self-help tape my mother gave me. Hay was an American self-help guru who claimed to have cured her own cancer, and her book *You Can Heal Your Life* was my mum's bible. As Daryl Hannah transformed into a mermaid, Hay intoned: *I trust the miracle that is my body. I love myself. I know I am worthwhile.*

I wasn't sure that my video was more than the sum of its parts. But it wasn't ironic either. It was a piece of wish fulfilment that I presented to my tutor, hoping she could decipher what I couldn't.

Instead, she shook her head. 'Research the mermaid properly. Think about the mermaid across time and culture. This can't be about Daryl Hannah!'

'That tutorial always fucked me off,' I said to Anna. 'I mean, look at Mermaid Melissa here. She had her name legally changed to include Mermaid! She worked in an aquarium with dolphins! Look at her orange tail! *Obviously* this is about Daryl Hannah.'

I had my evidence, but it was twenty years too late.

'My tutor even told me to dress up as a mermaid and film myself,' I said.

'Did you do it?' Anna chuckled. She'd also been to art school — different school, different era — but she was less useless than me because she had never made video art and now owned her own house.

'No,' I said. 'Where would I have got a tail from? I wanted to be a real mermaid, not a cosmic joke.'

2.

The Waters of Life

Every day, mermaids rose towards me. Rich and I wandered along Lyall Bay on the weekend. The wind was rugged and cold. This part of the coastline was bitter, especially in winter, the dunes swept with flaxen grass, the sand deep and dense beneath your feet, fey little insects sometimes crawling out of it. Lyall Bay was where my father lived; it was the landscape of my teen years, of fraught weekends and holidays.

'If I was a mermaid anywhere, it would be here,' I said.

'You'd need a warm jacket,' Rich replied.

We walked to the rock pools. I kicked at large brown tangles of kelp, spongy and bizarre, stinking of shellfish and other things I didn't want to eat. I picked up a chain of brown beads, the size of olives, and burst one open. Invisible pus.

The rock pools were black, thick and jagged, splattered with slime-green seaweed. The tide sizzled in and out. Rich plunged his hand into one. 'Look.' He held up an orange starfish. One spangled arm had been bitten off, presumably by a villainous seagull with a tart red beak. The other arms of the starfish started moving, curling, like synchronised swimmers. 'It's alive,' I shrieked. Rich dished up the starfish on a pāua shell, an oil-slick rainbow caught in its curve. I took a photo of it. 'Poor little guy,' we said. Underneath, the starfish had fine little apricot-coloured feelers, like a mini bathmat.

Rich threw it back into the sea. He found a broken crab claw next and called it Mr Pinchy. In the sand nearby, multiple rusted pincers and shards, a crab's graveyard. Rich and I lined the broken crabs up on a piece of driftwood and I took more photographs.

'I'm happy,' I said.

'Good,' Rich said.

Next, we walked to the end of the long wooden jetty, a runway into the sea, and he took my photo. My mermaid hair lapping across my face, my red puffer jacket puffed out. Then he walked to the end, held out his arms and I took his photo, thin and wiry, a dapper sea otter.

Rich and I had met years ago, in Norwich on Boxing Day, at a pub called the Ten Bells. He introduced me to scampi fries. 'I don't eat fish,' I told him boldly, because I like to list my weaknesses up front and because I was rotten drunk. 'Just try one for me,' he insisted. The packet of fries lay open on the bar. I pulled out the salty little stick and chucked it onto my back teeth. 'What did you think?' he asked. I thought he looked nice in his pale-blue jumper with a dragon stitched on it.

The next morning, I woke up beside him. Downstairs, I met Fishy, who lived in a glass bowl beside the fridge. Rich placed his finger on the outside of the bowl and Fishy swam up to it, her mouth opening and closing. 'See,' Rich traced his finger over the glass. 'Fishy follows me.' I assumed Fishy was a 'she'. I followed Rich too. We went to Sainsbury's, our arms linked. I wore his grey trackpants with the orange stripe down the side and watched him stock up on bottles of Evian that he later decanted into Fishy's bowl. He kept that fish in domestic bliss.

'Soon I'll be thirty-five and in the baby zone,' I told him. 'So watch out.'

Rich didn't watch out, but it didn't matter. Fishy eventually got swim bladder and swam permanently upside down, until she died and was disposed of in the Thames. And I dragged Rich to the other side of the world.

I left behind me a broken first marriage to an Irish actor, hours of useless retail jobs, mostly in bookshops, and a few choice nights riding waves of ecstasy. Now I was home, happy to watch the seagulls fly in on zigzags, the boisterous waves rush forward and then run out again, surfers dotted in them instead of seals.

I was like the mermaid I'd written about in an old poem, who had lured a sailor back to her underwater grotto. Rich was the shy obliging sailor, whose kisses sometimes tasted of pineapple. I had basked in his love, grown used to it. Normality was a taste I had acquired, and even though we still couldn't afford a house, and he didn't really read, and I couldn't swim to save myself, I was ready to have a baby.

~

The local writer's group was a mid-afternoon gathering of introverts, cat strokers, poets, drinkers of plunged coffee. Somehow, I'd got myself invited along. We met in the travel writer's retro-cool apartment to critique each other's work.

'The beginning has too many declarative sentences in a row,' the travel writer said, flicking through 'The Mermaid Chronicles', a poem I'd been trying to finish for years.

'I'm not sure about the stanza where the mermaid's corpse is kept in a vault next to the Roswell Alien,' chimed in a brunette from the kitchen table. 'You're telling an obvious fiction. That undermines the world building.'

I felt an urge to buck against received wisdom. The poem was about homesickness, feminism and boredom; it was only lightly about swimming.

'In this stanza where she lays an egg it's like you're channelling David Attenborough,' a poet said.

A compliment! My ego was as large as an ostrich's egg and tinted blue.

'Is the line about "fast men and even faster legs" a sexual reference?' he asked.

'Yes,' I said boldly, uncrossing my legs in their skin-tight jeans. I had spent my twenties working in a strip club and figured that gave me and me alone the skinny on sexuality and mermaids. The other writers were chronicling the discontents of modern life in their spare time and being as sensitive as hell about it.

'I don't know about the title,' the travel writer said finally.

A palpable um and ahhh. The rest of the group unanimously agreed. '"The Mermaid Chronicles" isn't good enough. It needs a more distinctive title.'

'Like what?' I asked.

No one knew.

'Have you ever read Adrienne Rich's poem "Diving into the Wreck"?' the kitchen-table brunette asked.

'No, but I've heard of it.'

'It is a classic feminist poem about a diver submerging to explore a shipwreck. I think you might like it. It might be useful,' she said.

'I'll look it up.'

Then an avant-garde poet in the corner spoke up for the first time. 'I wonder if you should try abbreviating it,' she said. 'Then it might do something stranger than just depict a tendency to myth-make.'

The group agreed, nodding sagely.

The comment — was she right? — stung my heart like a stingray's barbed tail. I felt as though she'd cut my tongue out, and I was only just learning to speak.

~

'I've let myself go,' my mum whispered. She began to weep.

She sat on a wooden bench in the spa, holding a small circular magnifying mirror in her right hand. It was her sixtieth birthday.

We'd had full-body massages, a manicure, a pedicure and now a young attendant in a white coat was trying to apply her makeup.

We were surrounded by upmarket stuff. White vials lined up in an orderly fashion on the shelves. Everything white and glistening and Mum weeping.

I brought her here because it looked sophisticated and expensive, a place for rich people. Now that I was a project manager with a business card and a briefcase, I wanted to spoil her, splash cash on her, as though we had it to spend.

'Sorry, dear,' Mum said to the child-like attendant, who took a step back, the eyeshadow brush poised in her hand.

The pampering package was meant to make Mum feel good, meant to be a treat at a place of glamour and escape where her skin could be cleansed, her toenails trimmed as though she were Cleopatra. Mum's feet were gnarly and untoward, flanked by chilblains, fit only for two pairs of fluffy slippers to ward off the cold. She always got cold feet.

'I've let myself go,' she blubbed again, staring into the mirror. Her mascara ran — all the effort of the pampering package undone.

It was true. Mum had let herself go. She had not been dieting and inhaling kale, she didn't pluck her eyebrows to perfection, her face did not say 'I'm proud to be me'. Instead, her cheeks and neckline were collapsing into jowls, her hair was short and blunt. She looked homely, like a woman who didn't consider herself to matter any more. Financially, she didn't matter — her salary was lower than mine, she still rented a house, had no partner. Her one dream in life had been to get married again and have a husband who loved her; instead, she had no possessions other than me, her only daughter.

I knew she'd recognised the death of something in that small handheld mirror. A vial of sadness had been uncorked like an essential oil and we could never get it back in the bottle again. It is a terrible shame for a woman to Let Herself Go.

She sat there, crying silently. Her chin and lower lip wobbled, in that pathetic way I hated.

My shoulders tensed. 'It doesn't matter, Mum,' I said. 'Don't cry.' But letting yourself go does matter.

~

When I returned to New Zealand, towing Rich with me, it was because Mum was getting older. She had already had cancer and lived alone. My funny little mother, with a penchant for purple — she put streaks of it in her short hair and carried a multi-coloured purple paisley handbag from Desigual. Mum also had chin whiskers that she got waxed at times, but I enjoyed tweezing the hairs out in private. They were now thick and white and as stubborn as me.

Mum lived in Auckland and we moved to Wellington, so she couldn't get too attached and cling to me like a barnacle. I sometimes gazed at daughters with sophisticated mums, walking arm in arm wearing swish attire, the mother as uber-cool as the daughter. These mothers didn't look like the poem 'Warning' (about turning into an old woman wearing purple) was their personal touchstone.

Mum had retrained as a counsellor and over the years tried to set up her own business. 'I hate my work. I'm not fulfilled in it any more,' she said periodically. 'It's good to have the income though, isn't it?' I reminded her, as I sat in my swivel chair, project managing, googling mermaids, trying to make the sums in Excel add up. We can't all live our dreams, can we?

When she'd ring in a flurry of tears, worn out with her own workplace dramas, I'd try to coax her back down to earth.

'She's a bully,' Mum said, about her own boss. 'What happened?' I asked, aghast. Why couldn't she keep a bloody lid on it? Had she never been pulled aside by an HR manager and given an A4 handout of a frazzled cartoon stick figure called ERIC? Emotional Reaction Impedes Control. Some things you can control, some things you can influence, but most things are outside your control and your influence, the HR manager had explained to me.

Mum was inside my sphere of influence, but outside my control. And vice versa. I was embarrassed by her efforts at self-fulfilment. She had once made a business card that consisted of a bad blurry photo of herself perched in a tree. I knew the tree was meaningful, standing outside of her childhood home in the small gold-mining town of Lawrence at the bottom of the South Island. But to anyone else, the middle-aged woman posed in a tree in the oval inlay of a budget business card would just look weird. It certainly didn't look aspirational. How could she sell a dream of happiness and self-fulfilment when she was sad, poor and desperate?

The day of the depressing spa treatment, we went out for a birthday dinner at a seafront restaurant. What a mismatched crew we were! Mum, short and mauve haired, prone to sweating even when she hadn't walked very far. Me in the floral backless dress I'd worn the night I'd met Rich, my mermaid hair flowing over my shoulders. Rich, shy and elegant as a seahorse, gently bobbing along beside me. Dad, tall and thin as a lighthouse. He had an impenetrable exterior, a strong bright mind, and a steep nose that had spent many hours deep inside books. His girlfriend was a kind, gracious non-reader.

'I'm ready to be a grandmother,' Mum told Rich and me.

'Roger that,' I said. Rich nodded. But if there'd been a kelp forest nearby, he might have dashed into it.

'I didn't use to be ready, but now I am.'

'I know.' I put my hand over hers on the table.

When I was in my twenties, Mum used to jump up and down like Rumpelstiltskin and chant: 'I'm not old enough to be a grandmother.' Now she was sixty. She was old enough.

But was I old enough? Technically yes. My womb was overdue. But emotionally? I was still invested in pursuing my artistic dreams.

I'd imagined a baby would be reeled in after I made it big. The writers' group hadn't invited me back, but I had signed up for a nonfiction writing class.

'I wonder what your baby might look like?' Mum said.

Dinner arrived.

Steak for me. Rich had the calamari, little wiry rings of innocuous squid. We took photos of the sea view, outside the large glass windows. The waters of Cook Strait, calm and blue-grey, waves endlessly lapping. How much did I even know about the sea and what was under it? Dad went to the bathroom, and Mum turned to his girlfriend and said, 'You two are lucky you have each other.'

Oh Mum.

At the end of the night, our waitress brought out the giant fuck-off chocolate cake I had bought Mum from a posh supermarket. It was studded with six candles — because sixty was too many — and we sang 'Happy Birthday'.

'Megan, would you like a set of my "Pearls of Wisdom" cards?' Mum asked after dinner.

She had recently made a new deck of affirmations.

'Yes,' I replied, because she was inside my sphere of influence, as I was inside hers. She handed me a dainty drawstring bag. I opened it and examined the deck. Her affirmations for self-care were printed in a sloping cursive text, the font black on pale blue. On each card was an image of an oyster half-open, like a makeup compact. In the centre sat one lonely pearl.

I take care of myself by following a healthy diet.

'I'll read them later,' I said.

~

'Your chances of having a baby at forty are five percent,' said the fertility specialist. He was old but because he was a man it didn't matter.

Rich and I were sitting on comfortable beige chairs in his office; the specialist behind the pale maple veneer of his orderly desk.

'What?' I said, laughing. 'But everyone's having babies after thirty-five now. Even lesbians are having babies!'

In London, my friend and her girlfriend each had an egg fertilised, using the semen of the same man from Amsterdam.

The specialist came out from behind his desk like the narrator in *The Rocky Horror Picture Show* and flipped open a chart shaped like a half-circle, as though he was about to sing 'Let's do the Time Warp Again'.

Instead, he pointed at the sliding odds of conception; after thirty-five the arrow shot down to near the bottom of the chart. His sunlit office exuded an air of not exactly sterility . . . but cleanliness and calm, the sense that, for the right price, life could be extracted from your womb.

It was time to have a look at my uterus.

Before I arrived, I'd skulled four glasses of water in preparation for the ultrasound. I was desperate to pee, but holding it in. Rich stayed on his comfortable chair. 'You can come with her,' the specialist said. Rich blushed, but I let him stay put — besides, he was already familiar with the path to my uterus. I darted behind a tasteful fawn curtain and took my knickers off, assumed a pose on the stretcher under the white sheet. The specialist and an elderly nurse — a vaginal chaperone — appeared. They put on plastic gloves. I put my knees up and spread my legs. 'Are you ready?' 'Yes.' My vagina braced to receive the inquisitive electric eel of the probe. I watched on screen as my womb was revealed like an underwater cavern. A dark sonar, black holes opened and stretched out, then closed again.

'What can you see?' I asked.

'A few fibroids,' he said.

The fibroids were shaped like kidney beans and reminded me of gallery furniture.

'What are fibroids?' I asked.

'Non-cancerous growths.'

'So, nothing to worry about?'

'Nothing to worry about.'

He explained fibroids can sometimes prevent pregnancy, 'but in your case that is unlikely.'

The investigation completed, I wiped the lavish amount of lube from my bush, put my pants back on and returned to my seat next to Rich. The nurse disappeared. It was time to get to the point.

'You have the womb of a forty-year-old,' the specialist said.

'That's not too bad,' I smiled. My womb was only one year older than me.

The specialist frowned. Then he asked how often we had sex. What did that have to do with the price of fish? I looked at Rich skittishly. A private truth was about to be revealed. Rich's orange Surly bicycle was the only thing he'd been riding lately. We squirmed and confessed, laughing. We'd been caught out languishing in the comfort of our long-term relationship.

'You need to have sex like you just met,' the specialist said.

The fertility clinic had answers. They just were not what I expected them to be.

I leaned forward in my seat, like a cartoon character — perhaps Jessica Rabbit — her eyes bugged out on springs. Surely there must be another way? The specialist explained that three rounds of IVF offered the best chance of a pregnancy, but that would cost $30,000 — with a discount.

'We could afford one round,' I said, turning to Rich. 'Maybe?'

He took my hand.

'And then when I turn forty, I will be eligible for government funding,' I said. I looked out the window and saw cloudless blue sky. It was time for some blue sky thinking.

Rich and I stood up. Eject. We left the Fertility Associates and walked down the street. 'I can't have a baby at forty, I'm not Nicole Kidman,' I said. Two lanes of traffic back-to-back and on the other side of the road, a bike shop. Rich gave it the side eye. 'Even lesbians are having babies!' I burst into tears. He held me, and I blubbed on his shoulder. 'Lesbians.' The smell of him, familiar now, the way his hair parts when he sleeps on it, his nice scratchy stubble, and his long piano fingers.

'I don't know if I want a baby,' I said. 'But I don't know that I don't want one.' It seemed an important distinction.

'We can try,' Rich said.

'And if I don't get pregnant, we could do a road trip across

America?' I sniffed. I had a vision of Florida swamps and bayous, an American crocodile rising from the balmy waters like a demonic log. I wasn't limited to my obsession with mermaids; I also had a longstanding thing about crocodiles.

At work, my latest project tanked — and went over budget. I made a PowerPoint about it and presented it to the board. The sky wasn't blue outside the windows that day. 'How did this happen?' the chair of the board asked, looking at the budget that didn't add up.

Back in the office, I flew out of my swivel chair and raged at Clive. 'We should have seen this coming. Where was the risk management?'

He went red in the face and screamed, 'Don't be such a diva!'

Anna cowered in her corner.

I retreated, like a boxer, to my swivel chair, and turned back and forth. How dare he call me a diva! I smoothed my maroon dress, trying to cool down, then I asked him into the meeting room to reconvene.

'Please don't give me gendered feedback,' I said, my legs crossed in my thick black tights. I faced him man to man.

He apologised, his blue eyes sincere, and he *was* sincere. Clive was a lovely man. He had hired me even though I had no experience as a project manager and had never worked in an office.

Maybe I was a diva.

'You're not used to being outside your comfort zone, are you?' Clive said. The water cooler stood sentinel in the corner. It glugged as it refilled.

I didn't know how to reply.

'How's the fertility treatment going?' Clive asked.

The Fertility Associates had given me a grab bag of hormones that I'd been injecting into my own stomach at timed intervals throughout the day. When I first picked up the kit from the nurse, she asked, 'How do you feel?' 'Like I am about to throw ten grand off a cliff,' I replied. The nurse looked alarmed.

'I have to keep the injections up for a week to two weeks,' I told Clive. 'Then we will know more.' My hormone levels would be tested again and hopefully there would be some eggs to extract. My fertility was up in the air. *Mermaid hair, don't care!*

~

Life began in the sea, so they tell me. But I don't believe this theory because for me the waters of life began as a blastocyst in a petri dish at the Fertility Associates office.

'Good news!' the specialist said. Seven eggs had been harvested from my womb, then lovingly fertilised by Rich's semen. In a lab-like white room, a female embryologist proudly showed me the specimen she had selected for insertion into my womb. I looked at the grey speck in the petri dish and tried to feel maternal. During the transfer I was drugged up, knees up, the revered specialist ferreting away at the other end with a torch, like a miner. The embryologist hovered nearby.

Afterwards, I sat behind a blue curtain in a discreet changing room. I was groggy and foggy. A disembodied voice in the cubicle next door — they had no eggs. Contained crying, whispered voices, the uterus like an empty cul-de-sac waiting to be filled . . . Rich escorted me home. So far my IVF experience had been uncomfortable but not traumatic. If it was a journey, it was like a short trip to the shops rather than *The Odyssey*.

A week later, we met the specialist again. 'Congratulations,' he beamed. We had hit the jackpot after one round of IVF. Rich and I looked at each other. The specialist wrote a note for our GP: 'The couple are somewhat shocked by the good news.' Understatement of the year. An embryo was now elbowing those fibroids for room in my womb. I was scared. What if I died in childbirth? Or had a baby with Down syndrome? I felt turbulent. Discontented. Now that I was pregnant, I was worried about the other risks. If I didn't want a baby with a rare genetic condition, did that mean I didn't want a baby at all?

I stewed over the increased risks for geriatric mothers; the rest of the time I was exhausted. My first trimester I could have slept all day on the couch, like a basking seal, if seals were prone to dozing off.

~

Then I turned forty and Dad's Russian wolfhound ate my birthday cake. Our small family had gathered in Lyall Bay to celebrate. Rich and I sat at the table, and I tried to look like it didn't matter that my birthday cake had been enjoyed by Dad's dog instead of me. My aunt made me another cake, but it tasted terrible. She thought that was funny. When you're forty and pregnant no one expects you to need an edible, delicious birthday cake.

My dad's house, a weatherboard villa that Dad had nicknamed The Shoebox, was by the sea. The wind whistled through the chimney and my heart heaved like the waves outside, grey and threshing. I looked at the higgledy-piggledy rows of paperbacks and hardbacks on his bookshelves. Some of their spines buckled, the pages thick and sandy yellow. Old books smell like old clothes, that fumey mothball scent of the past, of thoughts long out of fashion. Dad favoured Russian literature. Tolstoy. Dostoevsky. The classics. Serious stuff.

'This is what I want,' I told him, kneeling on the floor beside the bookcase. 'To be a book on your shelf.'

He sat in his armchair and nodded.

My aunt had given me a fortieth-birthday card that read: Queen of Fucking Everything. The card had a picture of a brunette in a twinset who looked like a hot fifties secretary. It was meant to be a compliment. Instead, it felt like a mirror held up to a diva.

'I'm so tired,' I said.

'Have you had a banana?' Mum asked.

'No, I haven't had a banana.' I rolled my eyes.

'Is it normal to be this tired?' she said, biting her lip. 'I don't remember being tired when I was pregnant with you.'

'Mum, that was more than forty years ago,' I sighed.

'Forty years old. You're no spring chicken any more, are you?' my aunt said, laughing. Mum's older sister was a thin crooked lady with a raspy smoker's voice. 'I suppose none of us are.'

'Megan, you've had nothing to do with babies,' Mum said, suddenly, as though it had just occurred to her.

No. I'd never imagined myself as a mother. A mermaid: hell yes. I'd have loved to be a beautiful mermaid cruising through the ocean with the commanding force of a great white, occasionally seducing a sailor just for the hell of it. But a mother? The literature about mothers was not compelling. I didn't read books about motherhood.

After my birthday lunch, we walked along Lyall Bay beach together.

'Mum is driving me crazy,' I told Dad. We strode ahead of the pack. Not difficult — Mum was short and not accustomed to walking far. 'She makes me feel incompetent.'

Dad was the rational one, a tall lighthouse throwing out its steady beam. 'It will be okay,' he said. 'I don't think you'll ever regret having a baby.'

I believed him, because that was what I needed to hear — striding by the rugged sea, the waves choppy as fuck. I was still hungry, so we got fish 'n' chips from the shop by the beach. I ate them next to the old wooden surf lifesaving club, sand sluicing into my teeth, my hair flying into my mouth, my mother following behind, out of breath even on the flat. The whole family was coming to terms with this new development: that inside my womb was a foetus, growing and developing, tadpoling into shape. Soon the baby would be born and take over my life.

Rich was also pragmatic. 'Everyone has babies,' he said. 'If everyone else can do it, we can.' Rich had given me a bright-yellow birthday card with three chickens on the front. A rooster, a mother hen and a baby chick. 'Two become three,' he wrote on the inside. I cried and cried.

My pregnancy was a hormonal whirlpool. I had expected the

process to be physical but it was also psychological. I googled 'having a baby'. Bought the notorious, Bible-sized instruction manual *What to Expect When You're Expecting*. Located not one, but two midwives, who worked in tandem — one was young and had a black bob, the other was an old, toughened hippy who had the bedside manner of a barracuda. 'I can't help you with that,' she snapped when I called one day, distraught about not being able to get a doctor's appointment for a rash. I put the phone down, cried again.

'You only need to eat an extra handful of almonds a day,' the midwife told me as I stood on the scales and the arrow sprang up up up. Good news if you like almonds. But someone needed to tell the baby, who was only interested in carbs and Nippy's chocolate milk. I sucked those carboard packs dry as I slowly climbed the small but pronounced hill to our flat, sweating. I was fine, except for the abstract feelings of sadness inside me.

I found an online checklist of 'essential' baby items to check off. Rich researched prams online. In stealth mode, we cruised the aisles of baby shops. My eyes glazed over nipple guards, transparent teats in all shapes and sizes, bibs and sterilisers, and breast pumps. Nursing bras that popped open, so your tits could hang out. The plastic paraphernalia reminded me of props from some nightmare contemporary art performance. I imagined a small audience of art-centric intellectuals watching as I placed a plastic funnel over my breast.

'Let's get out of here,' I said to Rich.

We walked home, hot and bothered. We didn't have a car, we didn't have a baby room to decorate. How much of this shit did we really need?

~

Mermaids and midwives. The weeks ticked down; no almonds fell through my hourglass. My red leather briefcase sat under my desk, holding sheaves of printed PowerPoint presentations. At work on the thirteenth floor, I opened the Excel files but the sums didn't add up. At home on the hill, I wrote a funny essay about my life as a bookseller at a doomed retail chain for the writing class, though what I really wanted was to finish my mermaid poem, as if it were a lifeline that could save me. I swivelled back and forth in my swivel chair, examining the wreckage, the mermaid in the bath and the bathos. The professional mermaids were evidence of some oceanic overwhelm that was taking place online, and only I was on to it.

Memories flooded back. I made my first mermaid in ceramics back in high school. 'It's a risk,' the teacher said, as I rolled the clay into a long tail. My terracotta mermaid was modelled on the publicity poster for *Splash*, the one in which Daryl is lying on the beach on her belly, her chin cupped in her hands, smiling and game. The art room in my memory is a dense underwater terrain, paintings on pegs move back and forth like waves. The sounds of kids, distant as breaking surf when you close your eyes, lying still on a towel at the beach.

I added a dribble more water and tucked the plastic around the clay, like a body bag. But my ceramics teacher was right. When I fired my mermaid in the kiln, her tail broke off. My terracotta mermaid. The one that got away.

~

On my lunchbreak I visited the barracuda midwife. She lubed up the fat plastic white wand, and rubbed it over my belly — boom, boom, boom, boom, boom. Fast as a techno beat. In the wildness of that moment, I started crying, startled by the surety of the sound, my baby's heartbeat, alive and pumping. The barracuda told me that babies have a faster heartbeat than adults. Then she scrolled the wand again over my rotund belly.

'You are having a girl.'

'Are you sure?'

'Well, I can't see a penis,' the barracuda said, and there she was on the screen — the white outline of a baby sleeping inside my womb, lying on a crescent. Joy burst open inside me. A daughter. I wanted a daughter.

'What about the name Sophia?' Rich said, at home later, trying to narrow down our list.

'No, that's a stripper name.' I frowned. I had worked with a stripper called Sophia, who had conical implants.

'What about Juniper?' I suggested.

He said nothing, but I knew Juniper wouldn't fly.

In another session at the hospital, we had to blow up a purple balloon and pretend it was a breast. Rich and I laughed till we cried — we'd arrived from work, tired and sober. A lean nurse took us through the basics of breastfeeding as though we were rehearsing an earthquake drill. The moment the balloons were passed around, we started giggling like we were on LSD. I drew a nipple on my purple tit as tears rolled from my eyes. Words like 'mastitis' entered my mind, only to disappear into the ether.

We signed up for our local antenatal classes. The baby was the exam and we were going to be prepared. The other couples were a mixed bunch of heterosexuals: a Kylie-Minogue-sized Texan with a husband in the army, a pair of seismologists in Patagonia fleeces, a banker and his good-looking wife. Even when the other mothers looked forty, they were thirty-six or thirty-two and I was intimidated by the atmosphere of middle-class superiority.

Once a week, we sat on chairs in a semi-circle, as though a campfire was blazing in the middle, calling us to our primal past as hunter gatherers, people who innately knew how to have babies.

We didn't know how to have babies.

Whenever anyone asked a question, the antenatal woman replied, 'Good questions!' cheerily. It became our catchphrase. Rich and I turned to one another constantly at home and said, 'Good questions!' One night the male seismologist asked what would have happened in the pre-industrial era when a woman went into labour but didn't fully dilate.

'Would she and the baby have died?' he asked.

A long pause. 'Yes,' the antenatal woman answered.

'Good questions,' I whispered to Rich. By this stage, I was dressed in a brown-and-black-striped sack that betrayed the number of almonds I was not eating. One night, another mother said to our gaggle how impressed she was that none of the women in our antenatal group had put on much weight. I was puffy and disconsolate. It was true. The other mothers-to-be were obviously eating the right volume of almonds. Arseholes.

We were given information about the drugs we could take during childbirth. Laughing gas. Electrodes. The epidural. Most women in the group said they wanted a natural birth. Fear, deep and reptilian, gripped my mind. I knew having a baby was natural, but it didn't sound natural to me. Kissing and sex were natural, too, but benefited from expertise. I was the one mother in my antenatal group who felt open to painkillers.

Another night we split into two groups — the mums and dads. We placed coloured cards, representing the hours of the day, on the floor under different headings. How much time would be spent breastfeeding? Changing nappies? Sleeping? Making food?

'Can you write and breastfeed at the same time?' I asked.

The antenatal woman frowned at me. 'Maybe, if the baby is propped on a nursing cushion.'

A nursing cushion? I put one on my list.

I noticed she hadn't turned to me and said brightly, Good questions! I worried that I was too selfish to be a mother. Selfish was the one thing a mother was not allowed to be.

~

At work, I typed data into Excel, wearing the stripy pregnancy dress. I only wanted to eat food that was yellow. I popped open the staff toastie maker in the small kitchenette. Sandwiched down the knobbly Vogel's bread and thick Edam cheese, pressed the silver lid closed. A man with curly hair from the office next door looked at my baby bump through the stripes. 'When are you due?'

he asked. I told him. 'I'm looking forward to finishing work and having a rest.' He laughed, a throaty cackle that set my hackles on edge. 'Having a baby will be the hardest work of your life.'

'Surely having a baby can't be worse than sitting through another blue-sky session at the board meeting,' I raved to the new office administrator.

She sat behind her grey partition and gazed at me with quiet, soulful eyes. Mia was a young poet who had just graduated with distinction from my creative writing school. Its master's degree was very prestigious. Now she sat at the front desk and answered the phone on the rare occasions it bothered to ring.

'They wanted me to get Lady Gaga as an arts ambassador! They told me to send her a tweet!' I rolled my eyes.

Mia smiled sympathetically. I'd never read her poetry but had heard it was very good. Despite that, I assumed that she was destined for a life of anonymity working in a job she hated on the thirteenth floor.

I had the horrible feeling I was annoying Mia with my jibber jabber — gate-crashing the privacy of her own mind. I returned to my desk to gobble my cheese on toast. Outside the window, a slice of ocean. Wave upon wave upon wave.

I joined Twitter. Other people were good at it, why not me? The Twittersphere was an eco-system heaving with local writers, unbound from the drudgery of their day jobs. One of them was Mia, who tweeted almost constantly from the front desk, her head bent down in quiet communion with her screen. I had always assumed she was working. In person, she was silent. Online, she was elegant, dexterous, insatiably witty.

When I published my first essays — about being a submerging artist, then a doomed bookseller — I tweeted out the links. Then I waited for the feedback of the online literati — dangling, squirming, on a hook.

~

Another day, another handful of almonds. I sat at home on our maroon couch with a pattern of fraying Egyptian figures on it, undone by my old Plunket book. On the cover was a stylised illustration of a retro fifties mother holding her baby. The book contained my mother's handwriting and that of an ancient Plunket nurse. They clocked my weight in ounces and noted my first mouthful of beef broth. It was a relic from a time of my life that I had no memory of, an era when my own mother and I were knitted close, my flesh from her body. I didn't feel well.

How had I reached the middle of my life so unprepared for what came next? Through the doorway, out the big bedroom window, I looked at the view of Wellington Harbour, the big white Interislander ferry cutting slowly across the horizon. I owned next to nothing, except books. Even the couch had come with the flat we rented. I liked it, because of the hieroglyphs, but Rich thought it was the most uncomfortable couch in the world.

I had never paused to wonder about my own babyhood before, the nine months I spent stored inside my mother's womb, the amniotic waters that swirled around me. My mum and dad had originally wanted to be sorted with a house and an income before they had a baby, but I came along unplanned. They got married because of me.

I'd waited until I was forty. I'd spent my life before that pursuing art — video art, then writing, for fuck's sake! — and now I owned no house either.

~

During my last week at work, I tidied my files, cleaned my desk, saved my poems to a hard drive, emptied my briefcase and threw away sheafs of printed-out PowerPoints, but I couldn't stop googling mermaids. I opened a new file and copied and pasted a photograph of Hannah Mermaid into it. An order was beginning to emerge in my Google searches: some mermaids were more important than others. Hannah Mermaid was parked in front of a shipwreck in a glittering sequinned tail and matching bikini top. She held the rusted stairwell of the boat, as two sharks flitted across the background.

The natural habitat of the mermaid is the shipwreck, the embodiment of the drowned world, whereas ships are synonymous with men, sailors and explorers from the eighteenth and nineteenth centuries, like Captain Cook who had 'discovered' Aotearoa, or Christopher Columbus who had allegedly sighted mermaids — or more likely manatees — off the coast of a Caribbean island. He thought them not very beautiful, but we'll never know what the manatees made of him.

On Hannah Mermaid's website, I found an old Kodak image of her as a child, dressed in an orange mermaid tail sewn out of a tablecloth and posing on a rock by her family swimming pool. Hannah Mermaid was my vintage — a Gen X woman who first watched Daryl Hannah in *Splash* at the movies. As a little girl, Hannah Mermaid obsessively drew pictures of mermaids and scanned her local library looking for books about how to be one. Nothing. She even wrote a letter to Robert Short, the special effects artist who had created the *Splash* tail, asking him how he did it. It was hard and expensive, he wrote back. But she didn't give up.

'Look at this,' I said to Anna. 'She watched *Splash* and really did turn into Daryl Hannah. Now she's the most famous professional mermaid in the world.'

The scales had fallen from my eyes. Hannah Mermaid stared out of the shipwreck, as though saying, *Yes, Megan, mermaids exist, and what of it?*

'Why don't you just Skype her?' Anna said.

~

Then we gathered in the boardroom for a final morning tea. The staff presented me with a beautiful book of first words for my baby. Clive thanked me for all my work, there was even a cake. 'We'll miss you,' he said. The book's bright-blue cover featured a little bird, its beak open in a perpetual squawk. On my way out of the office, I passed Mia sitting at the front desk and felt suddenly ashamed of my countless rants and demonic bitching. 'I hope I haven't been too hard to work with,' I said.

The world's best tweeter looked up. Her blue eyes were calm and steady. 'Dude, you are the easiest person to work with in this office.'

I take care of myself
by following a healthy diet

Pearls of Wisdom by Lee Dunn

3.

Another Mother

I arrived at the hospital to have a baby. I was induced at 7am and lay on the bed in my birthing suite, waiting. Rich slumbered in a nearby chair. He looked tired, worn out from work and my incessant worrying. Birth, like most things, was a protracted affair. I was a week past my due date, and our baby was still showing no signs of making an appearance.

The birthing suite had a spa bath in one corner. The walls were painted a creamy taupe. No art. I wandered into a cupboard and found a dark-blue container full of vaginal plugs, so I took a photo and posted it to Facebook. The plugs were contained in little plastic bags, sterile and ready to be plugged into miscellaneous vaginas for reasons unknown.

I had also rented a TENS machine on a wire stand and stationed it next to the bed. It looked like a miniature telegraph pole. The TENS would administer shots of electricity to circumvent any labour pains. I had to keep that electricity free-flowing.

The barracuda midwife turned up. I had acclimatised to her bedside style — a mixture of rough pragmatism and sudden humour. She had brought her knitting. Everyone was ready.

I texted Dad: 'Everything is fine.' Ditto Mum. I had refused to let her come to the birth, knowing it would only push me over the edge. I'd put a veto on her even coming to Wellington, the thought of her waiting outside the hospital like a deranged wombat didn't calm my nerves. And I didn't need another one of her pearls of wisdom either. *But Megan, you've never pushed a baby out of your vagina before!*

The morning passed as in an idyll. Waiting, waiting.

The barracuda took out her knitting, and I took out my book. It had a mustard cover and featured an illustration of the British comedian Richard Ayoade, holding a video camera up to one eye like a monocle. I lay on my stretcher in the birthing suite, cracking up. Surely I was the only pregnant woman ever to take Ayoade's book parodying contemporary cinema to an induction. In my favourite chapter, Ayoade had composed a list of tweets in the voice of the auteur film director Terrence Malick. The tweets were deeply silly, and it was this that made them funny, because I'd recently watched Malick's latest cinematic venture, *The Tree of Life*, and apart from the CGI dinosaurs I'd found it long and terminally boring. I had fallen asleep on the Egyptian sofa.

I cackled when I came across a passage about Ron Howard, the director of *Splash*. Richard Ayoade had a hotline to my pregnancy! It was like he was standing above me with a stethoscope planted on my baby bump, knowing that I needed an injection of *Splash* jokes.

Ayoade joked that he had written two collections of essays on Howard's early work, *Ron Howard: The Semiotics of Splash!* and *Splashback! The Hermeneutics of Howard*. 'Sadly, they are no longer in print, though they can be obtained by directly contacting Ron Howard himself who has bought up all remaining copies.'

I felt a rush of pleasure. It was another sign. I wanted to read *The Semiotics of Splash*; this was my cultural terrain. And

Splashback! Ayoade had perceived the nub of the problem — comedy is never taken seriously. I thought again of art school and my tutor who told me I couldn't make an artwork about the influence of *Splash*. 'Think about the mermaid across time and culture. This can't be about Daryl Hannah.' But what if it can?

Then my waters burst. A non-event. Pain began. Not sharp and shooting. The room turned grey. I felt like I was in a basement. I put Ayoade down, concentrated on my body as a vessel. The pain came in vice-like squeezes, constricting, grinding and slow. 'Fuck the TENS.' I pushed it away and it wheeled off to the side, forlorn as a Dalek. Rich put his hand on my shoulder supportively, only for me to shove that away too. I clutched the silver rail of the hospital bed. Crouched, rocking. A contraction sounds like it has a beginning and an end, like a sentence, but this pain just went on and on.

'I want an epidural,' I said. 'An epidural!'

The anaesthetist was summoned. He was a thin, muscular man who administered the injection into the base of my spine. 'You have a nice strong back,' he said.

'Thanks,' I said.

After that, I recovered enough to read Ayoade again.

The midwife knitted beside me, clack-clack.

Night fell. The birthing suite lay in silence. Rich was asleep in the chair by the dark window.

'I'm worried about him,' I said from my hospital bed. 'His white blood cell count is low.'

I looked at his face, his long black lashes, slumbering on the job.

'But the doctor says some people just have low white blood cell counts.'

I wanted the midwife to comfort me, to offer some maternal platitude, lightly rubbed with medicinal authority.

The barracuda looked at him and said, 'He does look sick.'

'I'm glad I had the epidural,' I said.

'Yes, that was a good choice for you,' she replied.

'I don't really have a birthing plan,' I said. 'All the women in the antenatal class had birthing plans, everyone wanted a natural birth.'

'It's better to just go with what happens,' she said.

The barracuda told me about the birth of her first child. 'It was the seventies,' she said, 'and we were hippies.' She lived in a commune, or at least a large shared house, surrounded by other women. They were feminists. When her labour pains started, the group rallied around her. In a room of soft furnishings, she moaned and groaned, pushing through each contraction with no pain killers. The feminist hippies cheered her on. A home birth! The barracuda felt proud of herself, determined. Three days passed. All the feminists had left. The doctor arrived. 'How close am I?' she panted. Her cervix was only three centimetres dilated.

We laughed.

~

A trio of female doctors came in occasionally to check the clipboard at the end of my bed. I'd been introduced to them earlier; they were young and polite, like head girls on their best behaviour. Nothing much was happening to my cervix either.

The brunette: 'I'll just have another look down there.'

'Sure,' I said. 'How's it looking?'

'Your cervix is only dilated by three centimetres. Four centimetres, if I'm being generous,' said the doctor, frowning.

An aura of concern descended on the birthing suite.

'We'll give it another half an hour,' she said.

I nodded. 'Okay.'

I felt responsible for the lack of progress. My reluctance to bear the pain of a natural birth was holding the baby back. I should have gritted my teeth and got through it without an epidural. Why didn't I have more commitment to an ideal birthing plan, to an ideal birth? I was failing the ultimate exam of womanhood: there was a right way and a wrong way to be in labour, but I had a block in my psyche, like a vaginal plug. I still wasn't ready to be a mother.

Half an hour went by. I lay on the bed, staring at my feet under the hospital blanket, unsure about what to hope. My cervix still hadn't come to the party, but the trio of sensitive doctors had. They examined the heart monitors again.

The brunette said, 'The baby is starting to show signs of distress.'

Our daughter had been docked at the entrance to my canal for some time. I imagined her head down there, trying to enter the pink gooey tunnel.

'Is it time to cut to the chase?' I asked.

'Yes.'

An emergency C-section was ordered. Rich and I had to put on blue shower caps and gowns — we were entering a sterile environment. I was wheeled in on my hospital bed. I had been given more drugs and felt about as ready as anyone can feel to have a baby cut out of their womb. A fleet of doctors in scrubs were introduced to me. It was all very cordial. 'Hhhhello.' My teeth chattered violently. A chalky hollow ring. The theatre felt like a freezer. A blue sheet had been raised above my abdomen like the net on a tennis court. I couldn't see below it, which I was grateful about. The doctor tested my reflexes before he began the incision. 'Can you feel this?' he said, prodding his way along my body.

'Nn-negligible,' I stuttered. My teeth were clattering so bad I could hardly get words out.

The staff in the operating theatre all cracked up.

'Wwwhat?' I asked.

'That's a new one. No one's ever said "negligible" before,' the doctor replied.

Rich squeezed my hand.

Then our daughter was lifted out and up above the net. She was crying. It was fast, so fast. 'Is she all right? Is she all right?' I managed. 'She's perfect,' the barracuda said. It was skin time, the mythical skin time, and I had skin in the game. My daughter on my body, my breast, this purple, oiled being, her hands crumpled and tiny but five fingered. 'She's beautiful,' I said, and started crying. She was the most beautiful perfect thing I had ever seen. Rich, still in his shower cap, held her and cried. The midwife took photos, and our baby was dressed and swaddled. We were all okay. The big event was over.

~

Rich left that evening and I was wheeled offstage. I lay behind a curtain in the dark, my daughter in a high plastic cot beside me. I felt like I was in a cavern behind a waterfall. Action was rushing on somewhere in another chamber of the hospital. I was recovering. In recovery. I couldn't turn and see her, couldn't look at my baby. She was higher than me. I couldn't move properly. Felt stiff and restrained. Pressed the button for the nurse. The door opened, a funnel of yellow light. A figure by my bed in a white uniform. 'Is she breathing?' I asked. 'Yes,' the nurse said, irritable. Another mother was wheeled in to recover, the curtain swept closed around her.

I couldn't sleep, but lay in the shadows in the cave behind the waterfall, tensed and listening for the rush of my daughter's breath. When I couldn't hear it, I pressed the buzzer again. 'What is it this time?' the nurse snapped. 'I'm sorry,' I said. 'I just can't see her. Can't see if she's breathing.' The nurse rolled her eyes — she was so brisk, I was shocked. I got a peek of my baby's face in the cot, her head turned to the side, then she was gone and I was lying down again. I wanted to call out to the mother behind the next curtain for consolation, but instead I lay there and said nothing, just listened for my baby's breathing.

~

A text from Rich in the night: *I love you two.*

~

'Megan, why did you have a C-section?' Mum asked in the morning. The light in the hospital room was grainy, as though we were underwater. A grey dishwater day outside. I held my daughter wrapped up in her swaddle. My baby. Mum stood at the foot of my hospital bed, short and awed. Dad was tall and pragmatic, his cliff-hanger nose pointed down at me, his colour a tinge ashen. His girlfriend stood beside him. They had brought me a bunch of flowers.

'I failed to dilate,' I said. 'The baby was showing signs of distress.'

She had lived inside me, stored in my tummy as though I was the oyster and she was the pearl. Then the doctors shucked me open and there she was. We loved her. Adored her. Couldn't believe we'd made her.

'Thank God you're all right.' My father looked relieved. I was relieved, too.

'I wonder why you didn't dilate?' Mum queried, as though it was a question I could answer.

Mum had flown to Wellington in secret and been staying at Dad's house. The three of them had kept vigil together during my labour, obviously worried out of their minds. I was grateful Dad had kept this information to himself.

'I wanted to be here,' Mum said. 'Isn't she beautiful?'

Mum reached out and stroked the top of her head. I gasped. The sacred fontanelle. I whisked my daughter away.

'You can hurt the top of a newborn baby's head,' I scolded. Everyone in shock. I was in shock.

Mum was bewildered, flummoxed. 'Sorry.' She bit her lip, looked around the room at the chorus of disapproving faces.

~

I paced the room, holding my baby to my breast, desperate to get things off on the right foot. I knew the importance of getting the right latch. The milk had to come down. The short-bobbed midwife appeared. 'Look at you!' she said, approvingly. I was proud. She asked me how many times I was feeding her. 'I don't know,' I said. 'As much as possible.' She gave me a printed-out Excel spreadsheet so I could write down the feed times, keep track.

Rich and I were alone again in our hospital room with our baby. The three of us getting used to each other. I knew the second night was meant to be worse than the first. Rich had brought my laptop so I could watch *The IT Crowd* again. It featured Richard Ayoade as Maurice Moss, a bumbling computer nerd with a nest of black bushy hair and thick-rimmed glasses. I needed comedy. I put our baby in her cot beside my bed to sleep on her back. She had one fist raised, and her lips curled in a snarl. 'She looks like Billy Idol,' Rich said. 'She does,' I said, laughing, and took a photo. Then I got out of my hospital bed to go to the toilet and shrieked. Rich and I looked down at my swollen legs. My ankles had disappeared. 'I'm a Yeti!' I said.

'It's just water retention,' the nurse assured me.

~

The second night was diabolical, but the third was even worse. Imagine a siren that won't ever stop. I cradled the siren to my breast. 'Shhh, shhhh.' I had the siren constantly attached, but was the siren latched? Why wouldn't the milk come down? How would I know when it did? Was it obvious, gushing, rushing? My nipples wet my blouse. Was that milk or stress? Or salt water, bleeding from a rock? I rocked my daughter. I held her. I put her down to try and sleep. 'You need some rest,' a nurse cautioned. 'Have you taken your painkillers?' The nurses rotated in shifts — some nice, others not. In the daytime they popped up like pieces of toast.

A nice one wanted to know if I would like some cheese on toast. 'What?' I said, sitting up in my hospital bed, dumbfounded.

'Cheese on toast. Would you like it on Vogel's bread?' she said. Vogel's was my favourite — how did she know? Was she my mother? 'And what about a hot chocolate?' I hadn't been treated like this since I was a teenager living at home with Mum. I drank the warm drink, cupped it in my hand and crunched into the heated cheese, and felt content.

Then night-time. Blackout. Richard Ayoade and the laptop went home with Rich and nothing was funny or cosy any more. I wept, broken, beached on the side of the hospital bed. What was I doing wrong? A calm, kind old lady with a hooked nose came and sat with me on the bed. She had brought a portable breast pump, with a handle like a toolbox. She plugged it in at the wall and it made a whirring sound like a fridge freezer. I sobbed silently and my daughter cried loudly, louder, loudest. 'Are you sure you don't want to try formula?' the lady asked. 'Just a bit of formula?' 'I didn't bring any formula,' I sobbed. The antenatal class had not given us any information on formula. Breast is best. I felt like the lovely old lady was asking me to give my baby a shot of absinthe. Just one shot.

I rocked back and forwards. 'No,' I said.

The lady turned the knob and the breast pump began to chug. I sat with a funnel over one breast, then the other, as the machine systematically pulled at each, straining to suck out milk. I had become the sole performer in an abject performance piece about the difference between nature and nurture.

The kind old lady left. 'You need some sleep,' she said, as though saying it was a spell that could make it come true. I lay back on the bed, but I couldn't relax while my daughter was crying. I rang the bell for the nurse. No cheese on toast on offer this time. She had a hard, tense face like an acorn.

'I can't sleep,' I said. 'My baby won't stop crying. I just need some sleep.'

My milk still hadn't 'come down'. My breasts hadn't got the message. The nurse took my daughter from her cot and walked round the wards with her, then put her back in the cot. We repeated this process three times. Each time the acorn appeared her face was even harder. Closed to pity. I could hear the cries circling the ward, then returning to me, ripples on an endless ocean of sound, coming closer. Closer. Now the nurse was wild eyed, too. 'This baby is REALLY HUNGRY!' She put my daughter back in her cot for the last time and swept back out to the wards. The siren still going full bore.

~

Motherhood had sent me out beyond myself. I navigated the long wide corridors of the hospital ward, holding my daughter, as though I was on board the *Titanic*, the walls lurching around me. I finally found the right room for breastfeeding support and sat down. A beautiful Japanese woman with long black hair appeared in the doorway — another time traveller from the maternity ward — holding her newborn. The baby wore a magnificent white snowsuit with a hood rimmed with white fur, as though it was a polar explorer. I was dressed in a slippery pale-blue floral nightie with thin straps that I bought specifically because it went down to my feet.

The teacher was a thin dogmatic woman past childrearing age who had suggestions for this and that. It would have been easier to follow if I wasn't on board the *Titanic*. 'You look a bit tense,' she said, as I tried to latch my baby. Tears began to flow down my face. 'Lower your shoulder.' She pushed kindly on my shoulder, which I had been hitherto unaware was stiff and awkward, and it split like a piece of wood. I nodded as though her words were the guidance I needed. Relax, lower your shoulders.

To the other woman the teacher gently suggested, 'Your baby might be a little bit hot.' I glanced up and saw that its small round face was beetroot red. The baby was sweltering, boiling. The teacher began to loosen the string around the hood. 'There, that's better,' she said. The baby had a lovely swirl of black hair.

I tried to make eye contact with the Japanese mother — to commiserate, to share a laugh — but she was oblivious. I returned to my room and methodically filled in my Excel spreadsheet with feeding times and slippery black shits. I noted everything down in my Captain's Log. My hospital sojourn was coming to an end and I couldn't wait to leave. I had to be careful about my scar, to rest and recover. 'Don't let the painkillers wear off,' someone had said on one of those thick, endless nights of wall-to-wall crying. I had been given Tramadol after my C-section and was popping them several times a day. Tramadol rhymes with Panadol.

Rich and I finally decided on her name: Fearne. We chose it because we liked it, because it was beautiful, because it went well with his surname, and because it reminded me of Fern, the little girl who saves the pig in *Charlotte's Web*, one of the first stories I truly loved. And it wasn't pre-loaded with expectations. Mum named me Megan because it means 'strong'. *This little girl will need to be strong*, she thought. I loved my name, a classic that carbon-dates me to the seventies, but I'd always felt the weight of it. Megan also means 'pearl', it's the Welsh variation of Margaret. But I never liked pearls — I'd never worn them. Too oldy-worldy. And I didn't want to read my mother's bloody 'Pearls of Wisdom' cards either.

~

On the fifth morning, Rich and I waited for the doctor to come so I could be released. I checked my phone. The barracuda waited with us, restless and on stand-by for the next baby, until I let her off the hook. The doctor still hadn't seen me, but eventually they let us out anyway. We were free to go as a family of three. Rich had hired a car and we dispatched Fearne into a baby seat rented from the antenatal woman. Good questions! I felt elated, but also shocked. It seemed crazy we could just leave with a new baby and no instructions. Even a car required a licence, and I didn't have one of those. But I did have a printed Excel spreadsheet of feeding times and a bounty of Tramadol. I was ready to ride the high seas. First, though, I had to bend to get in the car, and felt my stomach clench. The C-section had done something under the white bandage.

~

Days and nights of baby bliss, loved up, on the ecstasy of swooning, rising hormones, everything easy-peasy, buckets of sleep for her and me. Rich gave Fearne her first bath and she scowled. Her first bath! We presented her with Pingu, a penguin rattle that squeaked, and a line of knitted finger puppets that she could barely squint at, let alone see. Her first toys! When the midwife came round at the end of our first week we said, 'This is so good. We don't know why people find this hard,' pleased at our surprising capability as new parents.

Rich held Fearne on his forearm each evening like a butler of milk, while the theme tune to *Cheers* played in the background on the TV. He burped her and we lay her on the octopus changing mat for nappy time, and I put her down in her pinewood bassinet, the same brand Brad Pitt and Angelina Jolie had allegedly once used. Fearne always had a daft secret smile on her face when she slept. The Captain's Log was up to date. I popped another pair of Tramadol.

A few days later, we hit a tempest at sea. My face cracked open with red angry lashes, one tit swollen and pink, like a boil or a volcano. Even my nipples were cracked and split, one nearly hanging off like a toothpaste cap. 'That must be sore,' the midwife said during her routine visit. 'I can't feel anything,' I said. She left and I popped another Tramadol. That night, I sat on the toilet pushing and straining to get out a turd that felt like set concrete, as Fearne cried. 'I'm sorry,' I called to Rich from the bathroom, mystified and worried, clutching the windowsill.

'You don't have to apologise. I'm a parent now too.' His stern tone was like a slap across my lacerated face.

Fearne wouldn't stop crying, endlessly, a storm of unreason. I didn't know that sleep wasn't a natural state that the body would just succumb to, that a baby might need to learn how to sleep, or what a growth spurt was. I didn't know anything except that she was crying and I had to make her stop. It was like I had been asked to do a Rubik's cube in record time, except I had never once been able to do a Rubik's cube, even one side.

In the morning, we wound up in our doctor's reception, a pair of adults defeated by a baby. Fearne wanted to be locked on to one of my boobs constantly, and that would be fine if I didn't ever need a moment to myself and if my nipple wasn't on the edge of disconnect. The doctor took me into a room. Behind a blue curtain, I showed her my breasts. She winced.

'It can't be the worst you've ever seen, can it?' I asked.

'It's up there.' The doctor was a level-headed brunette. She could see I was in deep. 'We can fix this,' the doctor said.

'My poo is like concrete. I don't know what's happening,' I blubbed. 'I don't know what's wrong with me.'

It was the Tramadol.

'But isn't Tramadol like Panadol?' I said.

'No,' she said. 'It's more like morphine. It's highly addictive. What did they tell you before you left the hospital?'

'Not to let the painkillers wear off,' I said. 'But I didn't see the doctor before I left. We waited all morning and I couldn't wait to get out of there.'

'How many have you been taking?' the doctor asked.

'Two, several times a day, since the hospital.'

'For how long?'

I shrugged. 'Two weeks?'

The doctor frowned. 'Tramadol is strong. You should have been tapering off,' she said. 'I want you to stop taking it immediately. But once it wears off, Fearne might become a bit more . . . unsettled.'

Understatement of the year.

I came up with a new lullaby: 'Tramadol baby, off its meds. Tramadol baby, won't go to bed.'

~

When the cavalry arrived, it was Mum. 'Will you stay for a couple of weeks?' I wept down the phone. 'Yes, I will. Goodie!' I heard Mum clap her hands with delight. Like a harpy I had banished her from the birth, only to summon her back as first mate. Mum flew in and skipped up the concrete steps to our flat, clutching her purple paisley handbag and her floral suitcase. I had moved out of home when I was seventeen, but now Mum and I were reunited with a new project: my daughter.

Mum slept on The Worst Sofa in the World at night, claiming it was comfortable. She bottlefed Fearne — 'not too fast, not too fast'. If she pulled the teat away, Fearne would start wailing because she liked to smash her bottles back. Rich cycled to work each morning. Mum sat beside me during the day, as though the sofa was a sandbank. I pumped with her there, because it was less depressing that way. She sterilised the bottles for each round, the microwave lit up and spinning in its orbit.

Local mothers made me hearty things like pea soup and toasted baguettes. 'God bless you!' Mum opened the door and hugged one woman who was virtually a stranger to me, an artist and mother who knew what it was like to live on no sleep for days, in the doldrums, alone and drifting. She gave me a fridge magnet that read: 'Good things are to come'. But the good things didn't come. Not right away.

~

I visited a Plunket nurse with Mum, in a wooden villa near the sea not far from my father's house, the dim sound of waves crashing against the shore. The shrewd nurse watched my funny little mother dither over a plastic changing mat, looking for wet wipes.

'Do you work as a caregiver?' she asked.

Mum paused and looked up, a friendly manatee startled in the surf. 'I did once train as a nurse.'

I sat on a chair limply holding Fearne as the nurse explained how to latch correctly. I tried to follow her instructions. The room was in shadows. It had a feeling of total dreariness, or perhaps that was just me? I was dressed in trackpants and fatigued from the long-haul nights.

The lactation expert turned her attention on me. 'Even blind women can breastfeed,' she said. 'Close your eyes.' Somehow, I was meant to feel it.

Years ago, a pervy photographer had told me to *feel it*, as he took photos of me dressed up in fifties lingerie in a makeshift set in his warehouse apartment. I was a barmaid in a strip club at the time, hell-bent on being beautiful.

Salty tears rolled down my face. When it came to babies, I was blind and blindsided.

'It must be a terrible shock for a woman of forty,' my aunt said over the phone. Her comment circled around and around in my head like an animatronic shark. I hated how my age had become part of the equation — the wrong sum entered into the spreadsheet.

'I don't know if I would have been any better at this in my twenties!' I raged to Mum.

She nodded, empathised. 'I think I found having a baby very hard,' Mum said thoughtfully. Oh Mum. That annoyed me too. Surely post-natal depression wasn't another thing I had inherited from her.

'It's like a love affair,' the barracuda said on her last visit.

I held Fearne in my arms. She stared up at me.

'She knows you are her people.'

Mum sat beside us. It was a love affair. It was also a terrible shock for a woman of forty.

~

I lay on the sunken Egyptian sofa in the lounge and made the phone call. I was destabilised, turned over on my side, shivering, beneath a blanket. My voice sounded far away, muffled, as though coming from the inner recesses of a shell. I had to answer a series of questions. 'Do you feel like harming your baby?' said the woman at the other end of the line.

'No,' I said, aghast. 'I feel like harming myself.'

It was true. I was shipwrecked, boob-lashed, harpooned by lack of sleep. I wished I were dead because I couldn't imagine how else I might rest. Just a drop of sleep. One sip. 'Sleep deprivation is a form of torture.'

~

In seahorses, it is the male that carries the embryos in a pouch in its tail. After Rich cycled home from work each day, he'd strap on the frontpack and take Fearne out walking, walking, so I could rest. Then the nightshift, the seahorse asleep; Mum back on duty, joining me as I pumped through the night. We'd be in our dressing gowns on the couch, the microwave spinning until morning came. Then we did it all again.

'We're so glad you came here,' Mum said. 'We're so glad you came to our house.' Fearne lay on the baby blanket and stared up into Mum's hazel eyes. 'I found motherhood hard,' Mum said again. She had spent the first three months after I was born living with my grandparents. Perhaps when I was born and only a few months old, my own grandmother had said the same thing to me? 'We're so glad you came here to our house.'

Mum decided she would be called Nana. 'Okay, Nana,' I said. My grandmother had been a Nana too. Mum understood how tired I was, how I hadn't properly slept for days, so she sent me away for one precious night to my father's house by the sea. I woke only once that night, when the alarm went off, and pumped my engorged tits — they'd taken on a weird life of their own and were functioning like stars in a distant galaxy, about to fucking explode.

'Didn't you hear the storm?' my father and his girlfriend asked in the morning.

'What storm?' I replied.

~

Another night our flat on the hill shook from side to side. A catastrophic cry came from deep in the earth, this awful rolling sound. 'Earthquake!' Rich and I leapt out of bed and stood in our doorway. Mum sat up, dazed, on the Egyptian sofa. The hanging lightshade in the lounge zigzagged backwards and forwards, then the earthquake changed direction, rattling the house up and down. 'Megan!' Rich shouted, as I ran from the doorway to Fearne's room and snatched her out of the bassinet.

The earthquake had ripped through the South Island, collapsing the road to Kaikōura. No one in Wellington had died, but the next day no one went to work. Buildings across the city were inspected. I lay on my bed, unable to relax.

I'd dropped anchor and was finally hitting the bottom. Mum lay beside me and touched my face with the palm of her hand. 'It will be okay.'

~

'I think you've never needed help before,' said the kind blonde counsellor I found. She ended up seeing me once a week all through that first sleepless year, when I wore trackpants and a black sweatshirt that read AWFUL in white capital letters. The crying, the crying, my daughter like a Rubik's cube always handed back to me, and I loved her, adored her, but I also wanted to sleep for more than four unbroken hours in a row.

So many quotes from the abyss that wouldn't ever wind up on a fridge magnet.

'It must be a terrible shock for a woman of forty.'

'Sleep deprivation is a form of torture.'

'But Megan you don't know anything about babies!'

'If the mother is calm, the baby will be calm.'

'Have you had a banana?'

'Sleep deprivation is a form of torture.'

Sleep consultants are also a form of torture.

I wasn't calm one night when I woke up at 3am and Fearne was screaming like a siren next to me. Night terrors. I held her swaddled in a blanket, paced outside the flat in our tiny brick courtyard, looking up at the white moon. Fearne was startled into silence by the night air — the look of her soft cheek, in the moonlight, her eyes darting around, drinking in the world.

~

The doctor put me on antidepressants, though I refused to admit I was depressed.

'I just need some sleep! And people say that if the mother is calm, the baby will be calm,' I told the doctor.

She rolled her eyes. 'It's all bullshit,' she said.

I smiled with relief. Could have hugged her, but instead sat in her chair and bawled my eyes out.

'I'm not depressed, I just need more than four hours of broken sleep.'

Mum went home. Exodus of the Nana. I was ready to go at motherhood alone. Full throttle. Rich and I played Paul Simon's 'Graceland' every morning before he cycled to work. *I'm going to Graceland, Graceland*. I joined a Facebook group for women with post-natal depression — a dark echo chamber of sad thoughts — then a local group for new parents, called Space. I pushed Fearne there each week in her bright-yellow Bugaboo stroller. I had a banana en route. I was cracking on with motherhood, one nap at a time. 'Sleep when the baby sleeps.' But Fearne wanted to be awake.

Space was run by two women — one was a hippy with long crinkly hair who reminded me of Neil from *The Young Ones*, except happier. The older lady had a mouse-like quality; she was small and sensitive, highly attuned to our environment. She said one day on the mat, 'Having my first child was like growing a heart on the outside of my body.'

Yes. I understood. I was wearing my heart on the outside of my body too, under my black sweatshirt with the word AWFUL emblazoned on it.

That first year was full of anthropomorphic glee. 'Galoop went the little green frog one day! Galoop went the little green frog.'

I took home a booklet of nursery rhymes and sang to Fearne as I bathed her. 'I had a little turtle, his name was Tiny Tim, I put him in the bathtub to see if he could swim. He drank up all the water, he ate up all the soap, now he's lying sick in bed with bubbles in his throat. Bubbles, bubbles, bubbles, bubbles, bubbles, bubbles!'

I clapped my hands together. POP.

~

Finally, Fearne started sleeping through the night — once, twice, then again. My mind quickened. I stopped scrolling, scrolling, in the post-natal Facebook group, dabbling in its rivers of misery, and joined the MerNetwork instead. I became a junior member of the Oceania pod. The website was antiquated, it had obviously been made years ago, each forum like a sequence of interlocking rock pools. 'I'm interested in the history of professional mermaids,' I posted in one thread. 'Want to chat?' I pushed Fearne around in her bright-yellow Bugaboo, thinking about what mermaids do for work.

Fragments. Books. Poems. 'I have heard the mermaids singing, each to each. I do not think that they will sing to me.' Who said that?

I was going to find out.

4.

I've Heard the Mermaids Skyping

I hung the Waterhouse above my desk the day I started to call. She was my talisman, like the figurehead on the prow of a ship. The figure in *A Mermaid* by John William Waterhouse is the benchmark of what a mermaid should — or could — look like. I glanced up at her, seated on the rocky foreshore, her tail wound around her waist. Its silvery blue scales rose up her hips like a coat of amour. Her skin is almost pearlescent, belly slightly plump, and there's a faint hint of her bare breast, a peek of nipple showing beneath her arm. She combs her hair because she is in character. In the painting, the sea rushes towards her, foaming at its briny mouth.

She is an artist's model — perhaps Muriel Foster, the famous English contralto, who allegedly inspired several Waterhouse paintings. I don't know which fish posed for the tail, but it reeks of precision, of a specimen observed closely from life. The mermaid is young, but not a child. She is ready to lure sailors on to the rocks. The details in Waterhouse's painting all seem present and correct — yes, a mermaid is just like this. Her tail is a tad small, perhaps, but it's hard to tell because it is coiled around her bum, its full length unknown. Her mouth is open, but she has never — literally — spoken a word to me.

I had picked up the Waterhouse in Greytown, a small colonial town just over the winding Remutaka Range from Wellington. What the mermaid was doing in landlocked Greytown is beyond me. But we were on our first weekend getaway. Rich wore Fearne in the frontpack, slumbering, as I riffled through the stack of prints in a corner of the shop and found *A Mermaid* leaning against the wall in her plain black frame. I had to have her. Perhaps I liked her because she was alone? I might have felt differently if she was jacked up to a breast pump, sitting on a second-hand nursing chair, wearing an open chambray shirt with her tits out.

Waterhouse painted *A Mermaid* in 1900 and gifted it to the Royal Academy in London. He may — or may not — have been inspired by Alfred, Lord Tennyson's poem 'The Mermaid':

> Who would be
> A mermaid fair,
> Singing alone,
> Combing her hair
> Under the sea,
> In a golden curl
> With a comb of pearl,
> On a throne?

Quite a few people, it turns out. Waterhouse's mermaid is a babe, her mythology a convenient excuse for an artist in the prudish nineteenth century to depict a woman with her kit off. A mermaid combs her hair like a woman in a state of undress in her bedroom chamber. As Sophie Kinsella writes, the mermaid is 'the nineteenth-century equivalent of a page three girl, naked from the waist up but unavailable from the waist down'. And an early reviewer of *The Mermaid* had written, 'The chill of the sea lies ever on her heart; the endless murmur of the waters is a poor substitute for the sound of human voices; never can this beautiful creature, troubled with emotion, experience on the one hand unawakened repose, on the other the joys of womanhood.'

Whatever. I had still not experienced the joys of womanhood, even though I had been a woman forever. I thought the chill of the sea looked . . . inviting? Waterhouse's mermaid spoke to me of sadness, of solitude, of long walks with my father along the dense, freighted sand, the airplanes roaring overhead and the seagulls strutting around in the dunes, cawing at each other, and flying crooked on the wind. I saw Waterhouse's mermaid as a reflection of who I once was, or who I wanted to be. Beautiful, mysterious, sexy, arty. She could be sitting on the rocks at Lyall Bay, the scent of fish 'n' chips wafting in from the shop beyond. When I look at her, I'm drawn into the pleasure of being alone, brushing my long hair, having just drowned a crew of sailors and sent their vessel to the ocean floor.

~

The pixels clicked into place like scales, and Aysun swam into view, wearing fine-rimmed glasses. Her eyes so very blue.

'Hi, I'm nervous,' I said. 'You're my first mermaid.'

'I'm nervous too,' she replied. Her voice was soft and calm.

I felt like a passport officer in a booth at customs. I had a match. Aysun looked like Waterhouse's mermaid, but she was even more beautiful — vaguely Russian. She had long dark hair and a pale, otherworldly complexion. I could imagine her swallowing a shot of Stoli.

Aysun told me her real name was Carly Seaman. 'It was a terrible surname until I became a mermaid and then it became significantly less so.' She was a twenty-five-year-old Texan woman who worked each summer in the mermaid lagoon at a Renaissance fair.

'The first season we were supposed to speak a made-up language called Mermish, which was an awful idea. I have no idea how I made it through eight weekends just sitting there staring at people.'

'Can you remember any Mermish?' I asked.

'*Aslaoo* was hello. *Mucama mucama* was supposed to be thank you.'

I wrote down 'aslaoo' on my piece of paper, then 'mucama mucama'. Renaissance faires or 'rennies' are make-believe events, a big deal in America. Carly had started out as a punter at the medieval fair, then saw an advert for mermaids. She applied and joined the cast, choosing the name Aysun because it was the Turkish word for moon.

'If you want to be a believable mermaid,' Carly told me, 'you need to choose a tail that suits your colouration. So you look like a cohesive creature and not a person in a costume.'

She swung her laptop around and showed me the tail hanging on her bedroom wall, like a piece of taxidermy. Pearlescent blue, with two enormous eyespots in the fluke. She had designed it herself. It glowed in the dark.

Why would a mermaid have moons in her tail? Carly had looked to butterfly wings for inspiration. Eyespots are a camouflage mechanism to ward off predators by mimicking the eyes of the predators' own enemies. Many fish have them too. Carly had tweaked the eyespots in her tail to look like crescent moons — a detail that helped make her character believable.

'I'm an over-thinker and as a child this fact would have interested me,' she said.

'I'm an over-thinker, too,' I said. (Or did I just think it?)

Carly also makes a good truth sandwich. If a child touches her tail and says, *That feels like rubber*, she agrees. *You know what else feels like rubber? Dolphins.*

She told me there was a big debate in the mermaid community on whether mermaids had to have long hair or not. 'Some people say, if mermaids really existed, they wouldn't have hair at all, because water animals typically don't.'

I kept looking at her face and then mine in the square of

my screen. I put my hair up, then let it tumble down, trying to make myself look more attractive. I related to Carly as though she was a reflection of the younger me. 'What about merverts?' I asked, showing her I had done my research and knew the lingo — was sensitive to the workplace realities of the professional mermaid. At work in the lagoon, Carly told me, she once had to fend off the slippery kiss of an old man with a digital camera and a cane. He lurched up to her for a photo opportunity then planted a fast one on her lips.

'It was the epitome of all things icky,' she said. 'And I was mad because we're supposed to have back-up. In a mermaid tail, you can't get up.'

However, Carly's main problem was keeping her routine fresh. In her second year at the lagoon, she had developed a mersona as Aysun, a mermaid from the Black Sea. To the chagrin of some, she picked a Russian character, because that is the only accent she can do.

'Why chagrin?' I asked.

'Some people in the mermaid community get really angry about the issue of cultural appropriation.'

I sat on the other side of the screen feeling stupid. I knew the term from its application in contemporary art but had never thought about a mermaid being called out for it.

'Now I've grown into the role,' Carly said. 'I've started to learn Russian.' Her accent was now so convincing that many people believed she was from Russia. 'Some patrons are easy to fool.'

'Can you do Aysun for me?'

Carly clicked into character and her Rs started to roll.

'Hello, is good to be meeting you. Do you have any questions for me?'

It was a solid Slavic accent; she had it down pat.

'What do you think fascinates people about mermaids?' I asked.

Her face pixelated like a jigsaw puzzle broken apart.

'Do you think,' I stumbled, 'mermaids have to be beautiful?'

She reassembled on the other side of the screen, so lovely

I was amazed she wasn't a famous actress or model. 'People assume mermaids are beautiful, but I don't think they have to be. Mermaids are ethereal and otherworldly even if they're not typically beautiful. They're beautiful because they're almost human, but they're not.'

'What do you eat?' I asked.

'I prefer babies. I love milk-fed meat. Every picture I have with a baby is of me holding it under the ribs pretending to bite it. If people walk past with a baby all swaddled, I will say, "I see you have that one wrapped up to go".'

I could relate. Every picture I had of myself now was also with a baby.

'Also oranges, because oranges float,' Aysun said.

~

I hung up, saved the audio file, opened Excel and typed Aysun's details into Megan's Mermaid Log. I looked up at Waterhouse's mermaid, in her black picture frame. She was beautiful and evocative, but she wasn't on Skype. Nor did she know that oranges float. It was late afternoon, our small flat in shadows again. Fearne's toys tumbled over the carpet behind me. The soft toy Peppa Pig Mum had brought her lay on the plastic farmyard playing mat. Easy for spills. Her wooden rocking horse sat stationary. The plastic gate we had bought second-hand — red, yellow and green — was installed around the TV, waiting for her to return.

~

'Did she nap?' That was my number-one question to the all-female staff at Fearne's daycare, a short walk from our flat.

'Yes, she had a good afternoon nap.'

The daycare teacher, Lynn, had printed out a photo of Fearne wearing a tiger suit, with a long thick tail that trailed along the floor. 'She just loves dressing up as Tiger! This kind of role play is quite unusual for her age.'

'Is it?' I said, flushed with pride.

'Her language is very good too,' Lynn said.

'She loves talking,' I said. 'She talks a lot at home.'

The daycare regularly posted updates of Fearne's day in their sharing platform. They had recently posted a photo of Fearne pretending to talk into the phone. Mum was always the first to answer these posts. 'Oh thank you! I'm so delighted to hear these updates about Fearne's progress. Isn't she clever?! Love Nana!!!' It was sweet but annoying.

I collected Fearne's crocodile backpack and her jacket from the hook, then we walked home together, hand in hand.

Rich came in the door, taking off his bike helmet.

'Hello Daddy, did you have a good day?' she said.

Rich and I looked at each other, bowled over. Then burst out laughing.

'Crikey dicks,' Rich said. 'Where did that come from?'

Every day more words and even full sentences seemed to pop out of nowhere.

Bedtime was my time. I warmed her milk, and she twined her hand through my hair. I read her *Father Bear Comes Home*, a Little Bear book I got from the library. I got it out because I loved the Maurice Sendak illustrations, but I was surprised when I turned the page and discovered a mermaid. Father Bear has been out fishing in the middle of the ocean, where the mermaids are. In the story the mermaid is elusive, because she is shy.

'Mummy, why are mermaids shy?' Fearne asked.

'They're a bit like the cats next door,' I suggested.

'Is that mermaid shy?' Fearne pointed at a picture of a professional mermaid on my laptop.

'Yes, but not so shy she doesn't want her photo taken,' I said.

'Is that you?' Fearne looked up at the Waterhouse print.

'No,' I said. 'But she does have pale skin like me.'

'Is she your friend?' Fearne asked.

'Yes,' I said. 'But do you know who's my best friend?'

Fearne looked at me. 'Who?'

'You. You are my best friend.' I kissed the crown of her head, breathed in the lovely maple-syrup scent of her.

Rich called from the bedroom, 'LAME!'

I laughed. 'Shut up, Daddy Pig.'

~

Once I started skyping mermaids, I couldn't stop. I wanted one of every kind. I kept their stats in my Mermaid Log: name, date, location on the world map. Every time I opened my laptop, Skype's aquatic ringtone rippled out across the net. The blue circular icon pulsed, in and out.

'The number-one thing you do is interact with children,' said Mermaid Callie. Skype number two. I was disappointed. The idea of mermaids as children's entertainers didn't float my boat.

I gazed at Callie on Skype. She had long, curly brown hair and vivid blue eyes. Her mouth was quite toothy but she was still gorgeous, dressed in jeans and seated on her sofa somewhere in California. 'This is the furthest inland I've ever lived,' she said.

Callie had been a mermaid for three years, but was also a full-time counsellor. 'I have a wonderful job and I'm financially secure,' Callie said. 'I'm a professional mermaid because people pay me to do it. I have a hobby that pays for itself. It's certainly not a career. And I'm much older than most mermaids. I'm going to be forty-one in a couple of years.'

'I'm forty-two,' I confessed. My age had become a confession, as though I was trying to account for the fact that time was running out. I was doing everything, including motherhood, too late.

'What mermaid stories or films did you like as a child?' I asked.

'I really connected to Dante's *Divine Comedy*,' Callie mused. 'I liked the sirens in the Circle of Hell. I read *The Iliad* and *The Odyssey*.'

I was shocked. I hadn't read Homer's epics and I had not

expected the mermaids to namecheck any references older than Hans Christian.

I knew vaguely that the siren had started life in Greek antiquity as half-bird, half-woman, before morphing into a fish-tailed version. But the birdwomen didn't do it for me. I didn't want to hang Waterhouse's print of *Ulysses and the Sirens* above my desk — it wasn't sexy to see a woman's head pasted on to a bird of prey. In *The Odyssey*, the sirens are deadly, especially to mariners. What the sailors fear, however, is not their claws, but their voices, their song. Passing by the sirens' island, Ulysses tells his men to tie him to the mast of his ship so he can hear that song without being tempted to his death. The sailors stick wax in their ears. It is knowledge that the sirens' song bestows.

'I've never met a mermaid who wasn't a total attention whore,' Callie said.

I laughed in grim recognition. On the MerNetwork it was clear that some sirens had louder voices than others, but like Ulysses I was strapped to the mast, ready to listen.

'What inspired your name?' I asked.

'Many years back my family had a Creole name, Kalizere, but I shortened it to Callie. Mermaid Callie is easy for children to say and remember.'

Every mermaid surprised me, because every mermaid was a real woman. It was like I was shucking open oysters and finding pearls in every one.

Callie had originally dressed up as a mermaid for a local festival but got asked repeatedly — *Can I hire you? Do you do kids parties? Do you do events?* 'It's been non-stop since then.' Every year she attended the Pirate Invasion at Long Beach, with her mertender in tow. 'He's much bigger and burlier than my husband. It takes a lot of trust to let someone carry you around like that.' The mertender carried her on- and off-stage in her tail.

'How much does beauty matter?' I asked. This was the question that got under my skin, like a knife searing through a fish's stomach, pulling out the guts.

'I know people who don't consider themselves physically beautiful who are mermaids because it fills their soul,' Callie said. 'However, in a professional sense, I also know many mermaids who can't get hired, because they aren't viewed by society as conventionally beautiful.'

My favourite photograph of Callie on her Facebook page was a close-up of her face as she lay on the beach, reaching towards the camera, beads of sand on her tanned skin. It was a seductive pose, a siren's call.

'It's the idea of living in the ocean that's beautiful,' Callie said. 'I love the Pacific, like a person almost. When I dip my feet or my fingers in it, I feel like it washes away something. It's healing.

'I love the power of water, how you can have a single drop this small that's innocuous, or a tidal wave that takes thousands of lives. It's heavy and it's light — it's the most gorgeous thing in the world.'

~

T. S. Eliot wrote 'The Love Song of J. Alfred Prufrock' in 1915 when he was only twenty-two. Bastard — I hate an overachiever. His line 'I have heard the mermaids singing, each to each. I do not think they will sing to me' is one of the most famous mermaid refrains in literature. I vaguely knew the line from an old eighties movie, *I've Heard the Mermaids Singing.*

Eliot's poem is twenty stanzas long and has hardly any mermaids in it. They only make a cameo at the end:

> I have seen them riding seaward on the waves
> Combing the white hair of the waves blown back
> When the wind blows the water white and black.
> We have lingered in the chambers of the sea
> By sea-girls wreathed with seaweed red and brown
> Till human voices wake us, and we drown.

Most of the poem is about poor middle-aged Prufrock, his head grown bald, shambling through the streets in his rolled-up linen trousers. The poem is a stream-of-consciousness lament, a solid-gold modernist classic. It begins, 'Let us go then, you and I, / When the evening is spread out against the sky . . .' Prufrock is the narrator, though he may just be talking to himself. The poem winds along 'certain half-deserted streets', covering 'restless nights in one-night cheap hotels, and sawdust restaurants with oyster-shells'. Prufrock famously measures out his life in coffee spoons. I could relate.

The 'Love Song' was Eliot's first published poem — I couldn't imagine the immense satisfaction he must have felt after polishing it off, let alone going on to pump out *The Waste Land* next. It was packed full of existential cliff-hangers: 'Do I dare / Disturb the universe?' Prufrock asked. 'Do I dare to eat a peach?' Good questions! I definitely dared to eat a peach, though I preferred a nectarine.

Prufrock struck me as a certain kind of strip-club regular, shy and awkward, stewing in his own intellectual juices. He's being eaten alive by his own bad nature, his tendency to melancholy. But I also related to the women in the poem, the ones in the room who come and go, talking of Michelangelo. Perhaps they were art writers like me?

When the poem was first published one critic said, 'The fact that these things occurred to the mind of Mr. Eliot is surely of the very smallest importance to anyone — even to himself.' Time had proved that critic a moron. 'I have seen the moment of my greatness flicker,' Prufrock observes. Haven't we all?

I speedread Prufrock several times. I wanted the meaning of the mermaids to drop out of the last stanza like a coin: 'Till human voices wake us and we drown.' But it remained opaque. What did Eliot mean? Who drowns? Presumably Prufrock? But who else? Not the mermaids!

I had other reservations too. The canonical works of literature and art about mermaids were produced by men. Isn't that why Prufrock worried that the mermaids wouldn't sing to him? He was a turn-off, perhaps an early forerunner of the mervert. I had caught Eliot out objectifying the mermaids, basting them in the male gaze. As a middle-aged woman, I wasn't afraid of relating to the mermaids, each to each.

~

Skype number three was a mermaid who could eat fire. She had a red dragon-like silicone tail with black accents. She was also a blacksmith and a welder. But her real claim to fame was creating the first video tutorial on how to make your own mermaid tail. She had uploaded it to YouTube in 2008, when there were hardly any silicone or fabric tails out there.

I watched the video. In her kitchen, Sasha sat cross-legged in a pair of blue jeans on the floor, a length of blue fabric laid out at her feet. Step by step she talked through how to choose the right fabric (a dance or swimwear fabric that you can get wet), how to divide your measurements (by running a piece of masking tape along your foot to your belly button) and how to make space in the fluke for the monofin. Sasha recommended a monofin over separate dive flippers to get a better flow in the water. Then she fed the fabric through her sewing machine, working her way around the tail. The video ended with Sasha dressed in her new blue tail and matching bikini top, rather than her jeans. She waved goodbye with her fluke.

Sasha had once auditioned to be one of the legendary Weeki Wachee mermaids. Weeki Wachee Springs in Florida is the only mermaid theme park in the world, with a submerged underwater theatre where audiences can watch live mermaid shows. I'd seen the vintage postcards of early mermaids supping soda bottles under water, one fetching dame perched on a giant plastic seahorse as though she was riding a carousel.

But Sasha didn't get the job, even though she had the best swim time. Instead she was falsely implicated in stealing another mermaid's purse from the changing room. It was their loss, not Sasha's, who told me that working as an independent mermaid was more lucrative and she still had her creative freedom, too.

By the end of our Skype, Sasha was trying to convince me to skydive.

'You should give it a go,' she enthused.

'You're so brave!' I said. 'I hate flying, let alone skydiving. I'd never jump out of a plane even with a parachute on.'

If I'd thought about it, I might have realised I sounded like Prufrock.

~

I turned down the Skype ringtone. It was late at night. I was prepared to disturb the universe but I didn't want to wake Fearne up, not after I'd just spent an hour getting her to bed.

'Where was your first swim?' I asked. The Dragonfly Mermaid was the youngest mermaid I had interviewed so far, and my first mermaid who lived in the United Kingdom.

'At Stokes Bay. I got into the tail like I'd seen others do on the internet before. I learned from them and copied them. Even though the sea was rough that day, I felt so natural, as though I was part of the place. It was wonderful.'

'Who videos you underwater?' I asked. The underwater photographer played an integral role. It was hard to get good underwater images.

'My father,' she said. 'He's an optometrist. He gets quite worried when I swim without goggles on. He's never swum as a merman, but as a cameraman he's fantastic.'

The image of the Dragonfly Mermaid's father swimming beside her, keeping time with her dream, floored me.

'He goes deeper than I do,' she said.

'Mummy, mummy!' Fearne was awake. I heard Rich trying to hold her in the lounge, but she wanted me. My daughter stumbled hollering to the bedroom where I sat at my desk, lit by the white glow of the MacBook. Her eyes pink, her arms reaching for me.

'It's okay, it's okay. Mummy's just talking to a mermaid,' I said.

~

On my fifth call I hit the jackpot.

In 1983, Robert Short got the call from Ron Howard and was hired to work as a special effects artist on *Splash* because he was a certified diver and had a background as a creature designer. Robert had co-handled the makeup effects in the first *Piranha* film. He knew how to dolphin-kick. He could hold his breath for up to three minutes underwater. He could swim upside down like *The Creature from the Black Lagoon.*

For Madison's tail, Robert found a new product on the market called Skin Flex. It was a type of urethane; at the time it was being used in theme parks. Robert was looking for a product more durable than latex, but still flexible, so you wouldn't notice the tail bending at the knees when the mermaid was out in the open ocean. He and his crew tweaked the product's formula, getting the consistency just right so it would set. 'It was a state-of-the-art, cutting-edge material at the time. Since then, other companies have created dragon's skin silicone which people make commercial tails out of now.'

In 1983, Robert had no access to the internet. He sat in his one-room apartment in Santa Monica with a sketch pad on his lap and some ink markers. 'Hey, that's an orange tail. I'll flare it down that way . . . Yeah, that looks pretty cool . . . Hey, Ron — what do you think?'

Robert had become an unofficial godfather of the mermaid community. He attended events and conventions, spoke at mermaid conferences. All the mermaids knew him, Mermaid Raina from Halifax had connected us. Raina was a high-profile mer with her own business in Canada, a country that she joked was freezing and had few swimming pools — not obvious mermaid country. Yet she fell down the rabbit hole after watching *Splash*. 'Did Ron Howard even realise what he was starting?'

Robert had first met Daryl Hannah when she came around to have her body cast. I couldn't believe I was speaking to someone who had even met Daryl Hannah, let alone cast her body in a fibreglass mould.

'The *Splash* tail has been so influential,' I gushed. 'What role do you think the movie played in the modern mermaid movement?'

Robert was humble, but agreed that *Splash* and Disney's *The Little Mermaid*, released five years later, were touchstones. 'When I see someone in a *Splash*-inspired tail it brings a smile to my face. Part of the reason why so many people make tails today is the film . . . The ripples continue out.'

~

'Bounce, bounce this a-way, bounce bounce that a-way, bounce bounce all day, bounce bounce bounce.'

I watched from the sidelines as Rich twirled Fearne around the swimming pool in her togs and a pair of bright-pink water wings. The class was held on the top floor of a local hotel and was run by a Welsh man in a wetsuit, who sang the ridiculously catchy 'bounce bounce' song. Rich and the other fathers bounced their toddlers up and down in the pool, lightly raising the children in and out of the water. Rich sang along softly and shyly. He didn't like having his shirt off, felt his shoulders were too small, but he took one for the team.

I had noticed that swimming classes were often the domain of fathers. Occasionally I saw a bold mum in a bikini or a one-piece hop in with her child, whether she was wobbly or not, and God knows I admired her for it. I'd never had a beach body, but now on top of my white, freckled skin I had thick bubbly blue varicose veins coasting down one calf like tree roots and popping out of the other thigh.

I got my first varicose vein when I was only fourteen. The veins were a hereditary blip in my vascular system. Bad luck. I looked up the meaning of varicose veins in Mum's beloved copy of *You Can Heal Your Life*. Varicose veins supposedly represented being in a situation you hate, feeling overworked and overburdened.

Whatever, Louise. My varicose veins were simply a sign of age; my pregnancy had made them more pronounced. Resigned, I told myself it was okay to have ugly legs. Fuck! Maybe my thing about mermaids was because I hated my legs?

~

I set up a Google alert for professional mermaids and every morning new stories arrived in my inbox: 'Nurse fulfils her dream of becoming a mermaid'; 'Not a whale of a tail: You too can become a mermaid'; 'Fancy a career change?'

Another friend wanted to meet in town for a mermaid latte. 'I see mermaids everywhere now,' people told me. I saw mermaids everywhere, too.

Mermaids were coming at me from every angle, and I was coming at them slowly in a pair of trackpants, with a toddler in a blue Elsa dress singing, 'Let it go! Let it go!' It was our *Frozen* phase, and Fearne couldn't let it go. She watched bits of *Frozen* daily at home, stood in front of the TV and serenaded me. She loved to belt out the chorus with gusto: 'The cold never bothered me anyway.' It seemed to chime with something deep inside her. Small children can't let things go. She followed me to the toilet, she slept with me every night. I didn't care — at least she slept. I felt vaguely human again.

'It's not what you do after having a baby is it?' my friend the painter said. 'Do a lot of research into the history of mermaids?'

I laughed, delighted with myself. I couldn't shut up about the mermaids either. I felt everyone needed to know that there were woman right now across the world working as professional mermaids. And men too. And people who didn't identify with the gender binary.

Another mum I ran into at a café said, 'Did you get the idea from your daughter?'

I frowned. 'No. Fearne associates mermaids with me.' Fearne was interested in a lot of things: little stones she picked up on the street, me, Daddy, *Peppa Pig*, *In the Night Garden* reruns, *Meg and Mog* stories, baby dolls, playing baby dolls, ice cream, cheesy pasta, Nana, butterflies, and herself.

Another day I had coffee with two mums from the Space baby-group days. Ruth was a doctor, Esther worked in a government department. They both had boys and were a million times more sorted than me, but we'd bonded over 'Galoop went the little green frog'. Their friendship had kept me going when I knew no one else with a baby. Now, we saw each other infrequently — they were back at work — and the professional mermaids were keeping me going.

'I need to find a proper job soon,' I lamented. 'But I don't want to go back to project management. I can't bear it.'

Esther was my age; geriatric motherhood had forged an iron bond in us. Ruth the doctor was gorgeous and on to it. She was also ten years younger than us. I respected her and texted her for advice every time Fearne had a cold or minor ailment.

'I've got news,' Ruth said.

'What?' We looked at her expectantly.

'I'm having twins,' she said.

'You're joking!' I replied.

She wasn't joking.

'That's wonderful!' Esther gave her a hug.

But while Ruth was in the loo, I said to Esther, 'Thank God it is her. She's the only one of us who could handle it.'

'We're too old, hey,' said Esther, philosophically.

~

I booked a mermaid-themed birthday party for Fearne at a local indoor playground. Children's birthday parties are stress pits, with multi-coloured ball pits inside them. They also take planning. The cake, made by Rich, was a masterpiece, shaped like a hedgehog, with chocolate buttons instead of spikes.

Mum got out of the car, held Fearne's hand and started waddling to the front door, her bag held purposefully over her shoulder.

Fearne had been coaxed into a mustard top and a black denim mini skirt. She looked sharp. 'You're a fashion icon,' I told her.

The fashion icon hurtled through the doors and into the big inflatable play area. Her little friends from daycare started turning up. Time for bad coffee in Styrofoam cups and stalled conversation with other half-known parents.

Nana came into her own. 'I'm Fearne's nana!' she proudly announced, plonking down next to the other parents and asking them all sorts of questions.

'Megan, doesn't she just suit every colour?' Mum said.

Mini sausage rolls and chips eventually rotated out of the dire kitchen and the children dipped their fingers and chips into tomato sauce. Rich watched shrewdly as other children ate carrots. Fearne's taste for carbs and chocolate was not going down well with Daddy Pig.

Ruth and Esther from Space turned up. We watched our three-year-olds surfing the giant inflatable slide.

'They're growing up fast, hey?' said Esther.

'Someone has to,' I said. Then we all bitched about Esther's partner who left her when her son was only one year old.

'What a narcissus,' Ruth said.

'How are the mermaids?' Esther asked.

'Good,' I said. 'I've identified "the Mermaid Trifecta".' I told them about Hannah Mermaid, but also about the other two key pioneers I had discovered. 'MeduSirena is an aquatic performer who runs an underwater burlesque show at The Wreck Bar in Florida,' I said. 'And Mermaid Linden lives in Los Angeles and is a children's entertainer with her own YouTube series. She once performed as a mermaid at Jessica Alba's daughter's birthday party. And she performed at Justin Timberlake's kids' birthday too,' I said. 'They work separately but jokingly refer to themselves as "the Mermaid Trifecta".'

Nana tugged on my arm. 'Megan, do you think we should open presents now?' She looked tired and ready to go home. Poor Nana.

'Okay,' I said. This part of the birthday ritual was especially traumatic.

Fearne ripped open each present with zeal, barely regarding it before moving on to the next one. Ruth gave her a *That's Not My Mermaid* touchy feely book.

'I couldn't resist,' she said.

'Look Fearne!' I flicked through the pages. '"That's not my mermaid, her hair is too fluffy".' Personally, I didn't think her hair was too fluffy. I've seen worse. And how could her tail be too scaly? That didn't even make sense.

~

In the changing rooms, I stepped into my blue retro bikini, with the generous behind. Rich got into his swimming trunks. Fearne had a cute one-piece decorated with stylised waves. She loved to swim and I hated to say no to her. Together we trod past erupting fountains of ebullient water and terse-faced eaters at the indoor café.

We opened the gate to the toddler splash pool. Fearne adored the brightly coloured plastic balls — yellow, pink, blue — that floated in the toddler pool. She was not worried about how she looked in her sea-wave swimming costume. She was only three years old and I wanted her to enjoy herself. Then I spotted the banker from our antenatal group. Brilliant. My wobbliness exposed. My lack of assets.

The banker was good-looking in a semi-Patrick Bateman kind of way. His wife wasn't there. As always, the toddler pool was mainly dad territory. We waved and smiled.

In the mid-thigh water, the banker asked me what I was up to. I told him about my professional mermaid interviews.

'What do mermaids do?' he asked. His daughter barrelled into the water, confident. Fearne scooped a gathering of plastic balls into her arms.

'Most are children's entertainers,' I said.

'Figures,' said the banker, nonchalantly. 'It's either gonna go one way or the other.'

I knew, instantly, that he meant strippers.

'The mermaid has been associated with sex work since the Middle Ages,' I told him. 'But actually hardly any mermaids work in strip clubs.' I often passed the darkened windows of the Mermaid Bar, a strip club on Wellington's main drag. Once the club had allegedly had a tank but it became a health and safety nightmare and was removed. The billboard advertising on the side of the club read: 'Never ignore the call of the mermaids'. In my experience no one ever did.

~

At home, a letter arrived for Rich from Dawson, his best friend in the UK. He opened the envelope and a silver mermaid keyring fell out. Her fluke was embossed: 'Always be yourself, unless you can be a mermaid, then always be a *mermaid*.'

Rich passed the keyring to me. 'Disappointing,' he said.

~

Are mermaids feminists? Yes. But which wave?

My new pen pal, medievalist Sarah Peverley might be able to tell me. 'Belonging, not belonging, or straddling two worlds is at the heart of the mermaid's appeal,' she wrote.

Sarah was a redhead, around my age, who worked at Liverpool University and was writing not one but two mermaid books. I sent her a long list of questions and pored over her answers. *Once upon a time humanity believed in mermaids. We looked out into the sea and saw gods and goddesses reflected back.*

The earliest depictions of mermaids and mermen date to ancient Mesopotamia — the first mermaid with a known story attached to her is the goddess Atargatis. Once folklore began to be written down, mermaid sightings became popular and were reported in local newspapers. Artists — Waterhouse and co. — depicted mermaids, water nymphs and other magical creatures as fetching young women with their kits off, circumventing censorship. Then came the advent of photography and film. Mermaid performers surfaced in circuses, fairs and travelling curiosity shows, alongside bearded ladies. Mermaids also burst into cinema. The Australian swimmer and vaudeville performer Annette Kellerman invented 'aquaballet' and became the first woman to wear a swimmable mermaid tail on film — she even produced her own range of early swimsuits for women. Clearly a feminist icon.

Kellerman I knew about thanks to Mermaid Raina from Halifax. Raina had her own disabilities, and was inspired by Kellerman because she'd had weak legs as a child and first started swimming on her doctor's orders. 'I thought, if she can do it a hundred years ago, I can do it too.' Raina now had a tattoo of Kellerman — The Diving Venus — on her forearm.

We all had our favourite OG mermaid. Sarah's own personal touchstone was an early anime of *The Little Mermaid*. She empathised with the Little Mermaid because she didn't get what she wanted. But she understood why I was hooked on Madison and *Splash*, and agreed with me about the movie's influence.

'One of the reasons it's become a profession now is because girls who grew up watching *Splash* are now old enough and financially secure enough to purchase their own tails, but linked with this is increased accessibility. When I was younger, nobody of average means had a hope in hell of knowing a tail maker, finding one, or affording a tail. The internet has helped — now it allows professional mermaids to find an audience for what they do.'

Sarah showed me a photograph of herself swimming in a tail. The setting was dark-blue ultramarine, her tail a cold-water colour, her skin pale. 'Let's not forget,' she said, 'that these days, the rhetoric of living your dreams is very powerful.'

~

I wheeled Fearne to Rock and Rhyme at the library. In the children's section, the parents stationed their buggies around the edges of the room by the bookshelves. We sat on the carpet with our children and sang along to all the classic hits. 'The wheels on the bus go round and round' we sang in unison and disharmony, whether we had good voices or not, because we were good parents and we wanted our children to be happy. Then we launched into the terrible ear worm that is 'Baby Shark'. The song was as successful as the *Jaws* soundtrack, if not quite as revered.

'We tell ourselves stories in order to live,' Joan Didion once famously said. But we sing nursery rhymes in order to remember and also to pass the time and get some kind of socialisation happening. It was always good to get out of the flat and see other adults during the day.

I walked the library aisles with Fearne slumbering in the pram afterwards, stacking the bottom of the Bugaboo haphazardly with more *Meg and Mog* books. In the adult section I fished for books to help my mermaid quest. There were no books on or by Daryl Hannah. A shame. I longed to know what Daryl had to say about her own experience of working on *Splash*, and how that fed into her life now as an environmental activist.

'Megan, what are you doing?'

I looked up and saw a curator from the gallery. He was dressed in black jeans and a T-shirt, a tote bag slung casually over his shoulder. We'd known each other for decades, since I was a young video artist. He was the first curator to exhibit my appropriated videos and take me seriously. In the aisles of the film section, I pushed the Bugaboo back and forth, and gushed about my mermaid project.

'Great,' he replied, breezily. 'But what are you doing for work? We need someone to do some archival research at the gallery,' he said. 'It's a part-time gig though. I wondered if you'd be interested?'

'Email me,' I said.

~

The mermaids followed me down into the basement. I owed my job as an archivist to the king tide. The gallery was built on reclaimed land, near a lagoon. The basement of the gallery had flooded during a king tide. One night, water rose up through grilles in the concrete floor and drenched the analogue archive. After the floodwaters had subsided, screeds of old paperwork and ephemera had to be thrown away. Most of it was fine, waterlogged and crinkly but it dried out. Then I was sent in. I walked down the concrete steps, sorted out the past, one manila-box file at a time.

The basement had no natural light. The floor was painted a dense thick institutional grey. I sat in an alcove surrounded by box files. Inside each box were sheafs of photocopies, so many photocopies, and handwritten letters penned on flimsy blue paper that felt like forget-me-nots. I wore my black trackpants and a big, dark-blue sweatshirt that was adorned with a screen-print of a cabin in the wilderness and the phrase: HAPPY ALONE.

'This is like counting grains of sand on a beach,' I said to no one at all.

At lunch time, I climbed the stairs again to heat leftovers in the staffroom microwave. The conversation turned, as always, to mermaids.

'I wonder how mermaids have sex, if they don't have vaginas?' the curator blinked at me. It wasn't the first time he had pointed this out.

'Maybe that's part of the appeal,' I said. 'Limited availability.'

My mobile didn't get reception in the basement. I descended the stairs fretful, constantly strung out. What if something happened to Fearne at daycare and I missed the call? Days of treading water and sifting photocopies. Even down in the basement I could hear the mermaids calling. Not literally. I skyped when I got home.

~

Rachel was the Head Mermaid at Dive Bar in Sacramento. She was an illustrator who liked the Pre-Raphaelite Brotherhood and had a blue silicone tail nicknamed Huckleberry.

At the bar, Rachel's job was everything from costume repairs to the rosters, payroll and the two-month staff training process. Over Skype, we discussed the important things: *Splash* and the meaning of life. She grew up watching the film with her Dad. 'Daryl Hannah is so beautifully awkward. She's the perfect mermaid because she's just so out of place. She is discovering this world and she doesn't understand how it works — for her the traffic-stop light is beautiful because it lights up, you know? Just all of these really innocent, yet socially unacceptable things.'

Rachel worked alongside Barbosa, a batfish the size of a dinner plate, who did backflips if he got freaked out. 'He's actually been working at Dive Bar as long as I have.'

I had only worked with people and I had always found that hard enough, so I admired Rachel's compassion for her co-workers. A team of aquarists cared for the fish. They cleaned the tank at Dive Bar on Tuesdays and Fridays, scrubbing everything, and once a week they changed the water. As the Dragonfly Mermaid had also told me, the health and safety factors of running a mermaid show at an aquarium were a logistical nightmare.

Rachel gave me her view of the mermaid landscape: professionals have monetised and popularised the character. Diving centres now offered mermaid courses, and you could become a dive-qualified professional mermaid — completely legit. Recreational mermaids adopted their mersonas for cosplay, nostalgia or plain old fun. Sometimes this entailed helping the environment and sometimes it did not. And scholars, academics and historians were toiling away, trying to establish what the symbol of the mermaid meant.

Australia-based Philip Hayward was one of the academics, and the author of the book *Making a Splash*, an account of merfolk in twentieth- and twenty-first-century audiovisual media. It was a heavy read, even for me — its target audience. Philip was conceived in a guest house called The Three Mermaids, in an area north of Cornwall associated with mermaid legends — just down the coast from St Senara's Church at Zennor, with its famous mermaid chair.

His daughters have mermaid names —Miranda, and Madison, after famous mermaid films. Cute.

Philip also proposed that the sea monster in *The Creature from the Black Lagoon* was a butch aquatic hunk, the equivalent to the femme mermaid. 'The mermaid's tail itself is a phallus,' he said.

'I think you're on to something,' I replied.

'You should come to our Maritime Folklore and Mermaid conference in Copenhagen,' Philip said.

But the abstracts were due in under a week, and it cost over a thousand dollars plus travel and accommodation.

'Claire la Sirène is giving the keynote,' Philip said, reeling me in. 'She's from Paris.'

~

In the basement, I opened a box file releasing the scent of compressed time, that vague reek of paper that's been sitting around for decades. I found the last interview that New Zealand-born artist Alexis Hunter gave before she died. Hunter, also a redhead, had a day job in film animation and worked on the 1989 Disney film *The Little Mermaid*. Suddenly she surfaced in the archive, like a siren swimming up to my boat. 'I drew the foam,' Hunter said. I stopped and looked at her photograph on screen — a white-haired lady with a twinkle of mischief in her eyes. She had motor neurone disease and could no longer speak. She wrote her interview answers on an electronic pad. 'I drew the foam' was a feminist jibe.

I fished up a lonely, poorly photographed image by Alexis Hunter — a working drawing of a Melusine, a white goddess holding her two mermaid tails in each hand.

'Alexis, are you saying I should speak about *The Little Mermaid* and your work as a pioneering feminist for the conference in Copenhagen?' I said. No reply.

~

Some of my emails ran aground, but then the lawyer managing Alexis Hunter's estate sent me an email with a painting attached called *The Lure of the Sea*: a blue-tailed mermaid caught in an erotic embrace with the crest of a wave. The mermaid was pashing a man made of seafoam. And the painting was dated 1988 — the year before the Disney film was released.

I dragged and dropped it into my PowerPoint, then made my way upstairs into the light and told the curator my discovery over coffee.

Turned out, Alexis Hunter had seen one of my early exhibitions when I was still a video artist mashing up scenes from my own favourite childhood Disney films. 'Alexis really liked your videos,' he said casually. I blinked in the sunlight. Mermazed.

~

'Fearne!' Nana came running up the steps to our flat, with Rich following behind, carrying her garish purple floral suitcase.

'Nana!' Fearne cried, stood on the front step. She jumped up and down, a big unstoppable smile on her face.

Nana stretched out her arms and Fearne ran in for a hug. She'd arrived for a weekend visit, before we flew away to Copenhagen.

Rich boiled the jug and the rituals commenced. Her suitcase,

parked in the lounge by the TV. Her purple paisley handbag, plopped down beside the couch.

'Can I see your pills, Nana?' Fearne loved to play with Nana's pills.

'Oh yes, in a minute darling.'

The pills were a medical cornucopia that included anti-depressants and other bits and bobs that I assumed were about keeping her cancer at bay.

'Oh, that's a lovely cup of tea.' Mum blew on the beige-coloured water and sat the cup down on the floor beside her.

Fearne brought out her procession of baby dolls.

'Nana! You be the baby and I will be the mum,' Fearne said.

'Waaaah!' Mum sat on the floor with the baby dolls and played along. Her patience seemed limitless on these weekend trips. She always brought presents for Fearne. This time it was a copy of *The Little Mermaid*.

'Thanks, Mum,' I smiled.

'That's okay, darling. It's so nice to see you! And what's for tea?'

I felt my stomach tense. I neither knew nor cared what was for dinner. I could feed Fearne an endless buffet of pasta and grated cheese until the cows came home, but what about Nana?

'Do you have ice cream?' Mum asked.

'I'm not sure. We're out of everything. You don't like spicy food, do you? I better get to the shop and pick up some things.'

Fearne: 'I don't want to go to the shop.'

This cued a round of Nana's 'The Easy Song'.

'Let's make it easy,' she sang, swaying her arms back and forth in a jig. Rich said nothing but I could see the hair standing up on the back of his neck.

'Okay, that's enough,' I said. 'Let's get going.'

Nana said, 'You go on ahead,' even though we were only walking down the hill. On the way back up, I carried the shopping bags, but it was Nana who stopped every ten steps, and put her hand on her hip. 'You go on, darling.'

'Nana's having a wee rest,' she said to Fearne.

~

Before bed, Nana read Fearne *The Little Mermaid*, but Fearne couldn't bear the Sea Witch. 'Too scary,' she said.

Nana skipped that page.

'What did you think of the book?' Mum asked, when Fearne was finally asleep.

'It's a bit watered down,' I said. 'And I don't like the pictures.' The pictures were flippant, benign splashes of colour, no detail, or craft, the illustrator hadn't poured their soul into the book.

'Why? What's wrong with them?' Mum looked suddenly forlorn and offended. I had been caught off guard.

'But Fearne loved it. Do you want another cup of tea?' I flicked the jug on for her.

'Ahh that's a lovely cup of tea.'

'You always say that,' I told her.

'Do I, darling?'

'Yes, but then you don't drink it. You leave a trail of half-drunk teacups behind you wherever you go!'

Mum laughed, then got out her mint floss and started see-sawing a line through her teeth, as though Rich and I weren't even at home.

'Goodnight.' Rich slunk off to bed. I stayed up, my laptop open on my lap, Mum flossing alongside me. Sometimes she paused and looked at the floss, to see what she had gathered along it.

'Mermaid Rachel works with a batfish,' I said.

'What a hard case,' Mum said, laughing.

'Yeah, I had no idea fish had feelings and personalities. I'm getting great stuff, but I don't have time to transcribe the interviews. I barely have a minute to myself until Fearne goes to bed.'

'I can help,' Mum offered. Her hazel eyes sparkled. 'Send some to me and I can chip away at them at work.'

I chipped away, too, continuing my important research. A GIF of the animated mermaid from Disney's *Peter Pan* appeared in my Facebook stream. She lay on Marooners' Rock, hands behind her head, and fanned herself with her little feminine fluke. She was a dark-haired beauty, in a pale-pink shell-cup bra. The wanton, flirty little mermaid was exactly what I wanted to see. So serene on her rock, her arms tucked behind her head, daydreaming.

'Will you pray for our flights to Copenhagen?' I asked Mum.

'Yes, darling, I'll pray for you.'

Mum changed into her long nightie. She stared at her phone, beguiled by the blue-white glow from it, and I wondered what was so captivating inside her feed. 'What are you looking at?' I asked.

'Just Facebook,' she answered.

I was doing the same thing, staring at my feed like it was a handheld mirror. We were like the Disney mermaids on Marooners' Rock, idle and dreaming, barely awake to ourselves, feasting on something interior and insatiable, a private reservoir. We live to be seen. We live to share. We live to like.

I had quickly established that the number-one question children ask professional mermaids is, 'Are you real?'

'And are you real?' I asked one mermaid at the end of our Skype.

'I am real. I eat, sleep and breathe mermaiding,' she said. 'I'm as real as it gets.'

5.

A Selfie with the Selkie

I took a bottle of Phenergan on the flights. The aisles were dark and grainy, bodies twitched beneath airplane blankets, the shades were drawn down. We flew over expanses of ocean I knew nothing about. Our flight might suddenly plummet into the sea, our lives sink like coins to the bottom of the ocean floor, the black box the only clue to our fate. And when the plane reached that depth, I knew that Hannah Fraser would not flit past the wreck, her sequined tail glowing like a beacon of wealth and prosperity, because mermaids don't exist. Also, I still hadn't had the guts to email her and set up a Skype.

Flight two, the Phenergan didn't work. Fearne and I spent hours in the galley with the stewardesses, buckling and unbuckling Brown Teddy into a seat.

Fearne had a screaming fit at immigration when Brown Teddy was put in a grey container. 'Teddy! Teddy!' The screaming and sobbing escalated until eventually the immigration officer made a calculated decision and passed Brown Teddy back, unscanned. Fearne proceeded through customs, carrying him in her arms.

~

I was fourteen when Disney's *The Little Mermaid* came out and was already captivated by *Splash*, but for many women Ariel was their first mermaid. Of course, Disney had updated Andersen's original sad ending too — she doesn't lose her voice forever. Instead, Ariel is the plucky star of a lung-busting musical, in which she bags Prince Eric and everyone lives happily ever after. Even Sebastian the crab.

'We are the Disney generation,' Mermaid Jessica Pearl told me. She was an art school graduate, trained in underwater photography with a flair for the water goddess aesthetic. She and her best friend and muse, Amelia, were the Perth Mermaids. Their business had evolved from Facebook posts announcing their beach appearances. 'It just got bigger and bigger and bigger.'

Jess was the first mermaid I talked to who voiced a discomfort with her own body. 'When I started being a mermaid I wore a high-waisted tail, and a very covering bikini top and a net, I almost completely covered myself, but then slowly I gained more and more confidence, and before I knew it, I was wearing a bikini at the beach. I learned to accept my body for what it was. The effect on my self-confidence has been amazing.'

She also struggled with mental health. 'When you learn to freedive, it is very connected with mindfulness and anti-anxiety techniques. If you breathe out longer than you breathe in, your heartbeat automatically lowers. The mammalian dive reflex is a response your body has when immersed in water, that's why they tell you to splash your face when you are worked up, to plunge your whole face in water.'

I struggled with mental health too, but it was a secret.

I was impressed by what she said. I admired how this generation of young women were learning to turn the tide on their bodies and feel good about themselves. With her flammable hair and fetching green tail, cinched at the waist, Ariel, daughter of King Triton, is essentially a princess. At university, I'd been

— subliminally — encouraged to consider 'princesses' as inherently facile. Superficial. Unfeminist. But on the other hand, 'Ariel is a fully realized female character who thinks and acts independently, even rebelliously,' wrote film critic Roger Ebert in 1989, 'instead of hanging around passively while the fates decide her destiny.' I wanted Fearne to act independently and feel good about herself, too. I wanted that for myself.

I had expected the mermaids to be impractical airheads, or at least vessels waiting to be filled with meaning. Instead, I'd found Jessica Pearl, Mermaid Callie with her Dante references, Mermaid Sasha the blacksmith and Mermaid Grace from Reading, who owned her own small business. She was the first UK mermaid performer to become freediving certified. 'I had to swim five metres down to a cave, in bi-fins with the sea pulling me up and down. You're swimming under rocks where you can't go up if you need to breathe.'

'You seem very intelligent,' I said, averting my gaze from her boobs.

'Are you surprised?' she asked. I was.

~

At dawn, my good intentions were spiked with ill will. The air felt charged with raw emotion, the rush to find Ibsen's Hotel in the ethereal greyness, the cold swirling around us, the Bugaboo wheels sticking between medieval cobbles. 'Here, let me take it,' Rich said, snatching the pram handle, in his thick blue jacket with the collar turned up. I strode along beside him, in my knee-length khaki jacket from my London days, with holes in the cuffs. A jacket that preceded Rich and Fearne but was the only item in my wardrobe brave enough for a European winter. Why did we have to do everything together? Why could I never just simply walk out the door in the morning and go somewhere alone?

'Don't panic, we've got plenty of time,' he said, navigating Google Maps.

'I'm not panicking,' I lied, already livid at dawn.

We found the hotel. I was about to ascend the scalloped steps and disappear into the foyer. 'I'll see you at the end of the day,' I said.

'What time does the conference finish?' Rich pushed the Bugaboo back and forth, the resentment rose from him in waves. The bonnet shielded Fearne, wrapped up in her grey jacket and strapped inside like a mental patient.

'I don't know, I'll call you,' I told him.

'Bye-bye darling,' I bent down, hugged and kissed her, drank in her delicious scent, the smell of her hair, her skin, her youth; an elixir. I loved her, loved her, and she me. We had attached, but I also wanted to detach.

Fearne flung her arms out, 'No! I WANT MUMMY!' She thrashed in the buggy, convulsing and arching her back. Rich, sullen, his collar turned up, wheeled her away.

I stepped into the cool black hotel foyer, and took my name tag (Megan Dunn, independent researcher) from a table presided over by the co-convenor, Adam, and his teenage son. The foyer was populated by female academics ready for a mid-winter walking tour of Copenhagen. I did that barely perceptible microsecond scan — *who is youngest, thinnest, best looking?* — and realised if the group of sensibly dressed conference attendees suddenly transformed into a pod of mermaids and reconvened on the rocks, we'd be dressed in taupe, beige and black, with wind-resistant and water-repellent tails, built to survive the Baltic, but not to entertain Prince Eric. The most beautiful specimen among us was a calm brunette dressed in pale denim jeans and a matching denim jacket. An artist from Estonia, she was accompanied by a rugged bloke from Poland who might have been her partner.

I felt like Basil Brush in my big jacket, knocking everyone over with jokes. 'I guess only women come to a conference about mermaids,' I said. 'Go figure.'

But there were three men in our party. The polite co-convenor and his shy teenage son said nothing. Nor did the Polish bloke.

'I'm not an academic,' I kept saying.

I wasn't sure if I was trying to broadcast that I was too legit for academia or the opposite. That I was just some middle-aged woman in a muddle about mermaids with only her credit card earning interest.

I met a young Egyptian woman presenting a paper on M. Night Shyamalan's *Lady in the Water.* I wasn't the only one off on a tangent.

'Sounds interesting,' I said.

Next, I sidled up to an American early childhood anthropologist who was presenting on the mermaid as a symbol of gender transition. I'd already scoured the programme and circled her session as a point of interest.

'I'm looking forward to your talk,' I said.

Sally, the anthropologist, was chatty and upfront, the same age as me. She had curly chestnut hair and was not a waif like the icy Estonian.

She had a trans child herself and had been working with other trans children for years. The kids often spontaneously drew mermaid tails and related to the mermaid as a symbol of transformation, caught between two worlds. I felt that instant click, that familiarity of talking to a peer, someone with whom you can let your defences down.

'What are you going to talk about?' Sally asked.

I told her about my paper on Alexis Hunter.

'Alexis Hunter worked on the animation for Disney's *The Little Mermaid*,' I said. 'She also painted her own mermaids.'

'Everything converges,' Sally replied, and I felt something zip up tight inside me. She had summarised my PowerPoint in two words. *Stop it, stop telling your tale prematurely*, an inner voice cautioned.

Our tour guide, Paul, turned up in a grey sweeping Sherlock coat, with a silver ponytail. Brisk, a rapier quip at the ready. We marched out of the hotel, a shoal of tourists ready to be beguiled by the city's mermaid lore. Paul pointed at a mermaid trapped in the awning across the street. 'An example of eighteenth-century clip art,' he said. The group laughed. My eyes narrowed.

We were heading towards her. Everything else was just a rehearsal for the moment when I'd see the Little Mermaid, seated on her rock in the harbour, and we'd all get a selfie. And then what?

Claire la Sirène — a real professional mermaid — would arrive on the final day to give her keynote speech. I had been emailing her, trying to snare an interview. Claire was everything one wanted in a mermaid: blonde and svelte, with a regal beauty. She had a regular gig at the Aquarium de Paris. I had watched YouTube videos of her swimming up to the glass, blowing bouquets of bubble kisses to the children. She also had a master's degree in Disney archetypes and was writing a book about mermaids.

Most books on mermaids are anthologies, compilations of curiosities, packed with full-page Waterhouse reproductions and fragments of old-school poems, but René Magritte's *Collective Invention* (1935) always pops up — the antidote to too much fantasy. Magritte's reverse mermaid is stranded on the beach, with a fish head and woman's legs. The best article I'd found about the painting included commentary from chiropractic students — they'd found it flawed. 'The pulmonary physiology of a fish wouldn't support the energetic needs of land-based locomotion,' one pointed out.

Nailed it. Magritte's painting is more perverse than sexy. And that bush! What a thicket. Magritte was working in an era when waxing was less predominant. *Collective Invention* had prompted people to question what beauty is. It was the same question I asked every mermaid.

Paul stopped and pointed out the first mermaid on our walking tour: the Starbucks logo. Everyone groaned. A capitalist's talisman. Paul briefly outlined her origins in Melusine, the medieval two-tailed mermaid from France. Starbucks is named after the first mate on the *Pequod*, the whaling ship in *Moby-Dick*. The Starbucks logo, however, was the brainchild of Terry Heckler, a corporate artist, who found an image of a two-tailed siren in a sixteenth-century Norse woodcut. 'It's a metaphor for the allure of caffeine, the sirens who drew sailors into the rocks,' Heckler explained in an interview. He once had a sixteen-cup-a-day habit.

At the lights I wound up next to Adam.

'What did you study?' I asked.

'Legend,' he replied.

'The film?' A vision of Tom Cruise asleep in a dusky forest and Tim Curry in a gigantic pair of devil horns.

'Good joke.' Adam looked at me drolly. He was part of Island Dynamics, the organisation behind the conference. He'd studied the history of legends and folklore, *in general*. Not the 1985 Ridley Scott film.

I moved on and caught up to Paul, our tour guide.

'Will you speak about the history of vandalism attached to the statue?' I asked. Why had her head been chopped off? Thrice. First in 1964, again in 1990 and a third time in 1998. And whodunit?

'Yes.' He clocked my steely gaze.

Cyclists sailed by, their spokes whirring. I wanted our tour guide to hand me the keys to the city; to have a secret unlocked and placed in the palm of my hand. There, got it, the authentic detail that I came for.

Instead: disconnect.

On the street, I fell in beside another attendee with long blonde hair and a milky demeanour, like a hippy Waterhouse muse. We talked of our projects. Her grey-blue eyes were full of quiet regard, and her clothes wavered as she stepped along beside me. I suddenly asked, 'Are you a mermaid?'

'Yes,' the answer came back, half shyly. She sewed her own tails, was an artist too. 'You can interview me for your book if you'd like.' Yes please, I said. But something about the conference had thrown me off balance.

Here I was just one thinker among the throng. More cyclists, their spokes spinning.

Our group bought pastries from a corner bakery and stepped out into the morning air which had been lightly whisked into mist.

We plunged into King's Park as though walking into the illustration of a fairy tale. The path crackled underfoot. The trees were soft; everywhere a dappled hush as though we'd stepped back into the past. The park was built in the early sixteenth century, in a world not of our making.

My phone vibrated. A beautiful photograph of Fearne, wearing her fetching grey coat with the collar turned up. She faced the Little Mermaid statue. They had got there first! For a second, I felt taken down a peg, deflated, as though I'd missed my chance.

~

Hans Christian Andersen stood on a plinth above me, larger than life, his right palm held aloft as though in benediction or maybe simply saying: Stop it. Stop reinterpreting my fairy tale. Perhaps he was thinking, *Go home, Megan, and forget this wild mermaid goose chase. Also, you need to re-up your anti-depressants. Don't go off them cold turkey after the conference, that's a really bad idea.*

Paul pulled a sheaf of papers out of his large brown briefcase. We gathered in front of the statue to listen to a reading from *The Little Mermaid*. It had been years since I'd heard the story and I had forgotten how beautiful it was. I'd also forgotten that the Little Mermaid had so many sisters. One by one, on their fifteenth birthday, they surfaced for the first time. The eldest saw the lights of the city sparkling from the shore and heard the church bells ring. The second watched the sunset in a golden glow. The third swam up a river and saw nude children bathing in a cove. The fourth was shy so stayed out at sea where the dolphins did backflips, and the fifth sat on the hunk of an iceberg and frightened passing sailors. I felt the impatience of the Little Mermaid trapped in her underwater grotto, yearning for a piece of the action. Finally, it was her turn. When she surfaced, fireworks peeled across the night sky as she watched the prince aboard his ship, before it was struck twice by lightening, then sank in the storm.

It was spectacular. People used to the Disney version, however, are often horrified by the sad ending in the original. 'Hans, Hans, Hans, you sick fuck,' begins one dismayed review on GoodReads.

Paul asked us if we had any questions.

I put my hand up.

'Would Hans Christian Andersen have seen a real iceberg?' I asked.

I had bought a blue-bound hardback on Hans Christen Andersen years earlier as though storing it for some future emergency. On the flight I flicked through it, releasing the scent of old pages thick with deep academic thoughts. The first sentence of the first chapter read: 'Hans Christian Andersen spent his life pursuing fame.' He had apparently wanted to be known for his stories for adults, but it was his children's tales that had taken off.

Andersen was the only child of an illiterate washerwoman. He grew up and entertained nobility, never married, had no kids of his own, might have been gay and wasn't especially attractive, having a rather large and sloping nose. I felt that his yearning — for sex, for touch, for love, for fame — had been poured into the character of the Little Mermaid, who wanted what she could never have, and gave away her own voice for it.

Walking on, a flock of six wild geese flew over our heads, their wings beating, a mechanical whirring sound. The dark air was briefly aloft with magic. We gazed after them, and I felt like the Little Mermaid surfacing for the first time.

We waited for an older woman in our party to catch up. She walked as though she had a peg leg. Her face grey and crumpled. I fell into step beside her and asked what she was talking about at the conference. Nothing. She was just here as an attendee. She thought the conference might help her PhD.

'What's your PhD about?' I asked.

'Shipwrecks,' she said.

'A lot of mermaids do underwater photoshoots in shipwrecks,' I said.

She nodded.

I took a snap of the street sign pointing in the direction of the

Little Mermaid statue. It depicted two people, walking; below their legs, the silhouette of the mermaid on her rock was going nowhere fast.

'For most Danes it's a point of pride not to visit her,' Adam said. He told me he once surveyed a hundred locals and discovered ninety-eight percent of them thought the statue had a mermaid tail. She doesn't, of course — the Little Mermaid is captured in transit, her legs sprouting fins. Technically she could get up and join the cyclists that dominate Copenhagen's byways, but she doesn't need to. *A woman needs a man like a fish needs a bicycle.* I had noticed on social media that many mermaids referred to themselves as 'fish'.

~

Then we rounded the corner, and there was she was, plain as daylight and quite small too. On her rock, the mermaid was a fish and a tourist. She didn't have an ocean view, but perhaps it didn't matter. The Little Mermaid wanted to be a part of our world, and she was.

'It's a story of love and sacrifice,' Paul said.

The Little Mermaid is one of the most passive heroines. Yet every day, hordes come to see her.

'Why? When this story is just so horrible?' he asked.

Everyone laughed.

A boat drifted past so other tourists on it could take photos. Snap. Snap. Each year the Little Mermaid attracts more than a million visitors who take more than five million photos of her.

The statue was commissioned in 1909 by the Carlsberg heir, enchanted by a ballet of *The Little Mermaid* at Copenhagen's Royal Theatre. The heir asked ballerina Ellen Price to pose for the statue, and she agreed, but refused to go nude. So the body of the Little Mermaid is based on the sculptor Edvard Eriksen's wife.

I asked again about vandalism. The Little Mermaid is a locus for activism. She had recently been doused in red paint as a protest against whaling in the Faroe Islands. Since 1912 she's been decapitated three times, had a dildo whacked in her hand, had her head covered in a burqa and been blown off her rock by dynamite. Locals? Paul told me the Situationist artist Jorgen Nash claimed to have been behind the 1964 decapitation. According to Nash, he had secreted the statue's bronze head in a sealed lead box, which was now on exhibition at a museum.

Paul paused to open his bag and pull something out.

'And here's her head,' I quipped.

The group laughed.

I felt wonderful for making everyone laugh, but also like that one annoying person in the group who couldn't keep her big trap shut.

Paul quoted Karl Marx. '"The first time is drama; the second time is comedy." Be careful when you take a selfie with the selkie,' he warned. Many take a wrong step and fall in.

Yes, the story is unfeminist, but surely what matters about the Little Mermaid is that she has never gone out of print. Her tale has been translated into multiple languages, recycled in books, films and animations, over and over again. She has not stayed put in Copenhagen, either — now there are thirteen replica statues around the world.

I got my careful selfie with the mermaid, then the blonde hippy asked me to take her photo. She looked better in front of the statue. More windswept, more beautiful.

I didn't feel a particular connection with Andersen's mermaid, but I did look at the statue's legs with more investment. Her sadness was as integral as the salt in the sea. She longed for a man who didn't love her back. Sometimes a fish wants a bicycle so fucking bad. My mother had spent her life in love with a man who didn't love her back. It had defined her. My twenties were craven with longing for men who couldn't care less about me — even my stint working in the strip club had not improved my market rate. I had worked hard not to let it define me. Now I had a man, and he even had a bicycle, so I had won.

But why does the Little Mermaid have to be little? Why can't she be the Oldest Mermaid or even the Somewhere-in-the-Middle mermaid? What about the Little Mermaid's five older sisters — what happened to those fish? I have never been little. Even when I was little, I felt gargantuan, fed on my mother's emotional discontents, forever dining on adult daydreams.

We continued on. Around the corner on the promenade was a statue of a life-size bronze polar bear and her cubs. Paul told us that during World War II the statue had been shot by a soldier who saw it through the mist and thought it was real. It was disconcerting. Then he stopped our group by the statue of a huge buxom wench on a rock, built to promote a seafood restaurant that promptly went bust.

The Not-So-Little Mermaid wasn't famous. No tourists jostled for a selfie with her. The new owners had come and gone — the restaurant kept failing but the statuesque mermaid stayed put. Hans Christian Andersen had not legitimised the emotional discontent of the Not-So-Little Mermaid. If she wanted a prince, she probably wanted him in the salacious way of Nicki Minaj in her music video for 'Anaconda'.

'She's had some work done,' Paul joked.

I got my selfie with this mermaid, too. I wasn't going to shun her for putting that sad fish restaurant out of business. She was wanton with longing, and I was wanton with longing too — for fame and fortune. Like Andersen, I wanted to be seen and recognised for my voice.

~

As we left the waterfront behind, I remembered Pania of the Reef, a statue of a young Māori maiden sitting on her rock on Marine Parade in Napier, New Zealand. I had flown all this way, when there was a mermaid myth right in my own back yard. Pania is often compared to the Little Mermaid, because of her pose, and Pania too has become a national symbol and a tourist's trinket. A neighbour kept a miniature Pania replica on the dashboard of his car.

The statue of Pania came about in the late 1940s as part of an effort to lure more residents and visitors to Napier. Civic enthusiasts seized on the story of Pania Reef, important to local iwi Ngāti Kahungunu. Pania was a beautiful sea maiden, a marakihau, who swam to the shore each night, and returned to the sea by dawn. One evening, she met Karitoki, the son of a chief. The pair fell in love. He had never seen a woman so beautiful, and in secret they were married. She lived in his whare, but every morning Pania returned to her sea people. Only the ruru, night birds, saw them together.

Karitoki boasted to his friends about his beautiful wife. Some stories feature a custody battle over their son Moremore, but in others Karitoki lived in fear that Pania would return forever to the sea people. He consulted a tohunga, who suggested placing cooked food in Pania's mouth while she slept. If she ate it, she could never return to the sea. But when Karitoki went to place the food in her mouth, a ruru cried out, waking her. Pania fled to the reef. Karitoki never saw her again.

If you look into the ocean now, at low tide, you might see Pania, lying on the rocky shelf of the reef, her hair still black, her arms outstretched.

I had overlooked Pania's statue because she was presented with legs, but not every mermaid myth was about fish. Selkies are seals who slip out of their sealskins and become women. Selkie folklore is known in Scandinavia, Iceland and the places of my ancestry, Scotland and Ireland — countries that as a child I always imagined were populated with freckled redheads.

In one legend from the Faroe Islands, a selkie is trapped by a fisherman who steals her sealskin. She marries him and they have two children, but as soon as she finds the hidden sealskin, she returns to the sea. The selkie leaves the fisherman a note asking him not to kill her selkie family, but he does. Bastard.

I liked selkies because they were ambivalent about marriage.

Years before Fearne, on my thirty-fifth birthday, Rich took me seal watching at Blakeney, along the Norfolk coast. Sea sprayed my cheeks, my khaki coat. 'You're not up for this job,' the cold whispered. We shared the boat with a group of Italian vixens on a school trip. The girl who sat next to me looked like Keira Knightley on her way to reject Captain Sparrow. A seal swam past, its whiskers above the waves, nonplussed about its photo-op. More seals rolled around on the sandbank, enormous as steamed puddings. Some were a speckled golden-syrup colour, others a spongy chocolate. They batted their eyelashes at Keira, their pelts snug as neoprene. Their eyes blinked, dark orbs.

Dear selkie, what do you remember of your married years? How much did you itch to have your sealskin back? Did you love your first husband? I didn't love the Irishman much either. Did you even love yourself? Now that's a question. How did it feel once you found your sealskin? I bet you couldn't wait to wriggle into it like a dress. The sea was calling you back.

~

In the shower at the hotel, we had sex because it was a requirement, like a session on the conference schedule. I often didn't want to. A problem that had deepened during motherhood. I wanted to still desire sex like a younger carefree woman with something to prove, but often I didn't want anything other than skyping mermaids and a block of milk chocolate. I couldn't explain this part of myself to my own psyche. The shower was a beige corner stall in the hotel. Sex in a shower can be complicated. A matter of getting the legs in the right position. I am bigger and we are about the same height (he is taller, a technicality of an inch). I wished sometimes that he weighed more and that I was the light sprite that a woman is meant to be. The shower drilling. I clawed his back. My tongue was quite clearly present in my mouth.

I loved Rich — didn't want to lose him, he was the man who had agreed to us paying $1500 to come to a mermaid conference in Copenhagen. Yet it was also as if someone had stolen my selkie skin, and I wanted it back, though I didn't even *have* a selkie skin and if I did, I knew Rich would never take it from me.

'I always thought your mermaid thing was about hating men,' a friend had said recently.

What?

~

Our hotel room was strewn with picture books, clothes wriggled out of, socks hopscotched across the floor, discarded plastic packets of crackers. Rich fell asleep in the hotel bed, next to Fearne who was splayed out like a starfish grinding its teeth. I opened the lid of my laptop, that creak of bright white light opening up. One of Fearne's first sentences: *I am doing my important emails.* Funny how your own words boomerang back. The starfish twitched beside me, snored and stirred — how I loved that sound.

The mermaid conference had given me a generalised sensation of panic. The fee for the conference had given me a sensation of panic too. I had to get something unique out of it.

The professional mermaids identified as artists and performers. That surprised me. The mermaids felt empowered; they were aware of their creativity; they had made the active choice to transform. A tail had to be earned.

My eyes had that white glitter behind them, as though the glare of the laptop screen was flickering behind them. Was life online any less real? I felt a twitchiness in myself, a shiver of recognition: the professional mermaids were constructing the stories of their lives, one selfie at a time. It reminded me of my old art school days, dressing up as Alice in Wonderland and pretending to be critical about femininity, when really it was femininity I wanted and prized above all else.

The starfish sat up. 'Milky?'

I slid out of bed and put the jug on.

~

The conference took place in a brutalist building by an empty concrete playground. Inside, the tea and coffee were draining, the biscuits scant. Philip Hayward, the Australian academic, did an introduction called 'Into the Mer'. He began by writing two provocations on the whiteboard.

> A mermaid conference? That would be way too gay for me.

> How does your partner feel about you looking at naked women all day?

These were comments from male colleagues who worked at the same university as him. We all laughed because we were researching mermaids and therefore knew that no one takes mermaids seriously. Philip shared some of the criticism he had received about his book *Making a Splash*. One woman had accused him of misrepresenting mermaids. 'How do you misrepresent a representation?' Philip smiled. It was a rhetorical question. It was also an academic's joke.

I went next to a lecture by a short-haired brunette from Armenia who looked a bit like Pat Benatar. She stood up and gave an unillustrated lecture about a poet I'd never heard of who once wrote about mermaids. I could sense her nervousness, the complete nakedness of standing in this barren grey room, with no PowerPoint. I wondered what had motivated her to come here so unprepared. I assumed most of the other academics were bankrolled by their universities. Afterwards I told her I had loved her talk, and she said thank you. Her eyes brimmed with gratitude.

The conference introduced me to important locations on the global map of mermaids. Jennifer Kokai presented the keynote on her latest book, *Swim Pretty*, about the performance of mermaids in Weeki Wachee Springs. Jennifer was a professor and playwright who grew up visiting the park outside Tampa,

Florida. Weeki Wachee is quite literally the wellspring of modern mermaiding, featuring a submerged 400-seat theatre set into the limestone rock of a natural water source. The mermaids perform underwater by breathing through air hoses. Every single mermaid knows about it — visiting is on their bucket list.

The park was set up in 1947 by Newt Perry, an ex-navy frogman, ace swimmer and diver who also worked as a location scout for Hollywood films. (It was Newt who ensured *The Creature from the Black Lagoon* was filmed in Florida.) Newt cleared all the rusty cars and junk out of the abandoned pools and turned them into a theme park. He pioneered the air hoses and taught the first performers how to do tricks like eat a banana underwater. Then, a year later, *Mr. Peabody and the Mermaid* was filmed partly onsite; after that, the park mermaids began wearing fishtails.

Newt probably hadn't paused to consider what his performances might mean in the twenty-first century, but Jennifer had. She analysed several Weeki Wachee shows for us, including a submerged performance of *Alice in Wonderland*, and explained her theories on the taxonomy of water.

Humans display water, she told us. We pour it into pools that cut across the horizon lines. We tame water, make it do our bidding, fashion it into epic fountains and forget that we don't hold dominion. It is poured into theme parks and aquariums as though nature is under our control. At Weeki Wachee, apparently an alarm is raised for the mermaids if an alligator gets into the springs — a detail that scared the shit out of me.

So many mermaids. How could I get my hands on all of them? Someone else spoke about how Mami Wata was depicted in contemporary African cinema. Mami Wata is a water deity, often pictured holding a snake — a sensual and dangerous siren. I thought of Nicki Minaj and all the hours I had spent watching her sing 'Anaconda' on YouTube in a sultry swamp, water flowing around her ample body.

A Swede in a turban spoke about representations of mermen, from the fey fish boys in Japanese manga to the trident-toting

Poseidon. Another talk was about Picasso's Warsaw mermaid, which once graced the walls of a flat, until the tenants got so sick of tourists visiting that they painted over it. Someone else raged against mermaids' unethical use of coral in shell headdresses and jewellery.

I nodded sagely throughout, felt there should have been more biscuits. 'The conference needs better snacks,' I told Sally the anthropologist in a break. 'I mean we're paying a lot of money here.'

'Who do you publish with?' I asked an Australian novelist over coffee. To my utter surprise, a small UK publisher had just accepted my funny manuscript about bookselling. Trying to find a publisher who wanted to take on a book about professional mermaids was proving much harder.

'Why?' she snapped.

I bristled, but went to her presentation on the mermaid as eco-terrorist. 'How do you write fiction — the bourgeois novel — when the state of the world is in collapse and ninety percent of the ocean's fish stocks are plundered?' she asked.

Good questions! Her PowerPoint was packed with fin-tastic ocean trivia.

She flicked through a quick precis of the career of oceanographer Sylvia Earle. Why had I heard of Jacques Cousteau but not Sylvia Earle?

In 1969, the thirty-four-year-old marine biologist Earle saw an advertisement in the paper asking for scientists to take part in an experiment to live underwater. Earle led the all-female mission on Tektite II, an underwater habitat off the coast of the Virgin Islands. Four scientists and one engineer lived fifty feet below the surface for two weeks. It was the first team of women to conduct research of this type in the world.

In TV footage, the aquanauts were described as 'real life mermaids' and even aqua-naughties. Journalists grilled them: Did you wear lipstick? Have a hairdryer? What was it like to live underwater?

What *was* it like?

Earle watched a school of tarpon, struck silver, beneath a full moon. She saw light even in the darkness, generated by bioluminescent creatures, and said it was like 'swimming through stars'. 'I got to know the fish,' she said. 'As individuals.' She met five angelfish who got up early every morning, hung out together all day, and then retired separately to the same sleeping spots on the reef each night. She knew butterfly fish, two by two (they mate for life like some people do), and a beautiful green moray eel that the aquanauts called Puff. But in 2012, Earle revisited the site of the laboratory and described the reef as 'a ghost town'. Puff was long gone.

~

Claire la Sirène had arrived. I recognised her instantly. Dressed in a fetching red coat with gold buttons and a black skirt, her slender legs encased in thick black tights, she was easily the best-looking delegate at the conference. Not that it mattered. (But it did matter.)

'Hi Claire, I'm Megan,' I said, seizing the moment she walked towards the building, her boyfriend in tow.

She stopped and looked at me on the steps, confused.

'I'm the writer from New Zealand who's been emailing you,' I explained.

Claire apologised for not getting back to me recently. She had been busy.

'Perhaps we can connect at the conference, get a coffee?' I suggested.

'Yes,' she agreed. I felt relieved when she went inside. Confronted with my first live specimen, I was shy. I didn't want to haggle for a top mermaid's precious time. What did I really want to ask her? I felt something in my stomach. Not nausea, but fear. Could Claire la Sirène bear the weight of my fantasy?

~

I missed Sally's lecture on mermaids and transition. A real shame. But my lecture about Alexis Hunter was on at the same time. Inside, the big square room was near empty — everyone was at Sally's talk. I cringed through my presentation.

Hunter was famous for her feminist work, I explained, best known for her sexy and staunch, black-and-white narrative photographic series from the seventies. When she died in 2014, the Tate put on display her photograph of a manicured female hand burning a silver strappy high heel.

Claire sat in her chair, watching me. I showed Hunter's burning high heel. I knew I was being judged. I was judging myself.

In the eighties, I continued, Hunter had made the switch to painting mythological chimeras. Her intellectual credibility pancaked, but I thought these weird mash-ups mattered too. I showed the swag of paintings Hunter had applied to early computer motherboards — they included Tarot-like goddesses, monsters and a mermaid. Hunter's mermaid was an amphibious gill-woman, like the Creature from the Black Lagoon, trapped in the golden circuits of the memory board.

The connections felt whisker-thin. Tenuous, especially in the presence of a real mermaid. Most of Hunter's work — like my life — had nothing to do with mermaids. I clicked through Hunter's amphibious mermaid, and then ended on *The Lure of the Sea*, her painting of the mermaid kissing the man made out of foam.

'See? She painted the foam,' I said.

It felt like an anti-climax.

After my presentation, a professor from Hong Kong stood up and gave a talk on the transformation of the nereid to the mermaid in art history. There were so many different water nymphs, sprites and goddesses across culture and history it was hard to keep track. The nereids were from Greek mythology, and often accompanied Poseidon, the god of the sea, or his son Triton. I felt like I was playing a complex game of mermaid Guess Who? that I could never hope to win.

Then she flashed up a painting, *Triton and Nereid*, by the

German artist Max Klinger. I gasped. It was the same composition as *The Lure of the Sea*. Hunter had obviously based her image on Klinger's, except where he had painted Triton kissing a mermaid, she had painted the man as seafoam, dissolving in the arms of the mermaid. Everything converges.

~

'The belief in mermaids may have arisen at the very dawn of our species,' said the next speaker, a cool scientific dude, quoting from a factsheet on the National Ocean Service website, 'but no evidence of aquatic humanoids has ever been found. Why, then, do they occupy the collective unconscious of nearly all seafaring peoples? That's a question best left to historians, philosophers and anthropologists.'

Or the professionals. Claire la Sirène held the attention of the room from the moment she draped her blue silicone tail over the whiteboard. It hung there throughout her talk, emitting a mysterious power. Her PowerPoint included pictures of a steep dive pool where she trained for her work. The verticality of the pool was daunting; the athleticism of her work profound. Claire showed footage of her swims in the aquarium with and without goggles. The difference was stunning. She couldn't see a thing, let alone a dinglehopper. Yet she appeared to smile and wave to the children behind the glass.

Claire pointed out that the Little Mermaid wanted to grow legs and live on land, whereas professional mermaids are telling the same story in reverse — they want to don a tail and enter the sea. Claire showed images of the numerous mermaid tails available on the market, likening them to princess dresses. During question time I asked her what it was like being both a mermaid and a PhD student. Perhaps I was hoping for friction, but she'd had no trouble reconciling study and mermaiding — neither had her supervisors.

I asked her about mermaids and climate change. She thought

some, like the famous Hannah Mermaid, did a lot of activism, but for others it was just something trendy to say on Facebook. At the end of her keynote the audience surged forward to get a selfie with the real selkie.

Her tail was laid out on one of the banal tables and we took turns touching it. I stroked it, thoughtfully, and paused to say how heavy it was. It did feel weighty, but up close it was also quite rudimentary — the interior looked bare. A mum and daughter had their picture snapped beside her. I had not seen any other presenter asked for a selfie during the conference. Months later, a YouTube video of Claire la Sirène surfaced. In the video she sat on a rock beside the Little Mermaid statue in her turquoise tail, holding the same pose. *Why do we love this horrible story?*

~

On our last day, we walked the length and breadth of Copenhagen. It started to rain as we crossed the bridge to the Paper Mill. Fearne asleep, yet still managing to omit an aura of resentment from her Bugaboo.

'Hey, there's a gallery.' I pointed at the sign. Darkness swirled around the large concrete building. I sat on a bench watching *Gardien de la Paix* (2011), an aquatic video by German artist Lena Maria Thüring. Jellyfish orbited the deep astral blue, yet the subtitles told the interior monologue of a policeman trying to reconcile his profession. The policeman had inherited his love of the ocean from his family, yet had not known what he wanted to do with his life. 'If I'd been aware of my interest in the sea, I would have chosen a different path.'

I soaked in the blue light of the screen like a sponge. The jellyfish swirled their white skirts on screen. I kept trying to match the subtitles to the jellyfish. Sylvia Earle might have been able to see the jellyfish as individuals, to know them as something more than perpetual fantasia.

The footage switched to a school of large black fish with yellow speckled backs. One seemed to face the camera. The policeman visited the aquarium on his lunch breaks. 'You come out full of dreams, full of plans, full of ambitions . . . I'd like to be fighting for the sea and everything in it,' he said. Yet like the sea he also didn't want to be told how to behave.

His monologue held me, as though we were in the same lull. 'You end up believing that humans are bad . . . that they are the worst of animals.' I was not a policeman, yet I had ended up thinking this too. And I had started to wonder if the rise of professional mermaids wasn't a subconscious sign of self-hate, a rejection of the human. We wanted to tell another tale about our species, but maybe it was already too late, we were caught in a horrible story of our making.

~

We spent the rest of our holiday in England, in a little village called Brooke, outside of Norwich, where Rich had grown up. A dead tree rose up wizened and witchy from the field behind the back garden. The nights were long, the sun would not set, and Fearne tossed and turned, her forehead glazed with sweat. She kicked and called out, refused to sleep, I felt like Captain Ahab, caught in some wordless battle. Fearne was my Moby-Dick. Did anyone ever tell Ahab that if he was calm, the whale would be calm?

A tree of crows, light nights and that steep fucking concrete step designed by a man — obviously — that joined the kitchen to a cold hallway and the laundry. Fearne was irresistibly drawn to the step, trundling towards it, ready to pit her weight against it, and try it out.

One afternoon I shrieked hysterically on the driveway of my father-in-law's brick house, as Fearne thrashed in her pram. The lack of sleep had me turned inside out, a stranger to my own moods. Against Hans's advice, I had let my anti-depressants run out and did nothing about it. Instead, I stood mouthing off in the polite suburban cul-de-sac. My father-in-law took pity on me, strapped Fearne into the hired car seat and drove her around the block. She returned asleep. 'I don't feel like a natural mother,' I said to Rich's aunt over the dishes.

'I don't think any of us do,' she replied.

6.

Whale Watchers

Ben from Lazy Seals had told me that the static freediving session might be overrun with gurfers, girl surfers. I was sceptical as I left the house, night sky oily with indigo, streetlights winking, lighting the twisted branches of pōhutukawa trees a minty, Christmas green.

On the walk down the hill towards the pool, I was feeling nebulous and slow-moving, thoughts strobing over my consciousness like car headlights. To think, right now on the ocean floor, jellyfish danced in their fantasia world, freediving in oblivion, as human beings dined on noodles, chopsticks forked between their lips.

At the pool, we gathered on the benches by one lane. A man in tropical speedos walked past. Gurfers were present, looking young and lovely, like prime candidates to become professional mermaids.

'You're Megan,' Ben said. He was a tall man with a sense of humour and a look of keen intelligence. Anna, his fellow instructor, was an elfin blonde with a bad hip and a wooden crutch. She wore a bone carving of a whale fluke as a necklace.

Anna gave our group the pep talk.

First, we would hold our breath, then the twinges and twitches would start, she told us. (But not tonight, no one would get there tonight.) Then the cramps. As our bodies began to shut down, blood would leave our extremities and flood only our essential organs. We would black out. (But don't worry, no one would get there tonight.) Then we would die.

'Any questions?' she asked.

Someone asked what the purpose of the club was.

'We're just mad people who like to hang out and hold our breath together,' Anna laughed.

She also said freediving was the most peaceful and wonderful sensation, and that if you blacked out and someone woke you up you would only remember how lovely and peaceful it had been.

I thought back to Mermaid Callie, who'd told me: 'This is going to sound really dark. But I've nearly drowned three times and I gotta say, I didn't dislike it.'

The first hurdle for me was the wetsuit I had borrowed from Anna, who was significantly smaller and shorter than me. She said to put water and soap inside it and slosh it around. A lot. I took the wetsuit into the shower cubicle, feeling like I was the Creature from the Black Lagoon, and doused the inner suit in water. I was a chunky selkie getting back into the seal skin rather than taking it off.

I lumbered out of the shower cubicle, a slight lather of soap visible on the exterior of Anna's wetsuit. I was only half dressed, the top of the wetsuit flailing around my waist like a school jersey. Why is water so erotic in movies? It didn't feel erotic that night. A gurfer helped Velcro up my strap and then it was time for the next part of the jigsaw. The wetsuit had a hood with a little inbuilt hole so my face would poke out like the pope or a shrew. 'I feel like I am in a comedy,' I told Anna.

It didn't bode well that I found tunnelling into the dark interior of the wetsuit frightening, and kept retracting, already panicked.

'There's nothing I can do to help you. There's no advice I can give. You just have to deal with it,' Anna said.

'Just deal with it,' I echoed.

Ben told me to try again and helped roll the hood over my head and eventually my head popped through and I squeezed my arms into the tubes.

I looked sheepishly at Ben and said, 'I'm not even a good swimmer.'

I got into the pool and did my first starfish, floating on the surface staring at the pool tiles below me. Then came back up for air.

'How was it?' Ben said.

'Yeah. All right,' I replied.

He laughed.

I tried again. Light wavered over the tiles on the bottom of the pool. A door slammed topside, and the thud travelled through the water.

'It's a bit like planking, isn't it?' I said, as I resurfaced.

'I want you to be very disciplined,' Ben said. I reached towards the side of the pool and drew my legs up slowly. 'I want you to be strong.'

I went under again and tried to hold my breath for longer.

'What happened?'

'Wetsuits are so floaty,' I said. Pleased with myself. I had managed to hold my breath for one minute and fifteen seconds!

'Have you had many mermaids sign up to this class?' I asked.

No. Ben said that people were attracted by freediving's rhetoric of freedom, of finding your inner dolphin or mermaid, but that actually holding your breath for a long time is hard. It hurts. People had to want something badly to push through it. Freediving started out male dominated, full of spear fishers. The gurfers wanted to work on their breath holds, on not panicking. I wanted to know how it feels to be a mermaid. It did feel calmer under the surface.

'It's fun, isn't it?' Anna said, standing beside the pool. She invited me to join another group she belonged to and go out 'ghost fishing' next, then she left on her lone crutch like a pirate with a wooden leg.

~

I never went ghost fishing.

~

I'd come back from Copenhagen with too many loose threads to follow up — freediving to try, sea creatures to research, books to read, movies to watch. I'd been meaning to watch *Miranda* ever since Philip, the guy who ran the conference, told me he'd named one of his daughters after her.

In the British hit film from 1948, Glynis Johns plays a mermaid hooked by a doctor on a fishing holiday in Cornwall. When he returns to his wife in London, he brings Miranda home too.

'Did you catch any big ones?' The wife asks.

'A whopper,' the doctor replies.

The whole film was a big hoot about the perils of marriage. Miranda got all the men hot under the collar, while she slept in the bath and was trundled around town in a wheelchair, masquerading as an invalid.

Some academics propose that *Miranda* is about the troubling agency of women in society following World War II. My favourite scene was the one at the zoo. The ever-carnal Miranda is wheeled up to the seal enclosure at feeding time. She catches one of the fishes meant for the seals, directly in her mouth and swallows it whole. Gulp. Then she barks back at the seal who is miffed she has stolen his lunch.

In the end, the good doctor doesn't leave his wife, and Miranda dives into the Thames, only to surface in the last frame, holding a merbaby in her lap. But whose baby is it? No one knows.

Of playing Miranda, Johns said, 'I was quite an athlete, my muscles were strong from dancing, so the tail' — reportedly made out of rubber, whale bone and nylon fins — 'was just fine. I swam like a porpoise.'

The same year *Miranda* was released, the Americans made *Mr. Peabody and the Mermaid*, another vintage classic tonnes of mermaids were into, so I watched that too. Ann Blyth is totally charming as the mermaid, but she doesn't say a word. The plot was another dodgy mid-life crisis, 'a mermaid nearly ruined my marriage' story. Arthur Peabody tells his shrink all about his Caribbean holiday, and how out fishing he caught a mermaid, named her Lenore, and kept her in a pool at the resort where he was staying with his wife. In the end, the shrink convinces poor Arthur his mermaid was a hallucination, despite the fact he still has Lenore's mermaid comb and hairpins.

Lenore's dainty little tail was a nice contrast to the big flukes that now dominated the market, but my favourite thing about the movie was a photo I'd found of Frankenstein holding Blyth in her mermaid tail on the set at Universal. Two myths colliding, the alluring mermaid mixing it up with the big freaky monster in down time between films.

The deleted Sea Hag in *Splash* was part of this mythic universe, too. The film originally had Daryl Hannah visit a wizened old Sea Hag, played by the actress Marilyn Moe-Stader. The Sea Hag had billowing white hair, an octopus adorned her seashell brassiere, and her tail was covered in barnacles and purple. Robert Short and his team had poured a lot of love into that costume, but in the end, Ron Howard edited the Sea Hag out. Bad call, Ron! Every story needs a sea hag. At least for a while.

~

The sea was full of rugged beauty, but also ugliness and just plain bizarreness, too. I thought back to Sydney Fish Market, which Rich and I had visited on our final holiday before we had Fearne. I didn't care about fish but wondered if the market had something to teach me about mermaids.

Our tour group had gathered at the warehouse entrance. We had to change into blue shower caps and jackets and put on plastic shoes as though we were hospital orderlies going into theatre for a C-section. The rank stench of the ocean's bowels all around us, that aggressive lingering smell of brine. Raw and nasty things were being manhandled and packed on ice.

Our tour guide was a young jovial chap in overalls. He led us across the concrete floors, damp and wet. Our plastic feet sloshed. Ice melted in gritty clumps along the aisles. We walked the wet floors, past rows and rows of big-game fish, swordfish stacked in lines like impossible rows of timber. The fleshy red-pink meat in the middle was ringed with lines; their round flat eyes were glossy, disbelieving. The tour guide told us that the Australian fishing industry was regulated and sustainable, yet it was hard to believe the sea could serve this up every day.

Our tour group stopped at the buckets of bycatch. The creatures no one wanted, the fish killed inadvertently.

'Do you want to see the ugliest fish in the sea?' our guide asked.

He reached into a bucket of ice and hauled out a blobfish.

'The blobfish has been repeatedly voted the ugliest endangered animal in the world,' he said.

The group laughed dutifully. I didn't. White, pearlescent, spilling like a beanbag in his hand, the blobfish was a deep-sea fish, designed to live at least 2000 feet beneath the ocean. On the surface, its body collapsed. Its face and mouth were pallid and gooey; its nose drooped down like a snubbed phallus. It reminded me of my old boss from the strip club. 'All this one here needs is a boob job,' the boss used to joke.

The blobfish was served up as the butt of the joke at the end of our tour — no one was bidding on its sweet meat. Yet I looked at it and felt only tenderness. Then the tour guide thrust the blobfish back on ice.

~

'What did you do today?' Rich asked.

We were side by side on the sofa, in our adult aquatic dreamtime, Fearne snoring softly, the two of us supping Chardonnays.

'I watched *Miranda*.' I showed him the DVD case. 'It's about a mermaid who nearly ruins a marriage. When are you going to buy me a ring?' I teased.

'I'm not sure I believe in marriage,' Rich said.

'Lots of men find me very attractive,' I said to him, channelling Miranda, as though I could hook someone else and swim off any day . . . even though I was dressed in pyjamas, fluffy dressing gown and wearing the designer, knitted slippers he had bought me last Mother's Day. I had more in common with the Sea Hag at this stage of my life.

'And lots of women, who have not yet expressed it, also find me very attractive,' Rich replied.

I looked at his sensitive little ears, the lobes ever so delicately covered in hairs as soft as down.

'If you try and leave me, I will hobble you,' I said.

We sank the rest of the bottle.

~

Miranda stole a fish from the seals, and chowed it down whole, and I asked every mermaid what she ate. It is a question children ask. Seaweed salad and sushi were common answers. Many mermaids are vegetarians, or aspire to be. More creative answers included barnacle burgers and kelp cakes. But occasionally I hit an iron rod of pragmatism. Morgana Alba, the founder of Circus Siren pod, said, 'I'm meat and potatoes all the way.'

Alba was a kick-ass small business owner, who quit a soul-crushing job at Microsoft and worked first as an aerial dancer, then became a mermaid performer as it was gentler on the body. 'Did you see that post about the tourist who damaged the coral in Thailand taking selfies?' she said, as we veered off topic.

'That really crushed me. Coral is unbelievably fragile, and it's so vital to the eco-system. Coral's in a lot of trouble right now.'

Most of the mermaids had the health of the world on their agenda, or at least on their mind. I also had the health of the world on my mind, but my own health was on there, too. I had spent countless nights grazing on that sunken sofa, eating Tim Tams and Mint Slices.

When I got back from Copenhagen I went on a Jenny Craig diet. I was ready to rejoin society, start wearing something more than a pair of black trackpants and the AWFUL sweatshirt. I was ashamed of the dieting, but I wanted to look good in a pair of jeans again.

The Jenny Craig office was next to the central Wellington police station. I'd never have joined if I didn't know someone else who had, an old workmate who'd lost tonnes of weight. It doesn't cost much to join — it's the special Jenny Craig food that costs. I began to spend around $130 a week, but as a fussy eater the diet was perfect.

I rode the lift up to each weekly meeting and liked the young woman consultant who I saw. She was cool and good humoured — I felt better just for seeing her. Eventually she got a job in real estate and left, but not before the kilos began to budge. It was hard to go from necking a bottle of wine and eating chocolate biscuits every night, to nothing. 'Just give it two weeks. I promise,' the young woman said. She took a photo of me wearing a big white T-shirt emblazoned with the catchphrase 'Feminist as Fuck'. The small, designed portions did their magic, and I lost two kilos in two weeks.

As well as the pleasant-enough Jenny Craig meals, I was allowed to eat as many green foods as I liked. Oh, to be a woman who loves a peppery salad leaf! I have always thought lettuce tastes a bit like dirt, as though you can still trace the snail tracks over each leaf.

To keep me on track, I thought of the mermaid I most wanted to embody: MeduSirena. I had seen her post on Facebook once: 'I love pizza, but I don't *eat* pizza, because PIZZA.' I knew exactly what she meant. Except in reverse.

One day at the front desk, picking up my plastic bag full of Jenny Craig food, I noticed that the black microwaveable trays were not recyclable. I mentioned it to one of the women in black.

She commiserated but said something about the cost of providing recyclable packaging. I thought of all my Jenny Craig meals, consumed, their unrecyclable plastic trays bobbing about in the sea. Then I reached my target weight and was set free.

~

'Call me Ishmael' is the first line of *Moby-Dick* by Herman Melville. I knew that chestnut from my bookselling days.

I fastened my seat buckle, then opened my book as the plane sliced through clouds above Cook Strait on my way to Christchurch. The ether and water meet to produce the horizon line and I wanted to know what happened below it, so I was going on a whale-watching expedition to Kaikōura with the writer Philip Hoare. It was a special field trip as part of the writers' festival.

'Tea or coffee?' A calm, lipsticked smile, from the hostess.

'Just a water please.'

I folded down my tray table, placed the transparent plastic cup on it.

'And would you like the cookie or the cassava crisps?' the flight attendant asked.

'The cookie,' I replied. To hell with Jenny. Besides, it was only 119 calories. I could swallow it.

The trolley inched down the plane, the woman asking the same two questions, as I unwrapped the plastic from the cookie.

I turned the page; crumbs collected in the folds. I was reading Hoare's *The Sea Inside*. I loved the title. Yes, we all carry it: the amniotic sea we are born into, but also the shore at Lyall Bay as glimpsed on lonely walks beside my father in rugged southerlies. The soupy onion waves that stirred the legs of Cromer's Victorian Pier, out of season, as Rich and I sat in the window of a derelict B&B. The sea inside me is a winter sea, brooding and melancholy.

Hoare's personal sea was at the beach at Southampton where he lived. It also sounded brooding and melancholy.

The mermaids I had interviewed carried the sea inside them, too — and, like Hoare, they bore knowledge of the whales that lived there. I'd been struck by how many mermaids I'd interviewed who had swum with whales — or at least docile whale sharks. If they hadn't, they wanted to. Mermaids performed with whales in the earliest aquariums, and at the opening of the first SeaWorld in 1964. Even the tip of a mermaid's tail was named a fluke, after whales' flukes.

I had first come across Hoare in 2009, when I was still a bookseller and he released his prize-winning book *Leviathan, or the Whale.* I remembered selling bucketloads of it. *Leviathan* caught a wave — the zeitgeist. Like *Moby-Dick* it was quite chunky. No one writes a novella about whales.

Herman Melville allegedly once said, 'To produce a mighty book you must choose a mighty theme.' Yet Melville had died in obscurity not knowing the long life *Moby-Dick* would have in the literary canon. His quote also went on, 'No great and enduring volume can ever be written on the flea, though many there be that have tried it.'

I took issue with that. In the Anthropocene, a book on the flea could be pertinent, but I was already overcommitted. I planned to take all my research and write my own book about mermaids, the equivalent of a book about whales. A girl's own adventure tale. A publisher in Auckland had shown interest.

I stopped reading and looked at the sea outside my plane window. Thirty thousand feet below our air-pressurised cabin was the Pacific.

'Any rubbish?' The hostess was back.

'Yes,' I handed over my cookie wrapper and plastic cup. She held out her hand sheathed in a rubber glove and dispatched the contents into a giant black bin bag. 'Any rubbish?' 'Any rubbish?' The question of our time.

~

On Hannah Mermaid's website I read about her experience diving with humpback whales in Tonga. It was a turning point in her career.

> *We were swimming way out in the ocean, rays of sunlight shooting down into the endless depths when a huge mother whale began to surface underneath me, larger and larger! I realised I could end up in her blowhole or mouth, but the whales were so aware of their size — the mother surfaced within a couple of feet of me. It was amazing how conscious she was of her effect on me, down to the swishing of her tail. You can feel intelligence emanating from the whales. You look them in the eye and there's this ancient consciousness looking back.*
>
> *The humpbacks started singing to each other. It was mind-blowing. This big mama's song was so deep and so rumbly, like standing in front of the largest speaker stack in the world, just this massive whale rock concert where your ribs vibrate. I felt like it was rearranging my DNA molecules, reverberating through every cell in my body. The calf was singing high-pitched trumpeting notes that were nearly too loud for my ears to deal with. And of course, water carries sound, so you feel it coming from every angle.*
>
> *When we got back on to the boat I cried, the emotional release was so powerful. I knew at that moment that I would put my life on the line to protect these creatures.*

Hannah Mermaid's description moved me, stirred some ancient part of my own consciousness that was evolving and turning in the gyre. I wanted to connect with an experience far bigger than myself, but how? I would probably never swim with whales. They seemed to exist pre-memory. As a child I'd made an early picture book about a trio of pastel whales who cavorted in the deep blue with mermaids. The majority of my plot, however, looked like it had been mined directly from Jim Henson's animated film *The Dark Crystal*. On the final page of my story, the whales closed ranks around a giant purple crystal shard.

~

I met Philip Hoare in the foyer of the writers' festival venue. He was slight and wiry, dressed in shorts and a water- and wind-resistant anorak — i.e. appropriately for a whale-watching expedition. He'd been on numerous voyages before, including the one to Kaikōura that we were just about to take.

'Hello darling,' Philip said, as we were introduced.

A two-hour bus journey lay ahead, then the boat to go and meet the whales. But before that we had to meet each other: the whale watchers. A small clutch of middle-aged women had gathered in the foyer — we all looked like writers' festival groupies. We were.

I got down to business. 'Have you come across any mermaids on your travels?'

'Real ones? No,' Philip replied. 'But did you see that picture of the beluga whale? I was almost convinced.'

I had seen the photo of the white beluga, shot from below, with what looked like two kneecaps poking out through its blubbery tail. It was disarming. The mermaid/manatee theory is also popular, though it has been long debunked as the source of mermaid mythology. But what about mermaids and belugas?

In the 1800s, the showman and entrepreneur P. T. Barnum put several ill-fated beluga whales on display in his American Museum. The last pair, horribly, boiled alive in their tanks when the building burned down in a blaze. Barnum was also the dodgy operator responsible for the 'Feejee mermaid', a desiccated monkey stitched to the torso of a dried fish. He advertised the specimen with an illustration of three fetching mermaids rising above the waves. 'Without promotion something terrible happens . . . nothing!' Barnum said. Our fortunes are so easily reversed: a creature of the deep sea can still be killed by fire — or perhaps just stitched up like a kipper.

'When belugas wash up,' Philip told me, 'their bodies are so polluted, they must be treated as toxic waste.'

We got on to talking about David Bowie, one of the figures in Philip's latest book about the sea, *RisingTideFallingStar*. He cited a lyric from Bowie's 'Heroes', about wanting to swim like dolphins can swim.

Brian Eno had once told Philip that Bowie was probably referring to dolphins he'd seen at Berlin Zoo. I'd never thought about this lyric as anything more than a neat simile, perhaps even a cliché; dolphins have become a new-age symbol of playfulness and creativity and freedom. In the mindfulness section of any bookstore, they leap beyond mandalas and jingling windchimes. For Philip however — and for professional mermaids — Bowie's wish was more than real. It was an imperative. Mermaiding is built around the dolphin kick, an undulating movement from the waist, arms arched forward, piercing the water with elegance and grace.

'Fish move their tails from left to right, whales and dolphins move their tails up and down, so we mimic the movement of mammals,' one performer told me. 'And whales and dolphins also have to come to the surface to breathe air.'

In *The Sea Inside*, Philip had got up close and personal with dusky dolphins off Kaikōura Peninsula. They leapt around him, fornicating wildly: 'With the males' two-kilo testes and penises that quick release from genital slits, and females whose receptivity is advertised by plump flashing bellies, dolphins mate continually.

'Everything is turbulence. The water is alive with clicks, as if a current were being passed through it. I feel the sensual power of their bodies as they race past. But the space between us cannot be closed. Nothing passes in between. As abruptly as they came, they are gone.'

I had gotten much more bang for my buck than I'd imagined, reading *The Sea Inside* over Cook Strait. I could totally see why John Waters had said that Philip wrote 'whale porn'.

My own knowledge of whales and dolphins was chin-whisker thin, but stubborn. A memory of my first favourite pop star surfaced. In 1981 Olivia Newton-John released 'The Promise

(The Dolphin Song)'. In the video she wore a mauve wetsuit — that was the bit I really remembered — and swam between a pair of dolphins, holding on to the base of their dorsal fins.

If I can only help to right a wrong
With my dolphin song
Then I'll have done what I set out to do
If I can only make one man aware
One person care

Then I'll have done what I promised you . . .

'The Promise (The Dolphin Song)' was the B-side to her hit 'Physical'. I loved Olivia Newton-John and the image of her heavenly young face smiling benevolently next to a laughing dolphin fit snugly in my mind, as though her grace and femininity were manifestations of the same spirit the dolphins embodied. The thought of myself swimming alongside a dolphin seemed ridiculous — I couldn't lend my physical beauty to their plight.

The small bus to Kaikōura pulled up outside and our throng of middle-aged women and Philip Hoare climbed aboard. No one wore a mauve wetsuit. No one looked like Olivia Newton John. The men were few and far between. In our midst, as well as Philip, was the driver, one miscellaneous boyfriend and the American author and journalist David Neiwert, who had recently published a book about right-wing radicalism but was also the author of *Of Orcas and Men*. Philip and David sat beside one another up front and passed a microphone back and forth, regaling our crew with whale stories.

Did you know there are only three species in the world who go through menopause? (1) Humans, (2) belugas and narwhals, and (3) orcas. That hit home. Orcas are a matrilineal society. If our group had been a pod of orcas, we would have had the post-menopausal women up the front, with Philip, David and the one boyfriend behind.

My seat mate was a pragmatic-looking woman who worked for a digital arts outfit in Christchurch. I didn't ask if she was peri-menopausal but she probably was. One of their projects was a seismic digital archive. In 2012, a box had been set up in a portable shipping container so that people could share their stories of the 2010–11 earthquakes. She said that people needed to share their stories, to feel heard, many felt that no one was listening. She also told me that the stories recorded in the box were mainly by women.

'What's the image that comes into your mind when you think of a whale?' I asked.

Rolling Colin McCahon hills scrolled by out the window.

She considered my question, then replied, 'The whale from *Pinocchio*.'

Monstro! The ferocious whale who swallows both Geppetto and poor Pinocchio was an early villain from the 1940 Disney film. As Jiminy Cricket warns Pinocchio, 'This Monstro! I've heard of him. He's a whale of a whale! Why, he swallows whole ships!'

My seat companion mentioned the whale at the Dinosaur Park playground in St Kilda, Dunedin.

'Yes!' I agreed. In an old family photograph album, there was a Kodak moment of me, aged three, leaning out of the concrete whale like Pinocchio.

'It's quite an unwhale shape,' my companion mused.

We discussed the likenesses. I wondered who had made the concrete whale. Had they ever seen a real whale? Perhaps the sculptor was inspired by Monstro? Our knowledge of whales was shaped by representations of whales but what forces shaped the representations themselves?

I had watched *Pinocchio* as a child. I remembered Jiminy Cricket, the dapper little talking cricket in the top hat whom the blue fairy appoints as Pinocchio's conscience. To me, Philip Hoare was a Jiminy Cricket character, appointed by the blue fairy to act on behalf of the whales.

Philip told the bus his own seminal experience with whales was at a safari park in Windsor when he was a kid. He described a group of dolphins swimming around an overgrown concrete pool, balancing balls on their beaks, in exchange for mackerel.

Philip thought, 'This isn't Jacques Cousteau. This is a circus.'

What he'd seen on TV had been recreated in the suburbs.

Next: Ramu, a young killer whale, jumped through a hoop in the small municipal pool. It's now the site of a Lego Park.

'It still shocks me,' Philip said.

David had got into orcas when he covered a local story about the endangered Southern Resident killer whales of the Salish Sea.

'Far-right writing is pretty limited,' David said. 'And I've got a pretty spry sense of humour. Everyone loves to read about killer whales. The orca book sold better than any of my books about crime.'

And what was happening to the Southern Resident whales was a crime. I had recently seen images flash up online of a mother orca and her dead calf. I didn't click through to the story. The mother was called Tahlequah, or J53, and her calf died shortly after birth. J53 carried the calf for seventeen days. David told me that locals believed she was not only grieving — as was reported in the media — she was also protesting. The calf was on display to a human audience: *Look, you are killing us, look, look at what you are doing to us*. The chinook salmon-runs in the Northwest had been altered by dams, and the killer whales were dying from starvation.

Before the bus stopped for a toilet, tea and biscuits break, I learned that the toothed whales — sperm whales and orcas — clearly exhibit cultural behaviour.

'Whales don't have mortgages and get into traffic jams,' David joked, as evidence of their superior intelligence.

Philip explained that whale culture was 5.5 million years old. 'Whales are profoundly empathetic. Using echolocation they can see inside each other, detect moods and feelings. Their sense of self is bound up in one another.'

Putting an orca into captivity not only reduced its habitat to the circumference of a pool, it also destroyed the social structure of the pod. Keiko, the orca who played the whale in the 1993 blockbuster *Free Willy*, was kept in captivity and liked to watch documentaries on wild orcas. He'd also watch *Monty Python and the Holy Grail* from beginning to end. He wouldn't, however, watch *Free Willy*.

~

'What do you think is going to happen to the world?' I asked one woman, as she sipped her tea in a takeaway mug.

She blinked.

'I think people will take action when the problem is bad enough,' she said.

It was a hard question to answer on the spot, as impossible as 'what's your favourite film or novel?'. The situation was dire, but at the same time here we were drinking tea and eating biscuits and going to watch the whales.

I conducted an informal audit of the crew. Why did you decide to come today? Have you seen a whale before? Have you read Philip Hoare? Most hadn't seen a whale or read Philip Hoare, but both were on the list. One, however, said she probably would never read Philip but wanted to see a whale. Fair enough.

We stepped back on the bus and resumed our holding pattern in the fug and earnest sweat of one another.

The turning point for whales came in the late sixties. The American biologist and environmentalist Roger Payne discovered the song of humpback whales, recorded by a hydrophone placed in the seas of Bermuda to detect Russian submarines. Payne spent two years recording the sounds of whales. *Songs of the Humpback Whale* was released in 1970 and is still the biggest-selling environmental album of all time.

'It's the single moment that saved the whale,' Philip said, 'The record of something poetic, a song, a lament . . . the voice of an animal that had been dumb until now.'

The subsequent 'Save the Whales' campaign helped kick off

other environmental efforts and influenced the ban on commercial whaling.

Philip wanted to know what stories whales might tell about humankind. He proposed that they might have their own stories, myths, religion. One hundred years from now, a pod of whales might be communicating their own thoughts on us — the whale watchers — to their young. I doubted the whales would have anything nice to say about us.

A huge brown bird of prey flew past the windows, its wings outstretched on a diagonal, as alarming as a siren of Greek antiquity.

'What was that?' Philip said.

'A harrier eagle,' my seat companion replied.

She seemed very knowledgeable about nature.

How do we know worlds beyond our own? If not through experience, then through stories — Melville's *Moby-Dick, Alice in Wonderland*, Hannah Mermaid's Instagram.

'But books can never describe that encounter,' Philip said. 'That great distance between ourselves and other species.'

Philip was right. The space between ourselves and other species had never felt more acute.

~

Towards Kaikōura, the tunnels were still surrounded by road workers and scaffolding, the infrastructure from the 7.8 quake that woke New Zealand at two minutes past midnight on 14 November 2016. The bus was now travelling along State Highway 1, close to the epicentre of the quake. The highway had taken months to reopen and even now the effects of the earthquake were still visible: orange high-vis vests, road cones. The bus funnelled slowly through the tunnel, before us a porthole of sea.

As soon as we could see the sea, Philip was transfixed. I took a sneaky iPhone pic of the back of his head. He peered out at waves, raking in and out, their endless uncertain geometry. There, gone, forever lapping, and below them the whales.

'What are the birds on the rocks — shags or penguins?' he asked.

'Let's say they are penguins,' I replied.

'Shags. Penguins only come in at night. They swim and fish during the day,' my seat mate said.

Her family was from Port Chalmers. She was a boat person by proxy, but had never learnt to swim. I had never learnt properly, either. Once I grew up, swimming was just about swimsuits. To don a swimsuit was to reveal how whale-like your shape was or wasn't. My mind flitted briefly to a girl in school nicknamed Whale. 'Save the whale,' the kids would call, as she lumbered past in the schoolyard.

Huge freighted white mountains rose up above the landscape, magnificent as the idealised scenes that once decorated my grandparents' matching dinner trays. When the bus drove into the one street that constituted Kaikōura, I noticed two black whale pots standing like sentinels beside the shops, the only clues to the town's past as a whaling station in the 1800s.

'Whaling was like Auschwitz,' Philip said. 'I don't mean that glibly. The mass killing, the desensitisation to slaughter . . .'

We disembarked. Inside the converted 'Whaleway Station', I found a whole spinner of mermaids alongside the cuddly soft-toy whales. Then I looked at the electronic board: Strong Sea Sickness Alert. My stomach dropped. I began to consider staying permanently at the Whaleway Station.

'I don't know about this,' I said.

'Do you get seasick?' an older blonde woman asked.

'Probably,' I said.

A representative from the writers' festival stepped forward and gave me a Sea-Legs tablet.

'Thank you,' I said.

Turned out the one boyfriend in our midst was hers. They had both seen the whales before but were keen to see them again and had learnt that Sea-Legs were required.

The blonde had seen the whales, too. In the early days of Kaikōura whale-watching, she had gone out in just an inflatable boat and witnessed the head of a giant sperm whale rise next to her.

'Holy shit,' I said. 'Were you afraid?'

'No,' she said, gamely.

I was glad to step on to a proper boat, with a large, enclosed cabin. I sat at the back next to the blonde and watched the video presentation about the local whales. Behind us sat two good-looking young Italian couples. The presenter up the front talked on her microphone about Big Nick and Little Nick. (Little Nick was the bigger of the pair, but the nick on his tail was littler.) The sea was much too wild. Huge slopes rose outside the window, the triangular waves looked as thick and solid as concrete. The pill was the only thing holding my guts inside my stomach. I gripped the seat in front of me. My conversation fell away. I didn't have a quip or a question left.

I heard the sound of chunder. A beautiful Italian man was heaving into his supplied sick bag, while his girlfriend went outside. We sped towards our destination, the whales. It was like hunting the Snark, only with better coordinates and more chunder. The woman over the loudspeaker asked us to look out to the right. Everyone who could, hit the deck. Cameras ready. 'Here are some whales I ordered up earlier.'

The sperm whale surfaces for approximately ten minutes, then dives down again for another forty-five minutes. It was a small window. I inched carefully towards the outdoor deck.

The moment I got outside amongst the lurching concrete waves, my iPhone battery died. I leaned against the boat cabin. David lowered a piece of kit on a black cord over the edge and we listened to the clicks and ticks. The whale was sending up hieroglyphics. *Clickclickclickclickclick* meant that it was feeding on krill or something.

I tried to look attentive. I *was* moved. But that was the boat. The sea was so . . . chunky. The choppiness terribly unruly. I wanted to peacefully assess the terrain of the whale without losing my own composure.

I kept inching, but didn't make it round the side of the boat to get the prime view. The whale's innocuous grey flukes rose up and then under; it sank below the sea it belonged to. The encounter didn't feel close. Everyone made the right noises and expressions of wonder, though. Some had managed the perfect shot: the flukes at the right angle. The tail so symbolic — a totem, a sign of the whale. The dark freight below the surface, the tourist's holy grail.

I returned to my seat inside, my guts intact. I had seen a whale in the wild but it wasn't a defining encounter. I was still hungry for more about the sea and our place in it.

The first sentence of *Moby-Dick* is a classic. But the last line of the novel is harder to digest. It drags me under its swell. 'Now small fowls flew screaming over the yet yawning gulf; a sullen white surf beat against its steep sides; then all collapsed, and the great shroud of the sea rolled on as it rolled five thousand years ago.'

7.

Aquatic Masculinity

Mum asked, 'Do you like the flat?'

Me, unconvincingly, 'Yes.'

I was staying the night with Mum before heading back home. The house was down a steep awkward driveway. I hadn't been there before — I tried to avoid staying in Mum's flats because it always depressed me. But since I'd had Fearne I was more willing to please her, to be close again. The flat was part of a bungalow, its exterior composed from insipid tan and white bricks. It looked like what it was: a rental, a dead-end; and it was damp. The house in shadow in the afternoon. The flat had an upstairs and a downstairs, where my half-brother Mike lived, which was part of the attraction for Mum.

I stood in the lounge and put my bag down. 'I can't find my copy of *Leviathan*,' I said. 'Maybe I left it at the whale-watching trip? I got Philip Hoare to sign it for me.' Still caught up in my own business.

Mum had an L-shaped grey sofa with a mauve shawl slung over it and a coffee table set up in front of the blank screen of the TV.

The evidence of her attempts at optimism were all around me. Knick knacks. Floral aphorisms. On one windowsill she had the word 'Nana' spelt out in freestanding letters. A garish turquoise bookcase.

'Where's the old white photo album?' I asked. 'I want to find that photo of me in the St Kilda Park whale, remember?'

'Oh Megan, I might have thrown it out.' Mum looked instantly guilty.

'What?' I said.

'The album was falling apart. I saved some of the photos and pasted them in my scrapbook,' she said. 'But I had to throw the rest out.'

'I can't believe you threw out the photo of me inside the whale!'

'I'm sorry, darling,' Mum bit her lip and winced in that way that riled me even more.

Mum showed me the scrapbook that now subbed for the white photo-album: *Lee's Memories*. My mother was named Cecilia after the patron saint of music. But in childhood she was nicknamed Lee Lee, and the name Lee stuck.

She'd sellotaped some of the remaining photos on the cover. A patchwork of old Kodak moments from my seventies childhood. Little pinafores and tiny sprouting pigtails, baggy homespun jerseys, jam on toast in bed, but no St Kilda whale.

Mum boiled the jug and made herself a cup of tea. 'Do you want one?'

'No.' I don't drink tea.

She looked pale, winded.

I felt that enveloping sense of dread. I hated being out of the city, deep in suburbia, it always brought out a feeling of panic in me. A desire to flee, as though whatever sadness lurked inside Mum's life might rise up and swallow me.

'Do you want to see my office?' Mum asked, perking up.

I followed her down the hallway, to a corner room where she had a desk, tidy files and folders. 'I always wanted my own office,' she said cheerfully.

Mum retrained as a counsellor after she turned fifty, but somehow her own practice had never taken off. She worked on a polytech campus, as a point of contact for students, and helped them write their CVs. 'I work by myself now on campus. I like working alone. I love my work,' she said. 'Mike prefers working alone, too, he's like me.' My half-brother Mike had drug and alcohol problems and had lived with Mum for the past ten years. He was a landscape gardener. I worried about her and him. I always wondered if his problems were due to her leaving him as a baby, then felt bad because I knew Mum loved Mike, had not been given a full deck of cards to play out her life's choices. I felt desperation under the seams of everything. Her need to be seen. And only me there to see her. A blue mesh drawstring bag on her desk.

'Do you ever read the Pearls of Wisdom cards I gave you?' she asked.

'Yes,' I said.

What did she know about pearls, for God's sake? Even the saying was a cliché. I didn't believe she had much wisdom to share with me or the world. It was the sadness underneath the false optimism that kept me away from her, the fear it might be catching, clinging to the hull of me, like a barnacle to the wreck.

The flat also had a veranda and a glass sunroom that led off the lounge and overlooked a clump of bush. Mum sat down in the sunroom to finish her tea. 'I like looking out here,' she smiled. Tall ponga trees, ferns.

I smiled back. 'It's nice,' I said, throwing her a bone.

A wooden dollhouse she bought from an op shop sat in the sunroom. It was painted purple and maroon. The dollhouse was musty and evacuated. No little dolls inside it, but a big doll with long strawberry-coloured hair sat outside. She had blue eyes that blinked open and shut.

'Fearne is a doll player from a long line of doll players,' I said.

'Yes,' Mum chuckled. She had a sepia photo of herself aged eight, holding a baby doll. It must have been the only one she ever owned. In her adult life she often found and brought home dolls that reminded her of this original. They were always ancient to me, relics from the fifties that seemed at once old and young, like the elderly people Mum used to care for when she worked as a nurse aid at 'the manor'.

The doll and the dollhouse were plodding signifiers of Mum's inner life. Mum cherished Fearne and me, but she also cherished her own inner child, whereas I think I hated her inner child. The whole flat had a feeling of inbuilt sadness, a wrongness that was never going to be made right.

'I think I'll lie down,' Mum said. 'I'm a bit tired.'

'Okay, you do that.'

I scanned her bookshelf for the whale photo again, then slid a book off the shelf, *Playing Big* by Tara Mohr, and stood in the glum lounge, reading it. The words 'Playing Big' were in a teal font designed to look like handwriting. 'A practical guide for women like you,' the tagline read. I usually didn't like to have too much to do with Mum's bookshelf. I didn't want to give her emotional life that much power. Mum and me and self-help books go back a long way — to that flat I grew up in above the manor, where she discovered that the musician would never marry her and started reading self-help books instead.

'Mum,' I called out. 'Do you still have anything to do with that old boyfriend?'

'We call now and then,' she said, hollow. 'But no, not really.'

'Do you still wish you had married him?' It was the question that continued to burn inside me. She had never been able to let him go.

'No,' Mum answered.

'Really?' I said.

'I realise, looking back, that I needed to love myself more,' she said.

I sat down on the sofa with *Playing Big*. Maybe Mum had gotten over him after all? The book was about women choosing to be more loyal to their dreams than to their fears. 'What's the gasp level action?' Tara asked in one chapter. It was one of her cues to be bolder, and braver, to take more risks where they needed to be taken, rather than cowering on the couch, or hiding behind the rocks. It was also a pretty funny question for a fish. Yet I recognised myself and the professional mermaids in *Playing Big*. I took it to heart.

'Mum, can I borrow *Playing Big*?' I asked.

'Yes darling, of course.'

In the morning, she dropped me at the airport in her little turquoise-coloured car — 'do you like it, Megan? I couldn't resist the colour!' — and I flew home to skype more mermaids and work part-time in the basement as an archivist.

~

I doubled down on my Skypes.

Rose, the New York mermaid, was an ex-aquarium educator, who got into mermaiding while recovering from a collapsed lung. The doctor told her swimming would be good for her. She kept two parrots in her apartment — 'they're the biggest loves of my life,' she joked. Rose, as a mermaid, had once unwittingly graced the shores of a nudist beach. A white Russian asked to have his photograph taken with her.

I skyped a pod in the Philippines — two mermaids and two mermen. If was my first and only pod, but the connection was terrible. A shame, because one of the mermen had got into swimming in a tail after a near-drowning incident as a child. He had conquered his fear of swimming through mermaiding. A shame, too, because the pod was the first community of mermaids in the Philippines. They lived on separate islands but met every fortnight to swim together. 'Why do you think people are fascinated by mermaids?' I asked. One member replied, 'Well naturally mermaids are beautiful, and beauty fascinates people.' Our connection cut out.

Nerdmaid Faith was a super-cute Canadian who swam in her local pool still wearing her glasses. She constantly got asked by her followers how many mermaid tails she had. 'The answer is nineteen, going on twenty, going on twenty-one possibly twenty-two. You know, it's a lot,' she said, laughing.

It's a lot. My Skypes were mounting up too. But not my transcriptions. It took so long to transcribe each interview. One mermaid begat another mermaid, then another and another.

~

'Fearne, would you like some grated cheese and carrot?'

'Okay Mummy.'

I used to eat grated cheese and carrot.

I whipped up a grated carrot bowl and lightly spritzed it with Edam — not Tasty, never anything more tasty than Edam — then presented this to her in a bowl while the pasta jostled around in its spa bath.

Fearne was seated at her green kids' table shaped like a dog, watching TV. Rich had bought it for her because we didn't have a proper kitchen table. I didn't care — I grew up eating in front of the TV, and it still made sense to me. Why not eat mindlessly, spooning grated carrot and cheese into your mouth and watching your favourite series or googling mermaids?

Fearne's little crocodile backpack slumped on the floor. Another hard day at daycare and the archive.

We heard the jostle of his key in the lock and the spinning of spokes as Rich wheeled his bike into the space under the house.

'Daddy's home,' I said.

He appeared at the door, a lean shadow, worn out from a job that he didn't want to be doing, but was doing. Every. Single. Day.

'Hello Daddy!'

'Hello. What are you eating?'

'Cheese and carrot,' she said, stuffing another fist in her mouth.

'Carrot is a vegetable, Daddy Pig,' I said. 'I'm just finishing cooking her pasta.'

'Heating it,' he said.

'I am a wonderful heater of pasta,' I said.

'Yes, you are. What's this towel doing on the floor?'

I had been at my computer all day, thinking about mermaids and preparing for an interview with an environmental scientist.

'It was just hanging out, enjoying some down time,' I replied. 'Towelling around.'

'Right,' Rich picked up the apricot-coloured towel, sniffed it, then gagged.

'Onions, my telltale stress aroma,' I said.

'Her food is a problem,' Rich said, glancing at the carrot-cheese medley. The seahorse wanted a healthier organic diet for its brood, less plastic consumption, less chocolate too.

'I'm still hungry,' Fearne said. 'Food!'

'I've nearly heated your pasta!' I shrieked.

~

Brooke Porter was an environmental scientist and mum who had spent the last four years living and working in the Philippines. When she got into researching the connection between mermaiding and blue tourism — interviewing participants at the mermaid school in Boracay — her mother was worried it would ruin her career.

'We need to be careful about the idea of Mother Nature,' she said. 'Gendering nature can actually be detrimental to the environment.'

Brooke told me how she and some colleagues in Hawai'i came up with a joke campaign called: 'Don't pee in the sea.'

Apparently, the estrogen from women on birth control pills goes right into the reef. 'A lot of reef fish are hermaphroditic,' Brooke said. 'They start as females and then shift to males, so estrogen really affects the fish.'

I hadn't peed in the sea recently, but I had done it, and probably while I was on the pill, which I took from the age of fourteen on because I had terrible period pains.

My defences were down, so I asked Brooke something that had been bugging me. 'How do fish have sex?'

'They just spew eggs and sperm out into the water columns,' she said.

'They don't even shimmy up to one another?' I preferred Philip Hoare's horny story about the racy dolphins.

~

'Christmas time, mistletoe and wine,' I sang along to the Christmas playlist on Spotify. Nana sat on the sofa in her long nightgown, next to the tinsel tree that Rich had wrapped in fairy lights. The lights blinked on and off.

Christmas was back on the agenda. Fearne's mound of presents had the obscene sheen of capitalism — virtually everything under the tree was for her.

Nana had addressed a few goodies as 'From Santa'. Or 'From Santa's elf'. A tradition I had kept going.

'Isn't she lucky, Megan?' Mum beamed.

The stage was set for Fearne to wake up and rip everything to shreds.

'Happy Christmas, darling!' I said, as Fearne came running out in her My Little Pony pyjamas, which she liked to wear though she took zero interest in my vintage My Little Ponies.

'Nana!'

'Happy Christmas, Fearne,' Nana hugged and smooched her. Big kisses on each cheek.

Rich and I knelt on the floor, Fearne's present support team.

Fearne chose the presents to open, one by one, and we passed them to her.

Granddad from England got her an Ariel doll and a Snow White. I picked up the Ariel doll in her glittery fabric fishtail and swished her beautiful red hair.

Fearne opened Nana's present — a traditional baby doll in a blue romper suit with a butterfly on the top. The doll came with a turquoise bathtub and a potty. 'Christmas Dolly!' Fearne hugged it and kissed its forehead.

Rich and I knew the doll was cheap as chips, and that we had got her something far more special. We sat waiting patiently for the big reveal. A huge rectangular box lovingly gift-wrapped by Rich — the ace gift-wrapper in the family, the only one with the patience and precision to do it right. Fearne tore into it last. It was as though she had been avoiding the present, perhaps sensing we had our hopes pinned on it.

'A Barbie Dreamhouse!' I exclaimed, ecstatically.

I'd always wanted one.

Rich crouched on the floor, reading the instructions, absorbed by the Ikea-like detail of sorting the parts and laying them out, ready for construction. 'Get me bag A, Fearne,' he said.

He spent Christmas morning erecting the three-storey structure. He fitted the shallow pool and added the purple slide from the first floor to the mezzanine. The mezz level also had a shower with a flimsy pink curtain and a toilet that flushed.

It's the details. The simulation of real life, and then the lack of it.

'Look at the toothbrushes, Nana,' Fearne said. The tiny fuchsia-pink toothbrushes had handles so they could be fixed to the Barbie dolls' plastic hands.

'They're so fiddly I can't even pick them up,' Nana said. 'I need my glasses.'

Mum dipped her hand into her purple handbag. 'Any chance of another cup of tea?' she smiled.

'I'll put the jug on,' I said.

Rich was preoccupied. He was like Bob the Builder, only specialising in Dreamhouses.

'Don't put the stickers on yet,' he cautioned Fearne.

We were both awed by the house's majesty and its illusion of indoor/outdoor living. The backyard area even had a circular fishpond filled with koi carp — it was a sticker, but still. Barbie could be a homeowner, even though we couldn't.

Fearne shoved Ariel in the outdoor elevator and we tried to get her up to the top floor, so she could slide down and into the pool.

'Can we fill it up?' Fearne asked of the pool. Then as soon as we had filled it, she wanted to put some pond snails from the garden in it.

'The pool is for the dolls,' Rich said.

One of Rich's colleagues had given him her old Barbie dolls. She had trained as a fashion designer and the Barbies came dressed in various homemade outfits, which explained why Ken was wearing a black velvet cape.

Rich was more interested in getting the oven in the dream-house to work.

Ken in his black cape stood in the kitchen sizzling some plastic eggs in a frying pan on the hob. Then he put the pizza into the Barbie oven. When he pressed the purple kettle down on the front element it whistled as though boiling.

Fearne wriggled Ariel out of her mermaid tail. She wasn't careful with her dolls.

'Pretend Ariel wanted to marry Ken,' Fearne said.

'Okay,' I groaned. Ken and Ariel shared a chaste peck. I started trying to shimmy Ariel's mermaid tail on to Ken to jazz things up.

'Why doesn't Daddy have to play dolls?' I asked.

'Men don't play dolls,' Rich said, flexing his controversial opinions.

'Because you're the best at playing dolls,' Fearne said. 'And Nana.'

Nana laughed. 'I'll play with you in a minute, darling,' she said.

'Thanks, Mum,' I said, getting off the floor.

'Nana, you be the baby,' Fearne said, cradling Christmas Dolly.

I looked down at Nana's cup of tea. High tide.

~

I looked into the ocean every day and saw the world reflected back. Mermen were high on my agenda. They've been complicated from the beginning. Oannes, a fish-headed god from ancient Mesopotamia, is the first known depiction of a merman. He had the head of man underneath his fish head, which I presume was worn a bit like a hoody. Under his feet, he had a fish's tail.

One merman I interviewed, Christian, had done a gender bend on Madison and created his own amazing replica chiffon tail. 'The fluke is the best part of the mermaid tail,' he said. 'It's kinda like your beauty spot.'

'Sorry if this sounds inappropriate,' I asked another merman, 'but how many mermen have you encountered that are heterosexual?'

'More than you think,' he said. 'I get the *Zoolander* MER-MAN joke all the time. There are tons of great versions of mermen, but they all get ignored because everyone makes so much of Ben Stiller.'

In *Zoolander*, Ben Stiller plays the naive but affable and vain male model Derek Zoolander, known for his penetrating 'Blue Steel' gaze and his matching trout pout. Derek is the hero of the story, but he is also a bit of a dork. 'Wetness is the essence of beauty,' he intones, as he paddles through an Aveda advertisement in a ridiculously flaccid, blue CGI fishtail.

Derek's on-screen father and brother are hardened coal miners played by Jon Voight and Vince Vaughan. Seated in a sports bar, a pair of men's men, they watch Derek in his merman tail on the TV. 'I'm glad your mother never lived to see her son as a mermaid,' Jon Voight says.

'A mer-man,' Derek replies, standing up for himself. Then he says it louder, more triumphantly, 'A MER-MAN.'

~

I kept chasing after mermen but there were fewer of them and they were harder to catch. In South Carolina, the Blixunami was landlocked when I called. He'd just had his hair retwisted and had to wait a couple of months before he could swim in the pool again. He swung his phone round and showed me seven inches of thick snow outside.

'We've never had this much snow before, ever.'

Blix called himself the 'Geechee' merm. 'That's the native tongue for most people that live here in South Carolina. It's like broken English, the older folks down here still talk like that — my mum's still got it in her, my grandma did, she looks very Geechee, a lot of my aunts are.'

In early online photos and videos, Blix often wore a rainbow silicone tail, with a clamshell over one shoulder, draped with pearls. Being a professional mer was more difficult than easy, especially for a black merperson in such a Republican state. Blix could count the number of paid events he'd done on one hand. He advertised himself as a merman for a while on an online portal, but people repeatedly contacted him to request Ariel. So Blix relied mostly on his social media accounts.

I watched a clip of him appearing on a TV programme with the comedian Daniel Tosh.

Tosh hooked Blix, using a fishing rod baited with Beyoncé concert tickets. Then, after clubbing him over the head, Tosh apologised. 'Sorry about that, I know clubbing a homosexual sea monster is considered hate-fishing.'

Tosh asked Blix how many black mermaids there were out there.

'Not as many as white mermaids.'

I became aware, following Blix, that my own social media bubble and the mermaids in it were largely white. Why? Every seafaring culture had its own mermaid or sea-woman myth. Pania and her son Moremore. Mami Wata, whom I learned about in Copenhagen, the ningyo of Japan, the Yawkyawk of Western Arnhem Land, Australia. But it was Hans Christian Andersen's *The Little Mermaid* that had stuck in the Western world's imagination, then Disney's Ariel had further colonised the image of the mermaid as white — until the 2023 remake starring Halle Bailey. I thought Bailey made a wonderfully convincing Ariel, but the online haters circled with the hashtag #notmyariel. 'Don't be a racist dork,' Daryl Hannah posted in response.

Blix loved Disney's Ariel, but as a child he had also loved a local story called *Sukey and the Mermaid* by Robert D. San Souci. Sukey lives with her Ma and mean step-Pa, 'Mr Hard Times' in a cabin, but one day she meets Mama Jo, a black mermaid, who promises her an escape from her life on land.

Blix was irrepressible — he had a wild streak. His identity was also fluid — he happily goes by the pronouns, they/she/it and merm. He called the hater mermaids in the community 'anchovies' and said he didn't like people acting like 'President Mermaid', telling everyone what to do.

It doesn't matter if you only have a fabric tail, he said. You don't have to have silicone to be a real mermaid.

~

Hasan Hai lived in Newfoundland and Labrador, Canada, and had spearheaded a merman calendar, MerB'ys, that went viral. Hasan was a voluptuous Blackbeard in a shiny fabric mermaid tail. B'y, he told me, is the local parlance for boy or dude. The calendar was like an Anne Geddes photoshoot in reverse. Instead of cute babies, it featured burly blokes. A salty-bearded merman laughed seductively, fondling a large ginger pumpkin in a pumpkin patch. Other mermen posed solo or in playful pods wearing their spandex mermaid tails.

'There's not a lot of muscle tone shining through in the pictures,' Hasan joked. The calendar had taken the world's media by storm and raised thousands for a local domestic violence charity. It also raised morale. The group nicknamed one of their most popular models 'Fish Sex'— chiselled features, trim beard, posing by some equally chiselled rocks.

Another model had never taken off his shirt in public before because he was so ashamed of his body, but at the launch he sat

in a photobooth all night — shirtless — having his photo taken with his fans. The MerB'ys calendar wasn't making a mockery of men, it was about showing the different shapes masculinity can take. 'We can be comfortable with ourselves, we can be holding hands, we can be blowing each other kisses and not be afraid or even care if people question our sexuality.'

Hasan told me the calendar had grown out of the Newfoundland and Labrador Beard and Moustache club that he set up earlier.

'It sounds great,' I said. 'You know, I get chin whiskers now, so perhaps I could join?'

'You know what? You're welcome,' he said. 'After this conversation you're an official member.'

~

'You're in a good mood,' I said.

Rich stepped through the door smiling, and removed his khaki bike helmet, which looked like an army helmet out of *M*A*S*H*, but with a visor. His eyes were sparkling. He looked . . . frisky.

'On the way home, I ran into this guy at the lights who said "Nice Surly".'

A compliment on his bike.

'He used to have a Surly,' Rich went on, but my eyes darted back to Facebook. A painting of an underwater grotto had appeared in my stream. The water in the painting was the bottle green of old glass; the mermaids inside it, slender and waiflike. They paddled back and forth in the water, their long lean legs sprouting swishy ankle fins.

'You should get a bike,' Rich said. 'Then we could ride together as a family. We could do a biking tour of Europe.'

I looked at him sharply, thinking of the feminist quote, 'A woman needs a man like a fish needs a bicycle'. I hadn't ridden since I was a kid. A cycling holiday was his dream.

'Let me show you something,' he said. 'Just quickly.'

I passed him my laptop and he brought up an image of a fetching green Pashley bicycle.

'This could be you,' he said.

'Hmmmm.'

Cycling seemed perilous and unnecessary. What I needed was a man, not a bike. Though I didn't mind if that man needed a bike. What I needed was to interview more mermaids.

~

A fish might not need a bike, however, but a little girl does. Rich was adamant that Fearne would not have training wheels. In his favourite bike shop, we found a lovely little balance bicycle with a white basket and a happy pink plastic flower attached to it.

'She'll love it,' I said. 'But what about that doll seat? Could we fit that to the back?' I stared at the cute range of doll seats and imagined her riding around with the pink flower at the front and Christmas Dolly on the back, living the dream.

'No.'

I stood in the shop, the third wheel of the project. The bikes were arranged in their aisles, looking lean and fit, their silver spokes shining professionally.

As the male staff member talked grips and stems with Rich, the pair of them lost inside their own enchanted grotto, I threaded my hands through a pair of glittering pink streamers to be added to handlebars for extra frills. They rustled, like waterfalls.

~

'I will never become a professional mermaid,' I said, standing on Papamoa Beach, the sea only a sand dune away.

We were staying at our landlord's beach house. A complimentary MerFin had arrived for me from Mermaid Mahina, another OG mermaid from Byron Bay who had created her own line of recycled rubber monofins for children and adults. Other mermaids had raved to me about swimming in them. The MerFin looked the business, too — it had a beautiful feminine shape, with a frilled bootylicious fluke.

I packed the fin in the boot of our rental car and Rich drove us on holiday to Papamoa Beach. We had a compilation of kids' songs and sang along to 'Baby Beluga in the deep blue sea'. Then Fearne chundered. Thick bubbly milk spewed out all over the baby seat. At least a litre of it. We stopped at a playground in Levin. Then stopped again every time she looked green, which was often. Baby Beluga, on replay. Rich fretted about the hire car. He bought a car cleaner and an air freshener from a petrol station, drove with the windows down.

My first pilot swim in the monofin was everything I thought it would be: embarrassing.

The waves at Papamoa were surprisingly powerful, salty burps and splutterings. A wave can move you, tip you sideways, plaster your hair against the side of your face like it's tarred with thick housepaint. It didn't help that I had an audience. Janet, the landlord's wife, sat behind me on a beach towel supervising Fearne's sandcastles. She had brought her camera down to the beach so she could photograph me swimming in the fin. I knew she meant well, but I felt like telling her to stop staring at me and go back to the house and finish her fucking orange juice.

I stood at the edge of the sea, the tide sizzling around me and tried to wedge each foot into the stirrups of the monofin. I stuttered on each leg, unsteady on the sand, aware of the ugliness of my varicose veins and the whiteness of my legs, once called milk bottles in high school. Rich came and stood beside me, thin, elfin and graceful. He was everything a woman should be, except for his chest hair and that fine pelt on his tight buttocks.

I leaned against his shoulder. 'I've got you.' He steadied me.

I was in the monofin, but now I had to get into the sea.

I felt fright! I had every reason to be frightened. I decided to try and hop in the fin towards the sea. Even though the sea was only ankle deep, each wave rushed in trying to knock my milk bottles over.

Rich told me to go backwards. That was even worse. I fell on my bum, laughing. Once, twice, then again! Sand on my tongue and up my nose. Sand is obnoxious. It doesn't care about your dreams.

Then I was in the lurching waves, waist deep but still flailing, and afraid to let go and swim. Rich stood beside me like a chaperone, 'You're not going to drown,' he said, then dove head first into the surf, rising a metre away.

Splash undersells the force of the ocean: its terminal power. Professional mermaids can really swim — that was now obvious to me. The mermaids described the experience as liberating, cathartic and healing, freeing. But anytime I found myself in deeper water, I felt a plunging, lurching chaos, as though the abyss was opening up beneath me. I hated not being able to put my feet on the ground — the sea can carry you out. I remembered a time years earlier when I got caught in a rip at another beach and couldn't touch the bottom. My friend Cassandra had swum alongside me and kept me calm. I might have drowned.

'Help me,' I called to Rich. 'I can't get it off.' He swam towards me, helped unhook the monofin.

'Do you mind if I have a turn?'

Rich slipped his feet into the monofin and swam several laps along the beach. 'It's quite difficult,' he said. Up the beach, Janet watched. Fearne was still preoccupied with building sandcastles. White glints on the waves.

I trudged towards the sanctuary of a towel, wrapped it around my waist.

'Well, it was your first time,' Janet said, good-naturedly.

Rich followed me ashore, holding the monofin in his hand.

'I thought you were very graceful,' she told him.

~

That night upstairs in our en suite, I ran a big bubble bath for me and Fearne. She sat on my tummy and poured cups of water in and out of the bath. She pretended to make soup. I had my fin on.

A mermaid in a bathtub is not a performance. The bathtub is the site of a private transformation. The woman shrugs off her legs and turns into her true self, announcing, *I am more than you can ever imagine.* My tail is something I lubricate by myself, for myself. I have a secret inner life. You thought I was just a chick, but really, I am a *myth*.

'Get a photo,' I told Rich. 'Get several,' I said, inspecting each one, before selecting the best one for Facebook.

~

I put down Jennifer Kokai's *Swim Pretty* and picked up *Playing Big* again.

'I have to go to America,' I told Rich.

Fearne snored between us, her forehead slicked with sweat, the hair on her crown wet. She got so hot at night. We lay on the double bed together. I was waiting for a tsunami to announce itself; instead, there was just the sound of waves crashing back and forth and the curtain wavering by the veranda.

I looked at him. His small ears. His petite nose. He was my sailor, my first mate, even though I didn't know a thing about sailing. Didn't want to try it, didn't want to go kayaking either. Rich was the adventurous one. He had once swum with piranhas and crocodiles and pink dolphins in the Amazon. He had walked the Inca trail. I had been to London and on a few Ryanair getaways to Europe.

'I have to meet the real mermaids,' I said. 'I really think I can make a book out of this,' I told him. 'I have to go and meet the Mermaid Trifecta. Hannah Mermaid and Mermaid Linden are both in Los Angeles,' I said. 'MeduSirena is in Florida.'

'Okay,' Rich nodded. He was the only one with a full-time salary. He cycled to work each day and worked in an expensive design store that meant nothing to him, then he cycled home to me and Fearne. 'We've gone this far,' he said. 'We may as well go all the way.'

'I want to go to the Coney Island Mermaid Parade in New York, too,' I said. 'But I don't want to leave Fearne. She might not cope without me.'

'She'll be fine,' he said.

'I've never been away from her for more than two nights. What if something happens?'

'Nothing will happen,' he said.

That was the problem.

On our drive back home, we stopped and stayed at a big ancient hotel in the middle of the North Island. It had a shallow pool in the basement, and I cruised the length of it several times in my monofin, building up my confidence, until a group of teenagers arrived and busted my fantasy. On the last stretch of the drive into Wellington, Fearne chundered again. Afterwards, she looked up at us both and said, 'Crikey dicks.'

8.

Dreams of Venus

At the author party the night before the Auckland Writers Festival, I got talking to a good-looking American with a strong jawline, who had just written a book about climate change. He was also a contributing editor to *Rolling Stone*. 'I'm coming to your talk tomorrow,' I said. He asked about my own books, memoirs about bookselling and my time at art school. I glossed over them. Despite being some kind of climate expert and an American, he knew nothing about mermaids.

'I can't believe it,' I told him. 'This is an American story. I'm going to the States in a few days to interview some of the top mermaids.' I finished my glass of white wine.

'You're really serious about this, aren't you?' he said.

'Yes,' I nodded. 'It would be a great story for *Rolling Stone*.'

'Perhaps when the book comes out you should pitch it,' he said kindly, a true gentleman.

'What else have you written?' I asked. 'You're probably really famous. I just wanted to come to your talk because so many mermaids care about climate change.'

The writer listed his other books. One was about coal.

He also told me he had swum the Great Barrier Reef with his daughter.

'Lots of mermaids have swum the Great Barrier Reef,' I said.

I discussed my fears for Fearne's future.

'What's going to happen to humanity?' I asked. 'Will we all die?'

He seemed like he might know, but instead he laughed. 'That's not the question most people ask me.'

'What is?' I asked.

'Most people ask me if they should sell their beachfront property.'

~

On my hotel bed, I flicked through Sky channels, fantasising that it was me, not the *Rolling Stone* dude, who was the high-profile literary guest at an important international writers' festival. I sat on stage, a lapel mic attached to my collar, and leaned forward to sup my glass of water, the hushed and reverent audience a haze on the horizon of the sold-out auditorium. My interviewer was the critic and poet Maggie Nelson.

'Good questions, Maggie,' I told her. 'But does femininity, like literature, have to be deep? Isn't part of life and language also pleasurably shallow? Why is feminism described in waves?' I'd ask, leadingly. 'I see the professional mermaid as a symbol of our relationship with the ocean and the internet and isn't it funny how one is described through the lens of the other . . .'

'Can you expand?' Maggie said.

Then I'd let rip on how it was a woman who first coined the metaphor 'surfing the internet' or explain that mermaids actually do have vaginas. Because their tails are simply costumes that they take off.

But in my wildest dreams, of course, I am on *Oprah*, seated on a blue kidney-bean couch. One by one, Oprah introduces the Mermaid Trifecta. They can't walk out, but they are decanted on the kidney bean in their signature tails: Hannah Mermaid in her hand-sewn sequins, MeduSirena in her red fabric and Mermaid Linden in tail 1.0 with the crescent-shaped fluke. And me, Megan Dunn, a nervous wreck.

Life is brutal and so was high school. A thick, incoherent memory of choking on chlorinated water, a crowd of my peers looking down, as my arm chopped through the sloshing blue in a frantic whirligig to the end of the high school pool, only to discover I had come last.

Not any more.

On *Oprah*, I am seated on the blue kidney bean in a pair of flared Rolla's, my favourite brand of jeans. I have a replica Madison tail next to me.

Oprah leans in, her brown eyes wide, brimming with empathy. 'Megan, is it true you don't even eat fish?'

'Yes,' I confess. 'But not because I am trying to save the world. I have always hated the scent. So vaginal and raw.'

The audience explodes into laughter.

Oprah is incredulous, but deeply interested. Her eyes widen. She grips her chair arms, and leans towards me, hanging on my every word.

'And you did all this because you watched *Splash* as a child and were enchanted by Daryl Hannah as the mermaid Madison?'

'Yes,' I'd reply. 'I couldn't let go of this tail . . .' I smooth my hand over the silicone orange tail and its scalloped scales.

Then the audience gasps and starts cheering as Daryl Hannah walks out, and I stand up, shocked, and crying. The crowd goes wild. My mum leaps up out of the front-row seat and starts screaming. She loves *Oprah*. We used to watch it together when I was a teenager still living at home.

It's a terrible thing for a woman to let herself go, but it's also a terrible thing for a woman *not* to be able to let go. Especially of a dream.

~

'We need water,' I said.

In the kitchen, I got out our glass Pyrex jug and filled it to the top with a blast of cold. Fearne fetched her plastic stool so she could stand at the bench beside me. She extracted the pale-blue clamshell from its kitsch plastic casing. I couldn't resist buying the 'Grow Your Own Mermaid' kit because Fearne loves things that hatch like eggs. It must be the suspense. Or is it the surprise? When you are three years old you haven't seen it all before. Each gift from the gift shop isn't just a cheap hoax.

'I want to do it myself,' Fearne manhandled the clamshell with her chubby toddler fingers.

'I know, I know!'

She leaned over the Pyrex jug and added the clamshell.

It sank to the bottom and promptly did nothing. A few bubbles attached to the surface.

'When will the mermaid hatch?' asked Fearne, a pint-sized P.T. Barnum desperate for her experiment to take hold.

'Not right away,' I said.

Fearne and I would both fail the marshmallow test. She eyeballed the Grow Your Own Mermaid as though it was a jack-in-the-box.

'It's going to take time, Magoo,' I explained.

Magoo was one of my many nicknames for her because she had started walking with the confidence and swagger of Mr Magoo.

I inspected the packaging. 'The mermaid won't hatch for twenty-four to forty-eight hours,' I said. 'Maybe tomorrow morning there will be a crack in the shell.'

Before bed, Fearne checked the clamshell one last time, watching it for signs but there were none. I read her *Meg at Sea*. 'Mermaid's tail, Lobster's toe, Octopus wriggle, Blow wind blow!' I chanted.

'I've caught a whopper,' Mog said, reeling in a giant orange fish.

'A whopper!' Fearne repeated with glee.

I wanted to catch a whopper, too.

On the last page, Meg and Mog and Owl appeared in a circle waving goodbye. 'Goodbye,' Fearne waved back.

Greetings are so important. I didn't want to say goodbye to Fearne. Ever.

~

After I had got Fearne to sleep, I returned to the Egyptian sofa, sat down and felt the springs creak. 'What if my plane crashes?' I said.

'Don't be ridiculous,' Rich said.

'There are crocodiles in Florida,' I said.

Rich turned on Netflix. The rest of that night passed in a haze of TV and musical beds. Fearne woke in the night and called for me, a distress signal from the other room. Then she climbed into our double bed, and Rich slipped out and went and slept in her single bed until dawn.

In the morning, the first crack in the clamshell had appeared. Fearne was excited! But still impatient. 'When? When?'

The answer: Right away. Fearne broke off the remaining bits of shell and there she was. Blonde, rubbery, and slowly expanding. But the mermaid had been evicted too early. She only ever grew to fit the size of the Pyrex jug.

I took a photo of her escaping from her clam shell, her hands primly clenched in her lap.

Yes, the Grow Your Own Mermaid is a metaphor. But it did happen. I know because I posted it to Instagram and that is how I know it is real. A day later, Rich and Fearne drove me to the airport, and I said 'Goodbye' and stepped on to the plane, wearing my heart on the outside of my body.

~

I strapped my seatbelt over my waist and sat in the foggy greyness, half-awake, half-asleep, on the next leg into New York.

'Megan?' A woman's voice.

I turned to the blank face beside me, uncomprehending.

'It's me, Amber,' said the passenger next to me.

A vague memory, from the dreamtime before motherhood, her body beside me behind the bar, both of us dressed in electric-blue hotpants, like a pair of exotic fish flitting about in the endless dark. Our nocturnal role in the strip club. A memory of her white knee-high marching boot slumped over and stuck inside the industrial washing machine out the back. Who put her boot in there? Not me. The relentless bitching at the club, the size of her behind. The size of mine. Everything hung out in those electric-blue hotpants.

'What are you doing these days?' she asked.

'I'm going to interview mermaids,' I said. 'I'm a writer.'

'Cool.' Amber was on the flight with a synchronised swimming team.

I told her I had a daughter, too. We talked happy families. Neither of us mentioned the incident when her marching boot had been wedged in the washing machine. I didn't do it, but I knew who did.

~

Then I woke at the Amsterdam Hotel. My room was tiny and I jolted awake, hyper-alert, to every tick and ping of the radiator. My upstairs room had next to no natural light. In the wishy-washy ambience I packed for a parade.

The silver clamshell bag was a gift for Fearne's third birthday. Wallet, keys, phone. I am now the type of woman who feels panicked without her phone.

I got the video camera out: a small, black, handheld Panasonic, bought especially for the trip. Rich had shown me how to use it, but now it was up to me. Before the trip, my father had suggested I make a documentary of the mermaids, that my video footage could be key. This intimidated me. I thought he was probably right (he was my father, he was always right) but I also knew me — befuddled, technically incompetent, unsure.

Sunscreen. Check. My cheap sunglasses with tortoiseshell frames and mirrored lenses. Check. Red Birkenstocks — I was dressed for good weather. My form had gradually returned under the auspices of the Jenny Craig diet and I was beginning to feel . . . not totally abject.

En route to the subway, I walked past Madison Avenue. The best sign of all. In *Splash*, Daryl Hannah names herself Madison after seeing the street sign. She gets to grips with New York City, charmed and delighted by the way the traffic lights change from red to green. She bops out with breakdancers on the street, eats pizza for the first time. I was close to something. The subway entrance.

I was going to the Coney Island Mermaid Parade, and mermaids I had skyped would be present today. Rose the New York Mermaid. The Blixunami, on a float somewhere, shaming the anchovies. Mermaids I wanted to interview. Cookie, the Harlem mermaid, in her orange tail, who wanted to be interviewed by me. Jennifer, a cat-mermaid and costume designer I'd friended on Facebook, had offered to bring a dress along for me, and let me join her on a pirate ship float in the parade. This upped the ante — I'd not only be at the parade, I'd be in the parade.

As the F train approached Coney Island, a guy with a shark floaty around his midriff hopped on. The train shuddered to a stop. How do you know when you have arrived?

Everyone gets off.

I wandered up Surf Avenue. The world was still waking up. I couldn't tell where the parade would begin or end. I passed a rotisserie of hot dogs. Cotton candy, real or imagined.

'Can I please take your photograph?' I said, spotting a couple in costume.

Him, a puffer fish holding a spotted parasol. Her, clad in a dark-blue body stocking, her face painted an iridescent green, her red-lipped smile fetching, black sunglasses, and on her head a topknot of white coral.

'Thank you so much.' I posted the photo to Instagram and let the likes rush in.

I doused myself in sunscreen.

The parade was swarming with photographers — stout, middle-aged men in walk shorts.

'That's it, to the right.' The men had big black lenses that zoomed in and out. Their faces were obscured by concentration, the focus had to be just right.

I took to creeping up behind the male photographers and taking a few of my own shots. It felt odd. Preying on women like this.

Yet who dresses up as an octopus because they want to blend in? The Coney Island Mermaid Parade was not an introvert's paradise.

The sun had risen and was making its intentions felt. The flat white concrete was baking and the armpits of my T-shirt already felt drenched. I ponged faintly of onion. I stood next to a skinny grey tree that was unprepared to offer me more than a modicum of shade. I adjusted the shoulder strap of my silver clamshell bag, sifted my hand through the rubble inside, tilted my smeared phone screen towards me. A black glint. No messages.

I had reached The Last Straw. Literally, which is just how I liked it — my inane literalism driving everything I did. Behind the silver barrier, a wooden pirate ship had been parked on wheels. The side of the boat was draped in a banner that read 'Costume Kult: The Last Straw'. It was a protest asking society to give up plastic straws.

Then I saw Jennifer, the purrmaid. In the flesh she looked just like she did online — busty and big-hearted. She wore a pink wig and was dressed in a pair of hotpants, like some dime-store Botticelli who had stepped off her clamshell. I admired her body positivity.

'It's so nice to meet you,' I said.

'You too!' Jennifer handed over my costume.

Standing next to the skinny tree, I changed into the long, turquoise-and-gold mermaid dress she had made. It had spongy gold clamshell cups as the brassiere, anointed with fake pearls. The clamshells were built for much larger clams than mine, but the good news was it was long and flared.

I stepped out from behind the tree, held the Panasonic in my right palm and began to record.

Jennifer introduced me to a woman dressed as an octopus and told me it was her birthday.

'Happy birthday,' I said.

'Thank you!' The octopus took a deep bow. Her purple ponytail flipped over.

'How old, can I be rude?

'Thirty-four,' she replied.

'Great age,' I said.

The octopus held up and jiggled her two front tentacles. Her tentacles were made from that sequined fabric that changes direction when you brush it. Black, then red. She had nice breasts, two plastic octopuses strategically attached to each nipple. Extra black tassels hung down from below their yellow eyes.

'Have you always wanted to be an octopus?' I asked.

'Yes.' Her lips sparkled blue. 'There's more to hold,' the octopus said. Two tentacles fondled each boob.

A black, bondage-looking harness held the tentacles in place around her hips. Yellow-tinted jellyfish hung from each of her earlobes.

'I like your jellyfish,' I said, then turned to Jennifer. 'Is it your first parade?'

A little pair of black cat ears nested in her shell crown.

'It's actually my eleventh.'

'What do you think the mermaid represents?' I asked.

'I like to think the mermaid represents female fluidity and feminine energy, but I don't want to exclude the mermen!'

Next to the pirate ship, a guy bent down and adjusted his sandal strap, gripped his trident. I got that on video, too.

'To me, the mermaid represents swimming through the waves of life. Everything in art is a metaphor and you can express that in costume. No matter how rough seas get, you can transform yourself.' Jennifer's hands glided and swooped through the air. 'You can flow with it, and ride with it instead of resisting.

'I'm a mermaid hybrid — cats can swim, too, and I am here with my assistant Gravity Kitten.'

I turned and aimed my lens at Gravity Kitten. She wore silver hotpants, her breasts armoured with stuck-on jewels. Beneath all the makeup, her features were angular and captivating. Opaque rubber jellyfish hung from her ears and wobbled in an impromptu *Fantasia*. Her eyelashes, too, were another species. Alien. A pale hue, not quite blue or white.

'What about you?' I asked.

'What about me?' she said, glacially. Cordial. But cold, like her eyelashes.

'I'm Megan,' I tried again, 'and I'd like to know what you think mermaids represent.'

She introduced herself as 'Gravity, Queen of Love and Hope'.

'Mermaids are artistic expressions, fantasy brought to life, just representing that you really can be whatever you want to be.' She was giving me a speech, but I wasn't sure she believed it. 'No matter how crappy you feel on the inside, like I do today, honestly.'

'Do you?' I was taken aback.

Gravity wasn't having a great start to the parade. Neither was I.

'What's wrong?' I asked.

'Mental health issues.'

I had just met her and I had the Panasonic aimed in her face. That wasn't right. Or it wasn't right for me.

Why? She was next to nude. I was there to look at her. I held the Panasonic cupped in my right hand; it was easy to hold. That's why I had bought it. But it wasn't easy to look through the lens.

I had evoked the terrible male gaze. I felt like a mervert.

'You can be all bedazzled, like I am today, but feel like a sea monster inside. Costuming is art therapy. Kids need to see that they can be what they want to be. I can be a mermaid. I can dress up. I can be on these floats.'

Her sadness intrigued me, the sadness of young women everywhere who feel like sea monsters inside. Then there was the sadness of the sea monsters — did they get sad? How do sea monsters feel inside?

My gaze cut away to the disenfranchised renters in the brick apartments on the other side of the white pavement. They looked like extras from *One Flew Over the Cuckoo's Nest*. A hospital worker in blue scrubs stared benignly at the fuss outside the pirate ship then shuffled back into the apartment's corridor.

'All I want to do is perform right now,' said Gravity, 'and drown the other bullshit out.'

'I want that for you too,' I said, and meant it.

~

I didn't fit in at The Last Straw, so I told Jennifer I needed to go and explore. I was desperate to capture the magic. I set off, soles slapping against my Birkenstocks, the Panasonic still rolling. I wanted to see something totally mermazing — to be wowed by spectacle.

In 1939 the inaugural World's Fair was held in nearby Queens, and had featured two pavilions that set the benchmark for mermaid performances. Billy Rose's Aquacade presented synchronised swimmers performing aquaballet in military-like lines and formations. 'The theme for this year will be water, WATER,' said Rose. 'Anything writ in water will succeed.' He was right — his Aquacade was the most popular exhibit of the fair.

But it was Salvador Dalí's *Dream of Venus* that I thrilled to and wished I could have seen. The surrealist's project was bankrolled by a 'rubber man' from Pittsburgh who wanted to fund an aquarium with rubber-tailed mermaids in it. Dalí's crackpot pavilion was half peep show, half carnival funhouse. The exterior was a bonkers sandcastle, painted coral pink, and topped with a cut-out of Botticelli's blonde Venus. Punters entered the building through towering spindly legs and bought their tickets from a booth shaped like an angler fish and covered in spikes.

Inside were two tanks — one wet and one dry — meant to represent the subconscious mind, which was male, with seventeen liquid ladies hired to swim in it. The 'lady god-divers' wore Dalí's kinky swimsuits, their bare breasts protruding from cut-out love hearts. In between shifts they sunbathed on the roof of the pavilion and waved to passengers on the elevated subway platform nearby.

I would have loved to perform in that fucking pavilion, pretending to type underwater or play a rubber mannequin piano, the black ink from my costume running. Or to lie in the dry tank on the bed of ardour, pretending to sleep, a bucket of champers and some lobsters at my feet.

That's what I really wanted to see in New York — a woman dressed as a lobster. In one publicity shoot for the *Dream of Venus*, a young model wore a lobster as a fig leaf, attached to a G-string. In the photograph, Dalí clutched her thighs, his head poked out from behind her buttocks. A haughty white handkerchief rose from Dalí's suit pocket as though he might dab the corners of his mouth after the all-you-can-eat seafood buffet. Oh, Dalí you made that lobster look like such a cad!

The *Dream of Venus*, for all its titillating zaniness, was a commercial and critical disaster — a flop. The day after the pavilion opened, Dalí returned to Europe on an ocean liner but he left behind a manifesto, an artistic 'fuck you', to be airdropped on to the streets of New York. It was titled: 'Declaration of the Independence of the Imagination and the Rights of Man to His Own Madness'.

~

There was plenty of imagination and madness on display at Coney Island, but I had trouble capturing it on film. The whole parade had the feel of a New Year's Eve party. I was waiting for the drugs to come on, for the fun to happen, for something to start, but it was like that time in my twenties when I ate a hash cookie and fell asleep before midnight.

Hungry, I passed hot dog vendors who passed out bottles of water willy-nilly to the crowd. We needed them. I needed one.

A girl dressed in a white seal-pup suit talked on her mobile phone. Then I saw Cleopatra with a black bob and gold jewellery, like an escaped extra from Katy Perry's 'Dark Horse' music video. It was one of the songs Fearne and I watched together at home. This Cleo was a young woman in her mid-twenties — I wanted to say, 'Look Fearne, there's Cleopatra,' but Fearne was at home asleep on the other side of the world. I missed her chubby fingers curled in my hair.

Instead, I asked to take Cleopatra's photo.

'Thank you.' I primly ran off.

I took a selfie, my purple and orange bra showing inside the clams. 'A melting mermaid', I wrote on Instagram. Like. Like. Like.

The boardwalk had transformed into a catwalk; the day had the stick and sheen of ice-cream, of tackiness and tarmac. I shot hours of footage of people I didn't know.

Prepackaged Ariels strolled around in packs, with the creative aplomb of microwave meals. A few Ursulas. Some would always prefer to be a camp and villainous mauve octopus. The Disney animators had based Ursula's character partly on the drag queen Divine, who starred in John Waters' cult-classic, *Pink Flamingos*. A group of boring witches danced to Beyoncé. Feminine energy was present, especially in the form of blue orbs jiggling, and I saw a lot of boobs, but no lobsters. Where was Dalí when you needed him? Non-conformity has its own system. Stilt walkers towered above the Parade, swishing metallic silvery wings.

Another young Ariel zipped past on a scooter. To hell with Ariel — I spotted two gill-people. The Creature from the Black Lagoon, wearing a bum bag, and her creature-child ambling along the street, casually. The child creature looked out through his or her green mask.

The Creature from the Black Lagoon was released in 1954. In the original film, the Creature was the villain who longed for the babe. The sadness of sea monsters, who just want to be beautiful or at least get laid. The Creature had been designed by Millicent Patrick, a gorgeous brunette costume artist whose achievements were later downplayed by her male bosses. Millicent was the Creature's mother; in old black-and-white photos she holds the rubbery mask tenderly and smiles at her creation. No wonder other people found the sea monster loveable too.

The film director Guillermo del Toro first fell in love with Millicent's monster as a kid. 'The Creature was the most beautiful design I'd ever seen,' he recalled. 'I saw him swimming under [actress] Julie Adams, and I loved that the Creature was in love with her, and I felt an almost existential desire for them to end up together. Of course, it didn't happen.'

Until 2017, when del Toro turned an amphibious creature into the hero and romantic lead in *The Shape of Water*. In del Toro's movie, the Creature is an aquatic hunk who falls in love with the mute lead, played by actress Sally Hawkins. The roles are reversed — she saves him. They also have amazing fish sex in her bathtub (where else?). *The Shape of Water* has since spawned a silicone dildo inspired by the amphibious man's imagined member.

I had been gassing about the film with loads of mermaids. 'I felt like the monster was a damsel in distress,' Triton Mahtlinnie told me, from their houseboat on Puget Sound, Seattle. Triton was a non-binary merperson with a degree in fashion design and had created their own black tail with purple accents and a purple fluke. They also wore webbed gloves. 'Everything is more fun in a costume,' Triton said.

But I was in a costume and I wasn't having fun.

~

Cookie the Harlem Mermaid sat on a rock and told me about how much she'd loved that *Mr. Peabody and the Mermaid* movie, starring Ann Blyth as the comely young fish.

'Meeting you is like meeting a celebrity,' I said.

'I'm an elder!' she said.

Cookie DeJesus was a ballroom dancer. She'd been abused as a child, was bipolar and agoraphobic, but then found mermaids. Initially, she worried she couldn't be a mermaid because she didn't have long blonde hair, but she'd broken the mould.

I'd recently watched a documentary that celebrated her life story. In the movie, *Mermaids*, Cookie marries her partner and mertender, the pirate Ralph, in a swimming pool. She keeps her tail on throughout the ceremony.

In person, Cookie was like a ball of fire, dressed in an orange sarong with glowing lips. She was so bubbly and sweet. How could you not care for Cookie? In the parade each year, Ralph pushed her along in a wheelchair.

'Facebook is where I live,' Cookie said. For her it wasn't a black hole, a dead zone, it was full of life. 'Then when I'm in the water, nothing exists but that.'

I felt the same about being online. It was endless, expansive, this constant lap-lap-lapping, each mermaid's post a message in a bottle carried in on the tide.

'The mermaid wants a hotdog,' Cookie told Ralph.

~

As I came across the beach that afternoon and saw the pod in the grey shallows I thought, *These aren't mermaids at all, just people in costumes. What did I expect?*

I took some furtive pictures of the mermaids at the water's edge. The mers came in all shapes and sizes — some as large as walruses.

Then I recognised Nikki, one of the mermaids in my spreadsheet, pending interview. Her tail, a green Mertailor design, thwacked as she lay on the beach and lifted it into the air. The velocity, the magnitude of it, the sound! Water leaked out of the drainage holes in the fluke. She gave me a big hug and showed me the tattoo along her arm. 'To die would be an awfully big adventure' — a line from *Peter Pan*.

When she was just twenty-four years old, Nikki suddenly, for no apparent reason, crashed her car. Afterwards the doctors told her she had an aggressive form of brain cancer. At the time she was pregnant with her second child. She lost her hair. Did two years of oral chemotherapy. Recovered, and became a mermaid.

'Captain Hook is my inspiration,' Nikki said. She showed me the map of Neverland she had tattooed on her back.

Nearby, Steve the sea creature stood on the beach in a pair of shiny leggings, his chest bare.

'I'm shedding my scales so I can get in the water,' he said.

He picked the silver glittering decorations from his face and chest one by one. Cheerily. Cheerfully.

It was sensitive of Steve to decant the scales, in case he lost one and a fish accidentally swallowed it.

Steve was involved with 'otherkin': dragons, witches, faeries and mermaids. He'd come into the New York mer community from a background in musical theatre and found it accepting. A lot of dramatic energy. He followed Cookie online because she was so inclusive, positive, upbeat.

Steve said he'd always been told in school that you can't just sing and dance your life away, but then wondered why not. 'People just want to be fun, beautiful and fantastic.' The sun struck his scales, wrought light from the sequins.

~

The shadows stretched as the afternoon wore on. I felt like I was walking through one of de Chirico's early surrealist paintings, the crowd dispersing, Dalí-esque *Dream of Venus* figures slipping away back into their real lives. The air pink and fuzzy like candy floss, the sediment of the carny. A Ferris wheel's white spiral hazy in the background.

I bought Fearne a Coney Island Mermaid t-shirt and a blue-haired mermaid doll in a beachside shop. Then I waded away across the warm sand in my Birkenstocks, following a trio of parade-goers, one holding a turquoise Mahina MerFin by the foot stirrups.

On the subway back into New York, five dancers burst into the carriage. They back-flipped and twirled around the silver poles in the train as though it was their stage. As we rushed along the tracks, all our lives were caught together in the can. One break-dancer flipped the trainer off his right foot and held it aloft, then tipped his trainer like a cap. I clapped, delighted. Feet can be pretty sweet. Then I tipped him twenty dollars.

~

At the hotel, I took one last photo of myself in the clamshell dress. The iridescent netting around the waist glowed in the dark — a detail I hadn't noticed during the heat of the day on Surf Avenue. The clams had fake pearls stitched around the edge of the bra, and one fat fake pearl sat in the middle, between my boobs, like a fortune teller's crystal. I hadn't found Jennifer again to give her the dress back. I promised to post it to her.

I lay on the double bed, the oily fumes of sunscreen still clinging to my skin in the dark. Bad memories were catching up. The last time I was in New York, I sat on the subway bundled up in my winter coat, not yet frayed, and asked my first husband: 'Am I beautiful?'

'You're beautiful,' he said, but his brown eyes twinkled so I knew a joke was coming. 'You're like a beautiful amoeba,' he said.

He drew out the three syllables of amoeba in his lovely lilting Irish accent. I stared at his wonky front teeth, my arm linked through his thick black coat, and felt contempt.

But I laughed, because it was funny.

I put my head on his shoulder in the shiny silver subway. The stubble on his chin was black but tinted red-gold in the flicking lights as we shuttled between stops. He was happy with his simile, and I was happy enough with him, apart from the fact that he was a drunk. Why was it so hard to give me a compliment?

I know little about amoebas except that they reproduce by fission — they split in two.

That day we had traipsed across cold New York, two artists in their late twenties with little money. We took obligatory photos outside the Chelsea Hotel, then caught the ferry to Staten Island, passed the Statue of Liberty, her torch held high for the immigrants, refugees and out-of-towners. We took photos through the ferry window, the statue in the background.

I didn't give mermaids a second thought on that trip. Once our marriage started falling apart, however, I wrote about mermaids all the time.

9.

Diving into the Wreck Too

I phoned Mum before I left JFK airport and told her to pray for me. I called Rich, too. 'I'm worried I'm going to die.'

'Of course you are.'

I sat alone on the Delta flight to Fort Lauderdale. The plane was half empty. I stared vaguely out the porthole window, my mind in a thrum with the aircon, alert to every tick and flex of the plane, listening for twitches, for signs we were about to go down. The landscape far below the window was meaningless. The sea, the anonymous sea. I didn't believe there were any real mermaids in it. But there were shipwrecks, ghostly with algae, strewn along the seabed and watched by the mysterious blobfish with its googly eyes.

I clenched the seat rests. *Please God, please, let us be all right*, I repeated over and over like a mantra.

I opened my book and tried to concentrate, my leg jiggling up and down in my seat. I had bought David Sedaris's *Calypso* at the airport bookstore; his name was so familiar, it grounded me. In the store, my hand had hovered over the embossed cover, three knots in the woodgrain formed rudimentary eyes and a nose, a thin black marker line for a mouth — *no, I can't afford it* — smoothed my palm along the tiny subtle ridges — *yes, I must have it*. I should have waited until the paperback came out. I pictured Sedaris in a pair of culottes — hadn't he written a story about his love of culottes? I once saw him speak. Sedaris was a frequent flyer, whereas I was afraid that my Delta plane might plummet to the bottom of the ocean and become a wreck, just to spite me.

I flicked open my phone and stared at the screen. The poem 'Diving into the Wreck' is Adrienne Rich's feminist classic, from her collection of the same title. In 1974, the collection won the National Book Award. It was the same year I was born. The wreck in my mind bloomed.

> First having read the book of myths,
> and loaded the camera,
> and checked the edge of the knife-blade,
> I put on
> the body-armor of black rubber
> the absurd flippers
> the grave and awkward mask.
> I am having to do this
> not like Cousteau with his
> assiduous team
> aboard the sun-flooded schooner
> but here alone.

On the internet I had listened to a recording of Rich's voice — American, confident, clear — give a no-frills reading. She spoke quite fast. In the black-and-white photograph in the sidebar, her hair was short, eyes small and discerning; she looked mischievous but resolutely unfeminine. Rich wore a jersey with a rounded neck, appropriate attire for a fishing trip. I knew she was a lesbian — had been married to a professor, had three children with him. When she left, he killed himself.

Like Rich, I was going to the wreck.

In my usual inanely literal fashion, I was also going to a real bar called The Wreck located in the B Ocean Resort, 1140 Seabreeze Boulevard, Fort Lauderdale, Florida.

The moment I saw MeduSirena hanging upside down in the teal-blue window of The Wreck's Facebook page, I knew she was 'the mermaid with hair that streamed black', straight out of Rich's poem. She was also the brains behind the aqua-burlesque show that had been going strong at the bar for years. By rights, I should have invested my time and money in going to Weeki Wachee Springs — that was the most famous mermaid site in the world — but I needed the wreck. A site at once mythic and timeless, a destination in the imagination or the collective unconscious. Atlantis, beneath the sea, a mermaid's playground. *This is the place.*

~

The plane touched down without a hitch. Outside, the passengers disbanded, swallowed into the airport.

I climbed into the backseat of an Uber, the aircon on full bore, and texted Rich to let him know I had arrived safely. No reply. At home it was the middle of the night, and he would be sleeping, Fearne breathing beside him, her hand curled in his hair in lieu of mine. Palm trees flitted by outside the darkened Uber windows. I could have been driven to a swamp and fed into the open jaws of an American crocodile.

As we approached the B Ocean Resort I was disarmed. I had imagined being able to see the hotel from a distance, like an ocean liner parked on the beach. I wanted the postcard view, to see a hotel still retro, like it was in the fifties, perhaps tinted coral pink by a sunset. Instead, the Uber suddenly pulled up beside a tangle of tropical vegetation and stopped. I looked out the window and there was a vast white building, another pair of electronic doors.

'Are we here?' I asked. The driver popped the boot. I stepped out in my London jacket, a corkscrew of thread unravelling at the cuff. The humidity held me in its fist.

A concierge in a black suit appeared, took my luggage from the boot.

'Oh, thank you,' I said.

I walked into the foyer feeling rugged up like a sausage roll. The hotel aircon a gasp of coolness, as though I was inside a large glamorous fridge. The receptionist was dressed in a black jacket and white shirt, her hair pulled back in a bun. Next to her, an attendant in the same uniform smiled at my thick khaki jacket, 'I think you're overdressed for Florida.'

'I've come from New York,' I said, as though that made any sense. My tongue felt furry from the flight; I was sweating. 'The Mermaids and Mimosas show is still on, isn't it?'

'Yes ma'am.'

'I'm a writer,' I said. 'I'm here to interview the mermaids.' I felt like a hermit crab inching out of its shell, about to get its legs snapped off by seagulls.

All the travel had taken its toll. Ceiling fans spun around on the ceiling of the glacial foyer. 'Your room isn't ready yet,' said the receptionist, suggesting I wait. I walked to an armchair in a cosy area festooned with a circular rug. The cushion on the armchair read: B Inspired! I sat on it.

The Wreck Bar was right there, in gasping distance of me. The ceiling fans spun and spun. I should have gone inside — I'd flown thousands of miles to see it — but I wanted to shower first. I didn't want to risk an encounter with a mermaid while looking like a sausage roll. This was my first chance to watch the mermaids in the drink — and perhaps to have a drink too.

In 2005, Marina Anderson, aka MeduSirena, walked into The Wreck, one of the last remaining porthole bars in America, and thought, 'If I don't do something this place is gonna go the way of the dodo.' The Wreck Bar is inside a historic hotel built in the mid-twentieth century when Americans drove their Fords across the country for holidays in glamorous locations without leaving the map. Originally called The Yankee Clipper, it was shaped like the Love Boat and planted on the beach in 1956. 'The Yankee Clipper' was also the nickname of baseball player Joe DiMaggio. Joe and his then-wife Marilyn Monroe used to visit the hotel back in its heyday. Allegedly, their names were carved into the bar.

MeduSirena saw the potential to revive the retro aquatic shows she loved from the golden age of tourism. She pitched her concept to the hotel management team. They sat at the bar while she swam past the windows and did a show for them. 'The porthole is like a camera,' MeduSirena had told me when I first interviewed her months earlier.

Underwater she wore a fabric tail that swayed, sparkled and shimmered like a cocktail dress. The hotel management told her thank you, but we're not hiring. However, they told her she could practice in the pool anytime she liked. MeduSirena posted her practice swims on her Myspace page each week. In two months, the bar was full, she was hired, and she had introduced an aqua burlesque show that had since gone 'gangbusters'. MeduSirena was a fire-eating mermaid; her signature tail was red. She could swim by the windows of The Wreck drinking a mai tai.

'I can hold my breath long enough to get paid,' she quipped.

Marina Anderson was born in in Puerto Rico. Her father and brother taught her to skindive at three years old, and she learned to belly dance from her Moroccan neighbours. She taught herself to perform underwater by watching her shadow move across the bottom of her high school swimming pool. Marina had done everything — worked in an aquarium and a zoo, Polynesian dancing, volunteer firefighting, she could fly single engine planes, and she also performed taiko, a form of Japanese drumming.

Her persona, MeduSirena, was an anomaly in the professional mermaid world. 'I'm not a mermaid — I'm a swimmer. I'm a dancer. I'm an artist. One of my ensembles just happens to be a fishtail, which is the most popular.' She called her performers 'aquaticats' and they did an underwater striptease, removing stockings and flashing their nipple tassels. The aquaticats had been known to wear tight T-shirts that read: *Don't call me Ariel*. 'This isn't Disney,' Marina told me, 'so don't expect extreme conservatism.' However, the animators of Disney's *The Little Mermaid* had once visited her show and said to her afterwards, 'Where have you been? We could have used you for the underwater scenes.'

I'd been her Facebook fan for months now. She owned a tight black singlet emblazoned with the words 'Sea Hag'. One spiral of her black hair was grey. Marina had a teenage son she called 'the boy'; she also had a bald cat and chinchillas. We were both Gen X women, and I felt she had a lesson to teach me about how to age.

Amazingly, Marina had once posed for the famous photographer Bunny Yeager. I loved Yeager's photos of Bettie Page. Marina had brought along a leopard-print fishtail to commemorate the anniversary of Yeager's infamous Bettie Page shoot — the one of Betty posed in a leopard-print bathing suit beside two sad-looking stuffed cheetahs. But when Bunny saw her carry the tail out, she said, 'Oh no, that won't do at all. I want you nude.' Marina was forty-two at the time, but *I gotta do this*, she thought. 'On my death bed, I'd regret it if I didn't pose for Bunny Yeager.'

'Totally,' I agreed.

'Arch your back. That's perfect, now sparkle!' Bunny said, as Marina posed on a lawn in front of a mansion in Miami.

'I got the command to sparkle,' Marina said.

I underlined it in my notes.

I was forty-two and I would never pose for Bunny Yeager, but I would regret it on my deathbed if I didn't go to The Wreck. I had received the command to sparkle. Maybe it was a gift I had given myself. And when I got to the bottom of the Wreck, I wanted to open the treasure chest and find the gold inside it, fucking sparkling.

I came to explore the wreck.
The words are purposes.
The words are maps.

I came to see the damage that was done
and the treasures that prevail.

In the daytime, the bar itself was awash with darkness. A wooden interior, wooden tables and booths, small aquariums of tropical fish set inside the cavernous walls. Everything was in shadows, empty, like a cleaned-out ashtray. The bar looked like it served burgers and prawn cocktails, the kind of joint that has a laminated menu to wipe away spills.

I was afraid to go into The Wreck.

I didn't dare look through the square windows above the bar that faced directly into the bright, aqua-blue pool.

MeduSirena wasn't working the day I arrived — I had arranged to meet her off duty later in the week, before I flew out — but there was a mermaid behind me. In the middle of the foyer a young blonde in a fabric tail sat on a corporate chair mounted on a circular table, plates of sweets at her feet — or rather her fluke. Little tiramisus and other bijou treats. A man in a straw hat approached her, like some elderly Gauguin.

I wanted her to radiate a mythic power, to quote Rich from stanza four — 'the sea is another story / the sea is not a question of power' — but it looked like the mermaid was just explaining the menu. Gauguin hobbled off with a tiramisu.

When Adrienne Rich won the National Book Award for *Diving into the Wreck*, she accepted the award collectively with her fellow nominees, Audre Lorde and Alice Walker. In their speech they dedicated the occasion to, 'the struggle for self-determination of all women, of every colour, identification, or derived class: the poet, the housewife, the lesbian, the mathematician, the mother, the dishwasher, the pregnant teenager, the teacher, the grandmother, the prostitute, the philosopher, the waitress, the women who will understand what we are doing here and those who will not understand yet; the silent women whose voices have been denied us, the articulate women who have given us strength to do our work.'

Quite a list. I took it to include me and the mermaids. Was the mermaid in her corporate chair a silent woman who had been denied a voice? I decided she was, and I was the articulate woman who had the strength to do her work.

The blonde looked into her phone and stifled a yawn. I bet she had never read Rich's poem. I felt sympathetic, almost maternal, remembering waitressing — the idleness and down time between orders, the customers who wanted you to always be turned on, like a tap dripping sparkling conversation.

A staff member walked by and smiled, 'You have a nice view, because you're going to see the mermaids.'

I looked through the open door at the dazzling blue windows of The Wreck. Then I saw it. A purple fabric tail, like a pansy petal, flicker in the window. I watched the fin spider away. Just like that, gone.

'Ma'am, your room is ready.'

I took the lift to the fifth floor and walked along an outdoor veranda, as though I was on the bow of a ship. Blue stretches of tarpaulin had been fixed to the exterior of the hotel, I guess they were meant to represent sails. I looked down at the pool below me. A blonde in a hot pink tail floated on the bright blue surface. Hot and bothered, I took an Instagram snap.

In my room the note pad beside the phone read: B Yourself.

I had a shower. Part of my soul still yearned to be a mermaid, drifting in the window of The Wreck, surfacing only to feed old men tiramisu. I blow-dried my hair, amused by the puny blast of the hotel hairdryer. I dressed in my long floral skirt, and my Creature from the Black Lagoon T-shirt, pushed my feet into my lobster-red Birkenstocks.

When I got back to the bar, the Mermaids and Mimosas had already finished — twenty-five minutes early! The pool conditions were cloudy and the aquaticats' eyes were getting cooked, the bartender said. The blonde I'd seen now sat at the bar eating something that looked like lasagne. She was no longer wearing her pink tail. I didn't want to infringe on her personal space, so I sat at the other end of the wooden bar, and politely ordered a mocktail. The bartender Mike was bald and gracious. On weekends, he told me, drunks often leapt in the pool and mooned the bar. 'I can imagine,' I said.

I asked about Marilyn but he said he had never found her name carved into the wooden bar, or Joe DiMaggio's. There was, though, a small, framed photo of Robert De Niro and Billy Crystal seated at the bar, with a gold plaque below it reading: 'Scene from ANALYZE THIS filmed here, 1999.' I had once watched the film with Mum. Billy Crystal plays a shrink who tries to help De Niro, a mobster with a conscience. It was a comedy. I was uncovering signs, but they were not the signs I was after.

Instead of anything about mermaids, I read a laminated display by the hotel door, about the local sea turtles' nesting season. Then I walked around the concrete exterior of the pool. Rows of empty white deck chairs and another sign next to the edge: *No diving.* If anything, it was a relief I couldn't dive.

I have to learn alone
to turn my body without force
in the deep element.

In the morning, I posted an image of a solitary palm tree on Instagram. 'Hello Florida.' The heat felt inches deep. I could grab a fist of air and wring it out like a rag. I opened the sliding door and stood on the balcony staring at the Atlantic. Volleyballers played on the beach. An oil tanker went about its ethically unsound business deep at sea.

Mum called. 'I still haven't finished transcribing Mermaid Rachel,' she warbled.

'It's okay, Mum,' I said, relieved to hear her voice.

Mum confessed she was handwriting each interview, before typing it up. 'For God's sake!' I snapped. 'No wonder it's taking you so long, Mum.'

Why I was torturing my poor mother?

'How's Fearnebot?' Mum asked.

'Apparently, she's all right during the day but Rich says she cries for me at the cat flap at night.'

'Don't worry darling. I'll be there with her next week.' she said. 'I can't wait to see her.' Fearne's daycare had made her a yellow chart counting down the days until my return. In the first square Fearne had pasted a cut-out from a magazine. It was of a blonde doll dressed as a mermaid.

I was also counting down mermaids.

One arrived in the afternoon, and I steered her up to the balcony of my hotel room, feeling like a low-rent porn director. She was an utterly beautiful young woman, from a dance background, and a very successful full-time mermaid. 'Just being in the water, you have to be friends with it. It's either against you or it's with you,' she said.

Her scuba training involved diving to the bottom of a lake to retrieve a brick. Repeatedly.

'Does beauty matter?' I asked, as I asked everyone. It looked to me like it did. Yet she didn't seem to consider herself particularly beautiful. Was she insane? I took a photo of her, outside on the balcony, wearing a 'Shell Yeah' singlet.

I met another blonde, shapely mermaid performer in the darkness of the bar downstairs. She told me she had also once been paid to dress up as Marilyn Monroe for a corporate function.

We sat on barstools opposite each other. 'I'm forty-two,' I said. 'I had my daughter at forty.'

'You look good for your age.' Marilyn was younger than me but already had two teenagers.

Safely contained behind the screen of my MacBook, I'd felt in control. In person, I felt like a fake. But the whole point of this trip was to meet real mermaids. 'Are you real?' I asked, as I asked everyone.

I retreated to my room, put up the 'do not disturb' sign, hopped into bed and read *Calypso* like a nesting sea turtle. The title story was about Sedaris feeding his own tumour (cut and removed by a doctor) to a snapping sea turtle near his beach house. The turtle didn't have to think about what it had consumed and where it came from, and whether it would ever write its own bestseller or be a character in someone else's book.

In the afternoon, I opened the gate to a community complex in Dania Beach, the interior lined by semi-detached terracotta apartments. Behind another safety fence and a gate lay an azure David Hockney pool, ready to be pierced by a bright-white splash.

I walked towards it for my next lesson.

'You're so pretty,' said Charlotte brightly. 'I love your mermaid dress.'

It was a violent Kermit green, and I was the wan ghost inside it.

Charlotte was slender, with long brown hair and a tan, but her manner reminded me of Nurse Ratched from *One Flew Over the Cuckoo's Nest*. Charlotte had two kids. She was a copyright lawyer who wanted to start her own mermaid business, so she found a franchise and got involved immediately.

I had signed up for a one-hour private lesson that included the use of a tail and a video of my underwater experience. I left my bag slumped against the wall by the changing room. I already had my blue retro bikini on under my dress, and wrapped a towel around my waist.

Charlotte opened a duffel bag of fabric tails. They were PG, totally beginner's level tails, not like the silicone masterpieces that I admired online.

'What colour tail do you want?' Charlotte asked, laying them out like beach towels.

'I don't know. Maybe purple?'

'Perhaps orange would pop more?' Charlotte mused.

Perhaps it would. Orange was Madison's colour. I also had ginger pubes, so technically I should have an orange tail. I'd once asked Rich what colour mermaid tail he thought I'd have and he'd answered drolly: brown.

Brown was not an option today. Not girlie enough. But the orange had a tear in it, so purple won.

I sat on the edge of the pool and placed my feet into the rubber footholds of the monofin — the absurd flippers! — then began to roll the tail on. Advised by Charlotte, I bum-shuffled to get it over my waist.

'I like your directive style,' I told Charlotte.

I felt a kind of release in letting her take control. I wondered if she was a Trump voter, but didn't ask. Mermaiding wasn't about politics.

'I won't put on a tail in case I need to save you from drowning,' she said.

I stood beside her on the first step. The water rose to my waist, swirling inside the purple tail. The pool made sense in this heat. Charlotte had years of synchronised swimming and dance training experience. She demonstrated how to undulate.

The dolphin kick is the mermaid 101 movement, but it's tricky for humans to master. I thought back to what Marina had said over Skype. 'We're not built like dolphins, we're closer to manatees in the way we move.'

My waist stiffly responded to Charlotte's directions, jerking forwards then backwards, as my mind tried to comprehend what my body was being asked to deliver.

'Remember your neck and head,' she said.

I undulated them as well. The waist felt silly enough, but trying to undulate my neck and head felt even sillier. I stood half in the pool, half out, see-sawing my neck and chin. I didn't feel like a mermaid. I was an absurd flipper.

Finally, I dolphin-kicked to the end of the pool. I had bought goggles from the B Ocean Resort swim shop as advised and they grasped my face tightly. The pool was white on the bottom and sides, and I was relieved to be submerged inside its predictable depths. I followed orders; my arms out front in the superman pose.

'Good!' Charlotte said, when I surfaced. 'You're doing great. Much better than most on their first try.'

I did some more dolphin-kicking, feeling stupidly pleased, like Flipper.

Then I had to try and stay under. Expel my breath and sink to the bottom. Except I couldn't expel my breath, couldn't stay down. The pool was like a magnifying glass. Nebulous feelings were caught in the flow. Old stuff surfaced.

'I want to know how you feel,' Charlotte asked when we came up.

'To be honest, I feel completely hideous.' I poured out all my old teenage neuroses: the stuff so many women feel about themselves, that deep sense of ugliness that has been my constant companion in life. 'I've never been a pool person, or a beach person. I don't tan. I can't even handle the heat. I hate my freckles and my varicose veins. They have got worse since I had my daughter. I'm not even a good swimmer. I remember coming last in my high school swimming competition. When I grew up it was the era of Brooke Shields in *Blue Lagoon* and there was another girl named Megan at my school who looked just like Brooke. People would sometimes get our names mixed up because we were both called Megan. It was awful.'

'You remind me of my best friend,' Charlotte empathised. Her cordial gaze brimmed with compassion — or was it pity? I could tell she wanted to help. That made it worse.

The pool water lapped soothingly around us.

I felt like I was offering Charlotte my skin, or she was offering me hers, but I was a selkie and she was a mermaid. She'd never know what it felt like to wear my Scottish seal skin.

Charlotte's lithe body sculled water and sank to the bottom with ease. She demonstrated the corkscrew and the torpedo, told me about the kangaroo, the jellyfish. I watched her repeat the instructions, but I couldn't reflect her movements. I felt like a haggis, surfacing at inopportune moments.

Chris Crumley, an underwater photographer who has run mermaid classes in the Gulf of Mexico, had told me there were two types of mermaids: sinkers and floaters.

Now I knew the truth: I was a floater. Only the thin descend.

Despite that, I tried to perform femininity underwater. Charlotte had me blow bubble kisses underwater, because that's

what mermaids do. With each lunge across the bottom of the white pool, large thunderous bubbles belched from my mouth rather than a dreamy little fleet of feminine circles and well wishes. I felt gargantuan, roiling, farting out bubble kisses. Charlotte, who was now wearing my goggles and holding the GoPro, seemed completely focused on the task at hand.

After we got out, Charlotte took even more control and I let her.

I posed for an array of pictures beside the pool, lying on the terracotta floor beside the changing room.

'You're going to love these photos,' Charlotte said. 'You're going to be surprised.' She plucked a fake pink exotic flower from her own hair and pinned it into mine. Then she handed her own lipstick to me. 'Put it on.'

The summit of the lipstick was shaped for Charlotte's mouth, not mine. It had a high rigid slope and a skinny, sharp peak. But I'd been presented with it, so I coloured my lips in as best I could without a mirror, sensing my way along the contours of my mouth. It was like waking in the dark and stumbling towards the loo without turning on the lights. When did I stop wearing lipstick? Foundation? Eyeshadow? Makeup? Somewhere in my early-to-mid-thirties that second skin had slipped away. And when did I start peeing several times a night?

'Wait,' I told Charlotte. 'Let me get my sunglasses!'

'That's not necessary.'

But it was. I reached for my bag and extracted my cheap pair of mirrored shades with green plastic tortoiseshell frames. I felt better the moment I put them on. Behind the shades, I was shielded from my own glare.

Afterwards, I aimed my video camera at Charlotte.

Her life as a lawyer with two little kids in diapers was hectic.

'What's been the feedback from your day job?' I asked.

Everyone had been supportive, she said. Being a lawyer might seem the antithesis of being a mermaid — legal work is serious, about drafting contracts and protecting people's rights, while mermaids are free-spirited, playful and sexy. But South Florida needed mermaid classes, and mermaiding had brought balance into Charlotte's work life.

'Putting on a tail and swimming like a mermaid makes me feel good, it makes me feel like a kid again,' Charlotte said. 'And I want other people to be able to experience that, too.'

I had experienced it, but it hadn't made me feel good.

'I'm tired,' I confessed. 'Do you have anything you want to ask me?'

'I want to know how you felt when you were swimming like a mermaid. Can you use some adjectives to describe what it made you feel?' Charlotte asked.

Good questions. But I was here to find the language to fit the mermaids' experience, not my own —

> . . . it is easy to forget
> what I came for
> among so many who have always
> lived here
> swaying their crenellated fans
> between the reefs . . .

The whole thing was hard to describe. 'I guess there's a serenity to it,' I answered Charlotte, 'and a peacefulness when you're underwater in a breath hold. But I find there's a lot of other stuff that interrupts, more adult stuff about being in the body and the self. It's the accoutrements and cutaways that interest me. You wearing my goggles, holding the GoPro. Coming up, coughing, having swallowed too much water — all the stuff you would usually edit out. That's what interests me.'

'I love it,' Charlotte said. 'I want to take a picture of you right now.'

And she did.

On the way out she also asked me if I had got my interviewees to sign a release. I hadn't.

~

After my lesson, I went straight to a Barnes and Noble bookstore parked along the highway. Every building was super-sized, Jurassic. Stacks of bargain books had accumulated in the aisles. Just as water is the mermaid's element, words were mine. I took the escalator upstairs and located the one copy of *The Mermaid Handbook*. A turquoise hardback, written by Carolyn Turgeon. I had not met Carolyn but had spent hours scrolling her blog *I Am a Mermaid*. Her compendium of mermaid lore featured everything from how to make a mermaid crown to postcard entries on famous mermaid cocktail lounges from the fifties and sixties.

I took the book back to the lair of the B Ocean Resort, then opened my MacBook and skyped two more mermaids, in a daze on the double bed.

How would I ever do justice to their tendency to myth-make?

Lila was a medium who now ran her own range of mermaid workshops in Hawai'i. She had a degree in marine biology and had once worked as a federal fisheries observer in the Bering Sea. 'I had always been rigid science. A plus B equals C. Now it's A plus B equals infinite possibilities.' The other Skype was a fire performer, recovering addict and newly minted mermaid who was twenty-one weeks pregnant. 'The world as we get older brings us down. We get torn down by the reality of adulting, but when we're mermaiding, we're back to being playful little kids, being carefree and fun.' She also ran a social media boot camp promoting healthy living.

'If I joined your bootcamp, what would you tell me?' I asked.

'I'm starting a salad challenge,' she said. 'I'm telling everyone to eat one clean salad a day and take a photo of it, it really does help with accountability.'

A lettuce leaf appeared in my mind, swaying underwater like a crenellated fan.

That night I called room service and ordered a burger. Then I called Rich and I told him about agreeing to wear the lipstick and the flower. 'I felt so ugly.' I cried.

He stared at me through the iPhone screen. 'We're all out of our comfort zone. Louis Theroux would have done the same thing,' he said.

His face soothed me, his voice, his familiarity, that pull back into the orbit of my real life where I had a place and a purpose, an anchor.

Before the trip I had consulted parenting websites for tips on travelling without your child. That's why Pingu was with me in Florida. Earlier, I had sent a photo of me and Pingu in bed together at the hotel, but it had backfired.

'Fearne won't stop going on about Pingu,' Rich said. 'She wants Pingu back.'

'I won't send any more photos of Pingu, then.'

'She's fine during the day,' Rich said. 'It's just at night she misses you. In the morning she gets up and watches the World Cup with me.'

I listened to him talk about the frustrations of his workday. The aircon was an arctic furnace that filled my room with its frigid roar. It was okay for Pingu, who was a penguin, but I couldn't hear myself think.

'The aircon is driving me crazy,' I said.

'Turn it off,' Rich advised. 'Try and get some sleep.'

I located the switch and the aircon fell into a resentful silence. Pingu and I lay under the covers, but I couldn't relax.

Five storeys below, The Wreck lap-lap-lapped.

~

I woke. A siren pierced the sassy tropical air. It kept screaming, on and on, from Homer's *Odyssey* to Fort Lauderdale. I got up, flicked back the bedcovers, *Calypso* fell on the floor. I threw on the hotel dressing gown. Guests, befuddled, emerged from doors on to balconies. If flames were about to ravage the hotel, I could at least jump into The Wreck. But it was a false alarm.

~

In the morning I walked the long white pavements of Sea Breeze Boulevard alone, no mermaids to interview.

I waded on to the sandy beach to take a photograph of a wooden plaque: 'Don't disturb the nesting sea turtles.' The layer of seaweed strewn along the edge of the sea reeked. What was I doing here, looking for 'the wreck and not the story of the wreck / the thing itself and not the myth'? I had come to B inspired! Not to B afraid!

I flip-flopped through the lukewarm water past families. The moon was still out, a half orb, in the indecent blue sky. I felt extraneous, connected only to my shadow, which made for the shade.

I steered towards a big sign along the beach: 'International Swimming Hall of Fame'. A little old lady sat behind the counter in the dusty foyer. The room felt like being inside a snow globe — tiny particles shimmied in the afternoon light.

'Where are you from?' she asked.

'New Zealand.'

'You've come a long way.'

Yes. I had come a long way for a little girl who always came last in her school swimming competition.

I knew nothing about the history of swimming, hadn't even thought about it as having a history. But here it was, jumbled up in memorabilia, fusty displays and replica oil paintings.

Polynesians surfed the waves of tropical idylls millennia ago.

The Romans and the Egyptians described their public baths as 'democratic melting pots' though initially the baths were closed to women. In the sixth century the Christians closed public baths and pronounced bathing, nudity and sex outside of marriage to be sinful. Swimming pools and baths then disappeared from Europe for the next thousand years.

I wouldn't have missed them, personally. I checked out a row of mannequins in out-of-date swimsuits that were about as risky as a closed-mouth kiss with your grandmother. Light years away from

Pamela Anderson in *Baywatch*. I admired an Edwardian bathing costume that looked more like a dour French maid's dress with matching pantaloons, and posted a photo of a modest Islamic bathing suit like a pretty pink raincoat to Instagram.

Mermaids had nothing to do with the official history of swimming. Yet a mermaid painting graced the wall, high above a light fitting like a buoyant afterthought. She had long hair and sat on a rock, in a dainty blue tail. She held a conch shell to her ear. A crab annotated the bottom of the picture frame, its pincers outstretched like castanets. Artist unknown.

'Sailors and fishermen have told stories of seeing mermaids for centuries. The first sightings were made in Assyria around 1000BC.'

A glass case represented the heyday of Billy Rose's Aquacade, another showcased the Diving Venus, Australian swimmer Annette Kellerman. Kellerman, I knew, was the first actress to appear nude on film, in *A Daughter of the Gods*. She launched her own range of one-piece swimsuits and wrote two bestsellers — one about swimming, the other called *Physical Beauty: How to Keep It*.

Then, around the corner, I discovered a tiny black-and-white photograph of a row of bodies lined up on a beach. Little Victorian boots poked out of long skirts. On 15 June 1904, the *General Slocum* had caught fire on a routine pleasure cruise. Nearly a thousand girls and women died. The difference between life and death was the ability to swim fifty yards. The tragedy helped create the twentieth-century demand for swimming pools and lessons. The *General Slocum* fire remained the worst disaster in New York until 9/11.

The photo of the drowned girls from the *General Slocum* stayed with me. They were:

> the ribs of the disaster
> curving their assertion
> among the tentative haunters.

It was my last day in Florida. I'd arranged to meet MeduSirena later, but first I had to swim in The Wreck, at least once, to justify my trip. I vacated my towel and walked into the shallow end, treading cautiously on each white scalloped step. The water was warm and thick and syrupy, studded with a skein of dirt around the edges. The chlorine was no good for the aquaticats. Saline was gentler; they did not wear goggles. Images of aquaticats past and present turned lazy corkscrews and somersaults. In my mind, MeduSirena the fire-eating mermaid glided by in her signature red tail, supping a mai tai. I blinked in the grainy pool and tried to focus on the line of black rectangles that I knew were the bar windows. I wanted to swim down to the glass and do an aquaticat drive-by but didn't have the guts to go that far. It seemed so deep.

I dolphin-kicked, I sculled water with my hands, but I couldn't stay down. I was one of 'the half-destroyed instruments' in Rich's poem, my life at least half over. I had too much air in my lungs, too much high-density fat.

But I held course to the vision of MeduSirena in a sequined tail, shimmering in the window of The Wreck. The command to sparkle dies hard.

She walked into the foyer in a black bowler hat, glamorous, cool, made-up. A bit rock'n'roll.

In the Naked Crab café, we talked for two hours, the video camera focused on her face; her hat slightly askew.

'I've been at this for twenty-seven years. I'm a techie underwater.'

The shows she created for The Wreck were atmospheric, rather than choreographed; when one mermaid goes up, another drops down into the window. There is never a moment during a show when one of the windows is not occupied. Zero dead air time.

She described the routines for The Wreck in aviation terms: barrel rolls, loops, inversions, a stall — that's when a mermaid stops and hangs in the window.

Everything was tactical. 'I exhale to regulate buoyancy,' Marina explained. 'Sea lions are the model animal 'cause they cruise, no strokes. They have constant buoyancy. They do lovely barrel rolls and just look right up at you, and that was my approach.'

I was a junkie for her lingo. She made the work real to me.

Training her aquaticats, Marina started with no fin, just herself and the trainee underwater, getting comfortable in liquid space. Sometimes she got the trainee to sit down the bottom and play pat-a-cake with her. Once that comfort in water had been built up, then she got performers trying other things. She knew someone was ready when they could do something completely naturally, like reach up and pretend to pull a can of beans off a shelf in a supermarket. Except underwater.

The game-changer was the 'wasabi hit' — a moment when the performer takes water right up their sinuses. 'Once they get past it, they are comfortable to do a lot more underwater than they could before.'

I told her about my trip to the Swimming Hall of Fame and seeing the Kellerman display. Marina respected Annette for her swimming ability, for her creation of aquaballet, but also because she helped popularise a user-friendly swimsuit for women. 'Kellerman should be in every history book,' Marina said. Instead, Ariel was a household name.

Like Kellerman, Marina had spent her life perfecting the art of performing underwater, creating and sustaining the illusion that she belonged in 'liquid equanimity'.

'Escapism,' she said, 'it's all about escapism. We need to get away from this thing' — she gestured to her mobile phone. 'I'm here to give you a little breath of fresh air. I hold mine, so that you can breathe.'

Her life was counter opposite to mine — so brave. Yet I was convinced that her story was somehow the key to my own.

We are, I am, you are
by cowardice or courage
the one who find our way
back to this scene

carrying a knife, a camera
a book of myths
in which
our names do not appear.

'I've always been comfortable with the concept of flight,' said MeduSirena, 'either in the water or in the air. I have dreams where I fly to a tree. The division is lost in my mind.'

When her son was about five, he once noticed her coughing and said, 'You've been breathing too much fire.' Not a metaphor. She does breathe fire. She was also a vegetarian. Had been a raw foodie for years. When I asked her why she had stopped eating meat, she replied, 'Believe it or not, I think I read an article and found out Daryl Hannah was a vegetarian. I thought it was really cool that the lobster in *Splash* was stuffed with mashed potatoes.'

MeduSirena's salty pragmatism enchanted me.

'I love your Sea Hag persona,' I said.

'The Sea Hag is funny as shit. The whole idea is, "Yeah I'm the hag." People say, "You're not a hag." "Yes I am." Every day takes me further to my goal. I think I saw three more grey hairs this morning. I'll get there, just you watch.'

10.

Touching Madison

In the June gloom, Brian Eno's 'Deep Blue Day' came on shuffle, as Mermaid Linden drove us into the winding Santa Monica Mountains. We passed curving golden hills cleared by last summer's fires. 'I'm a hippie at heart,' Linden said. She was easily the nicest mermaid I had met. Linden called herself the PG mermaid, and she had the interest of children, or as she called them, 'little sea fans', at heart. She pointed out the sign into the Canyon as we passed. A local had crossed out the population and added a plus one. 'Someone's had a baby,' Mermaid Linden said, as we began our descent.

The music lapped over me. One night years ago, by a lake, Eno's ambient space-age song matched the stars Linden looked up at, long before she had the idea to build a blue silicone tail with a crescent-shaped fluke in her parents' garage and add the prefix Mermaid to her name. She worked for months with a special effects designer to create tail 1.0. Weekends, nights. First, they made a fibreglass replica of Linden's legs, then moulded a clay tail around them. They created a fiberglass mould of the tail, injected silicone into it. Linden had nightmares, it was an expensive, tricky process, she had everything riding on that tail.

On her computer she kept a folder of fish pics hauled from Google. Nature knows best. Scale patterns. Textures. Tuna. Sharks. Most mermaids have a fluke that resembles an inverted heart, but not Linden. She chose a crescent shape. Thin, lunate or crescent-shape tails like those possessed by jacks and swordfish allow for great speed over long distance. 'I knew that if someone took a photo of me from below and you can't even see my face or the details of the tail or the colour — you will know it's me, because no one else has the crescent.'

~

In October 2013, eight-year-old Lauren Cosgrove spent the morning with her family at the Sea Life Glasgow aquarium. Afterwards, they were driven in a limousine to Loch Lomond, a freshwater loch. The lake sits in a depression carved out by glaciers during the last Ice Age. Lauren climbed out of the passenger seat and walked towards the darkly lapping waters. Beneath her sequined mermaid dress, she wore a central venous catheter that provided her with nutrients. In her backpack, her 'special milk' drink. Born twenty-seven weeks early, Lauren has a condition called short gut syndrome, a problem caused by the small intestine.

As Lauren stepped along the pebbled shore, she saw Mermaid Linden swimming towards her through Loch Lomond.

'As soon as I got in the water,' Linden told me, 'I felt like someone was stabbing me with a thousand knives. It was the coldest water I've ever been in. I swam around past the pier, and I'm, like, scraping myself on the rocks to pull myself out of the water. Then I got up on the shoreline and saw her running, and I just forgot about all of it.'

Linden told me that her niece, only nine years old, was being treated for leukemia. 'I've been doing the work with children's charities for years. But it's become very personal now.'

She started to cry. The veneer of the interview cracked and I felt love rushing in, the love I had for Fearne, the love we all have for our families. Linden wasn't just a pixelated mersona on Skype, an image I'd netted on a Google search, she was real. The hard definitions between me and the mermaids were collapsing out here. *Who did you want to be when you grew up? What kind of woman? And who did you become?*

~

Linden and I met for our official interview at a café, and talked for ages. I took a photo of her 'More Ocean Less Plastic' reusable bamboo utensil set and rolled-up tote bag. Afterwards, I'd planned to browse the boutiques along the street and find a present for Fearne, then Uber back to the hotel and collect my thoughts. Instead, I followed Mermaid Linden back to her car, past fences overhung with huge purple prongs of flowers. 'Lupins,' Mermaid Linden said. She knew all the plants, all the birds, and called each one by its rightful name. She also called everything cute a 'muffin'.

'Look at that little muffin!' She pointed at the mockingbird on the power line, opened her car boot, then presented me with a pink Mermaid Linden monofin for my daughter.

As well as designing and manufacturing her own range of monofins for adults and children, Linden is the board chair of a non-profit organisation run by volunteer 'citizen scientists' to promote sustainable reefs worldwide. She has her own YouTube channel and makes a series, *Mermaid Minute*, to edutain children about the ocean and sea life. She has the best mermaid puns, too, and called herself an 'entrepremer-maid'. 'The mernacular is real, Megan,' she joked.

Linden had been filming a documentary about freediving in the Cayman Islands, the Caribbean Sea lapping at her feet, when the idea of becoming a professional mermaid first occurred to her. She'd recently graduated from Emerson with a degree in film and environmental science. She was the girl at film school who repaired an old 16mm Bolex camera and bought an aquarium from Chinatown, then dunked the camera in it and started filming. She saw her first minke whale by bioluminescence on an old schooner off the coast of Massachusetts.

In the Cayman Islands, the silhouettes of the freedivers below the surface had reminded Linden of mermaids and mermen. She was addicted to freediving, but didn't want to compete. 'As a freediver you are surrendering yourself to the sea. A good friend of mine said, "You can't hide from yourself in the water", and that's true, you can't. If you've got stuff going on emotionally on land, as soon as you tread water you feel it.'

Back on the boat, Linden asked Mandy-Rae Cruickshank, the Canadian world champion freediver, 'Hey, can I try your monofin?' Sweet. They had the same size feet. She jumped off into the Caribbean. The boat was waaayyy over there when she surfaced. 'Oh my God. What if this is it?' Linden thought.

Being a mermaid was it. She had since trained the team at Dive Bar in Sacramento. She had also worked hard to diversify her mermaid brand, collaborating with Body Glove to design and market her monofins. The point for her was teaching and sharing the wonder of the ocean. Swimming through the California kelp forests, Mermaid Linden told me, was like being in an underwater cathedral.

'Instead of stained-glass windows there are gorgeous layers of green, filtered with light, and the beams are showering. When you turn to the sun and you're looking up into that canopy, the beams are shining on you, flowing and moving in slow motion.'

~

Linden parked outside the village shops in her canyon. We walked towards a large wooden building that reminded me of a two-storey log cabin. 'You can look for a present for your daughter.' The artsy gift-shop in the Canyon sold beautiful wooden toys for children, handmade clothing, crystals and soaps. Mermaid Linden saw the deep blue deck of cards first. On the cover a fairy reached out to touch the outstretched hand of a blonde mermaid who sat above a night sea, on her rock. The deck of oracle cards was called 'Magical Mermaids and Dolphins'.

'Does this speak to you?' Mermaid Linden asked.

I hesitated.

'I want to buy these for you.' She picked up the deck. 'I might never see you again.'

The oracle cards were by Doreen Virtue, a name I recognised from my research. I'd read Virtue's book *Mermaids 101* months ago and remembered next to nothing about it, except for one thing: Mermaids often have red hair. I didn't put much stock in Doreen Virtue's opinions, but when Mermaid Linden offered to buy me a pack of oracle cards I said, 'Yes, thank you, I'm touched.' And I meant it.

The till chimed. The doorbell chimed. The wind chimes chimed outside the artsy gift-shop in the canyon. The muffins flew from power line to tree.

~

'Boo!' I recognised Merman Jax from behind even though I'd only skyped him once.

I tapped him on the shoulder, and he turned around, startled.

He reminded me of David, my best friend from art school — the same impeccable posture, the same graceful walk. David had studied ballet, was elegant and handsome. At art school he was the style icon everyone adored, including me. David was also the friend who put up with my insufferable bullshit, who sat with me during long nights in the edit suite as I recut movies like *Splash* and *Labyrinth* into art videos. He always helped me get the right take.

Now I was in the company of Merman Jax. He asked me where I wanted to go.

'I need a drink,' I said.

'Do you mind if I don't record?' I asked, as we sat down at the Mixologist. I ordered a cocktail. It was tinged pink, like a species of coral. I sipped it through a plastic straw.

'I've interviewed so many mermaids,' I said. 'I keep posting that emoji of the blowfish to describe how I am feeling.'

Merman Jax was sympathetic. He was also rare — the merman is much rarer than the mermaid.

Jack Laflin performs as Merman Jax. A competitive swimmer, he is the son of Filipino abalone divers on his mother's side, and Irish whalers on his father's side. He grew up with the ocean in his blood. Jack moved to LA originally intending to act, but after he kept getting cast as either a gangster-thug or a sexy dancer in a nightclub, he realised he just didn't love it enough.

I ordered another pink cocktail in a large margarita glass. Sipped deeply though my straw. I worried I wasn't giving Jack bang for buck, should have been interviewing him, but I felt an exhaustion crowding in. I needed to be myself, I needed a friend. I wanted Jack to be that person — I trusted him. Jack ran his own boutique events company, Dark Tide Productions. I related hook, line and sinker to his company motto: *Inspiring a workforce disenchanted with emotionless work.*

Yes. Rich biked home from work on his Surly every day, disenchanted by emotionless work. I too had done my fair share of emotionless work. I was a mother of a daughter crying at a cat flap — my work was either emotionless or too emotional.

I knocked back my cocktail, ordered another.

'I partly got into this industry because I didn't see the type of performers I would hire — usually the main mermaid is a beautiful blonde woman. Black mermaids don't see representations of themselves on TV or in films unless as an extra, and a lot of people of colour don't think they can be mermaids, professionally or recreationally. We want to change the dialogue, but until people rise up, it's this vicious circle.

'I have a big spiritual connection to Yemaya the African goddess of water. A lot of black mermaids identify with her.'

Jack didn't work with people who wanted to turn him into a joke. 'It takes so much work to make what we do look effortless. It's awful and there's cramping and sun and chlorine, so many things. A thirty-pound tail and people say, "Oh you just sit there." No, I don't just sit there. Trust me, you couldn't do what I do. If it was so easy everyone would do it.'

I thought back to my Skype with Mermaid Raina from Halifax. There were very few professional mermaids in the world, she'd said, who earned their living solely from performing. I rarely asked the mermaids I interviewed how much money they made — too afraid to burst anyone's bubble — but I now knew she was right. There were of course exceptions to the rule, but behind almost every mermaid success story lurked all the obstacles, and other, sadder tales, of just how bloody hard it is to realise a dream.

'That said, I do genuinely think that anyone can be a mermaid,' said Jack. 'Whatever makes you happy. If you want to buy a tail and swim whether it's for exercise, or for recreation or if it just makes you happy, don't explain any reason why you want to do that. Have fun and enjoy yourself and grab whatever happiness you need in this life.'

~

My biggest moment of frisson with Jack was over *Labyrinth*. In addition to being a professional merman, Jack is an artistic director involved in the annual Labyrinth Masquerade Ball, an event inspired by Jim Henson's fantasy movie. The ball has run for over twenty years and is an immersive theatre experience. It originally had much more to do with the waltz ball masquerade scene from *Labyrinth*, but now it's become its whole own entity.

'It takes an army to run this event,' he said. 'I get to do an extension of my merman work — I am a rare male siren. It's my favourite thing I do each year. You literally get to run wild, it's improv for two days. I am so proud of it.'

'I wish I could go,' I said.

Labyrinth was one of the films I recut at art school. In my edit, Jennifer Connelly never escapes from the Labyrinth. Instead, she falls continuously through the tunnel in 'the helping hands' scene. I overlaid another Louise Hay affirmation soundtrack, so that the green grabbing puppet hands appeared to mouth the tepid mantras.

For a long time, that was me. I didn't know how to love myself, wasn't ready to grow up. In my psyche, I was still falling through the tunnel of green grabbing hands, but of course I couldn't tell that to Merman Jax.

'Mermaid Linden gave me a pack of Doreen Virtue playing cards,' I said.

Jack told me Virtue had denounced all her pagan oracle cards and told people to burn her packs. 'She's become a born-again Christian.'

'God, how weird. "Virtue" — that surname has to be fake for a start,' I said.

We gushed about how nice Mermaid Linden was, and fangirled over Daryl Hannah in *Splash*. 'She looked so effortless. I strive to be even a fraction of how elegant she was in the water,' Jax said.

He offered to give me a lift back to my motel.

En route to the carpark, we stood on an escalator and passed a poster for *Jurassic World*. The film represented by that steely logo of a T-Rex skeleton, its jaws open as though it could take a bite out of you.

'Have you seen it?' I asked.

'No. I always thought dinosaurs were like mermaids for men,' he said.

~

On my second-to-last day in America, I held the airbrush that had painted Madison. It looked like a marijuana pipe, something you could take a toke from. The airbrush was surprisingly small, with a dark-red handle and splattered all over with yellow paint. It had a bulbous pipe head where you put the paint.

I held it aloft, and hoped I looked appropriately awed. This was as close to Daryl Hannah as I'd ever get.

Special effects man Robert Short was across the table from me, wearing a dark-grey cap, sunglasses and a white shirt. He pulled out a swatch, an irregular offcut, pointed like an arrow. It was one of the original samples from the design of Madison's tail.

'I can't believe I am holding a sample of her tail,' I said.

I stroked Madison, running my fingertips over the scale pattern, and thought back to my conversation with Caribbean Pearl. A vivacious Puerto Rican woman with long spirally hair, she had started out as a pirate, but then got into mermaiding despite being told by her boss that mermaids can't be black. Caribbean Pearl took her tail on flights, draped over her shoulder like a mink coat, to avoid extra luggage fees. Everyone in the airport wanted to get up close to her and get a photo.

'What do pregnant bellies, fake boobies and mermaid tails have in common?' Caribbean Pearl asked me.

'I don't know. What?' I said.

'Everybody wants to touch them.'

On Madison's tail, the tiny dots were like Braille, and I tried to read them. I could see quite plainly that the surface was an odd amalgamation of sharkskin, which feels like sandpaper, and snakeskin. Most commercial silicone mermaid tails have small scales, which is biologically incorrect. A fish the size of a human being — a grouper for instance — would have large scales. Scales the size of a human palm. That was not desirable.

I know more about the making of *Splash* than anyone should. Ron Howard, the director, wanted the mermaid to embody a fantasy. He'd suggested the koi carp as a reference point for the tail, and Robert was tasked with bringing that vision to life. Madison has translucent fins just like a real fish.

'Can we drill down into the bath scene again?' I asked him. 'I really love the bath scene.'

Robert laughed. Sure.

He drew the set-up on a piece of paper, showed how the fluke was inserted into a funnel, built into the custom-made bathtub on set. The tail was controlled by a platform pulled up and down by cables. When the platform was pushed, the fluke unfurled up and out. The fluke itself was made from fine urethane and had a steel spring coiled around the edge —

'To make it go boing?' I said.

'Yes, if it didn't have that steel spring the tail would come out and just go . . . bloouup.' He mouthed something deflating, like a blobfish. 'The whole point of the project was that it had to be lyrical. Today if we did the bath scene, it'd all be CGI. But at that time, we didn't have an alternative . . . It forced you to think on your feet.'

'And because it was rare and difficult to achieve, that made people believe?'

'I hate to say it,' Robert said, 'but there's truly a little bit of magic lost.'

I was also obsessed with the story of the octopus. The subsequently deleted Sea Hag had a small octopus cast on her costume, modelled off a real octopus.

'What breed was it?' I asked.

'He was just a little brown octopus. There wasn't anything special about him,' Robert said. 'We used to bring in crabs for him. We'd put the crabs in the aquarium and the octopus was in the far corner and he'd take one tentacle, bring the crab up to him, split it in half, eat it and then throw the remains away.'

One day Robert and the crew came back from lunch and found everything in the tank was stark white, bleached of colour. The octopus had raised its tentacle out of the tank, pulled the electric socket above the tank out of the wall and electrocuted itself and all the other creatures in the tank.

God, how I related to that octopus.

The mermaid community was killing me with kindness. Robert gave me a thirtieth-anniversary DVD of *Splash*, the cover signed by him, and a giant Toblerone.

'Where are you going next?' he asked.

'To interview Hannah Mermaid.'

Robert perked up. Hannah Mermaid is the most famous professional mermaid in the world. She has also met Daryl Hannah. I've seen the photo of them hugging. Both blonde and beautiful, in sync.

'I will give you a lift.'

~

Out the back of the café, Robert folded the top of his forest-green Pontiac Solstice down, and we drove across Los Angeles, the wind in my mermaid hair. I was performing the role of writer. It was the best part I'd ever played in my life. Then Robert parked the Pontiac across the street from Hannah Mermaid's white bungalow and we both got out.

We knocked, but no answer came from within. Fortunately, another dude arrived — a good-looking, black-haired man. 'Are you here for Hannah?'

'Yes,' I replied.

He appraised us coolly, then disappeared, exit stage left. I assumed he had gone to tell her we had arrived.

In the foyer of the quiet, spacious bungalow Robert and I looked at one another. 'Does she know you are coming?' he asked. He looked nervous beneath his cap.

I texted her mobile, and then she appeared from upstairs, in a floaty black linen dress, padding barefoot towards us. The Beyoncé of mermaids, the mermaid who had inspired the whole movement of professional mermaids. The one who had swum with whales and manta rays. Like me, she was a little girl who had wished she could grow up to be just like Madison, but in Hannah's case, she had. 'I literally lived my dream,' Hannah said in 'Turning Fantasy into Reality', her 2015 Ted Talk.

She greeted us, hugged Robert, they chatted, then he left.

I fooled around setting up my video camera.

'You nearly had it,' Hannah said, offering me a glass of water with lemon juice in it. She was much more tech-savvy than me. She was also comfortable in front of a camera.

Outside the French doors was a blue kidney-shaped swimming pool — apt and appetising. Above my head hung a photograph of Hannah swimming with a whale shark, her body posed with its body in the deep-blue element. And now I had my video camera pointed at the most famous professional mermaid in the world, the mermaid every other aspiring mermaid wanted to be.

We immediately got talking about *Splash* — that was her starting point too.

'I love the publicity image of Daryl sitting in a giant fishhook in her orange tail,' I said. For me, the image epitomised the appeal of the mermaid — the timeless hook.

'I had that poster in my bedroom,' Hannah said. 'I guess at that age all I wanted to do was look exactly the same as Daryl Hannah.'

She told me how her mum helped her find a plastic orange tablecloth that was the right colour. They traced the tail, cut it out and sewed it into shape. They padded the fluke with pillow stuffing. 'And then I just spent hours and hours, painstakingly drawing tiny little gold scales over the entire thing, and hand-painting the black lines. I had my poster of Daryl Hannah and I basically tried to copy her tail as closely as I could. Then I was like, right, well now I'm going to swim.'

Hannah was now as close to a real mermaid as anyone could get. Being a mermaid was about much more than fantasy. The role gave Hannah a platform to advocate for the ocean environment, it gave her life purpose. She was authentic, a vegan, who lived by her values and had campaigned with success to improve the lives of cetaceans. She had taken part in the surfer paddle-out in the documentary *The Cove*, putting herself on the line to save dolphins from slaughter. Lots of people didn't want to watch *The Cove*, Hannah told me, because they didn't want to see dolphins being killed. 'Many of us are unwilling to face reality when it is ugly.'

Sitting across from her, I was impressed but removed, somehow still so distant from her reality. Her beauty and authenticity and athleticism set her apart from me — she seemed so comfortable in her own skin.

'I got to live my dream,' Hannah said, as she'd said in the Ted Talk.

Hannah had filmed that talk in Spain, just after her father had died. Before she walked on stage, she realised, 'I just have to surrender. To surrender.'

Surrender was a part of the mermaid's calling.

'The stories of sirens calling sailors to drown in the depths is like a metaphor for humans surrendering to the great unknown,' she said.

'I did a mermaid lesson when I was in Florida, to try to understand a bit more,' I said.

'To *feel* things,' Hannah said.

'Yes, to feel things . . . My body was so buoyant, I just floated to the surface. It made me more aware of how specialised mermaiding really is.'

'Totally. You have to move properly and manage your buoyancy, and look good all at the same time. It's infinitely more challenging with video than photos.'

She looked up at the photograph over my head.

'When I look at that picture up there, I see it as absolute freedom. It's weightlessness. I believe that our spirit has a life and experience beyond our bodies. When we are underwater, we get a sense of what it feels like to not be in such density in the body. It's about attending to our spirit form a little bit, which is like going home.'

Before I left, Hannah opened the brown cushioned table in the centre of the lounge. It was a mermaid's treasure chest, filled with bags of colour-coded sequins, ballet slippers that could be weighted down with steel and conical contact lenses that give seventy percent visibility when you are under water. Hannah used these in her video, swimming with tiger sharks. 'But they are blurry as fuck on land,' she said.

This was the side of her I wanted to see. Her saltiness, her humour, who she really was. Hannah took me upstairs past her bedroom, and I walked into her walk-in wardrobe. Litres of clothes and shell crowns made just for her and, high on a shelf, a stuffed toy Grumpy Cat. 'I love Grumpy Cat,' she said, and I was surprised — it didn't seem to fit with the serenity she projected — but I respected her even more. I loved Grumpy Cat too.

Outside, by the pool, she showed me a white plastic trunk — there were her tails. She draped a few out for me. Each one took at least six months to make, the sequins hand-sewn on. They were one-offs.

I couldn't believe that, like the little girl painting in her bedroom, she still had the patience to create these tails. But when the underwater shots came back, her efforts were worth it.

'Someone is going to make the story of your life into a film some day,' I said. 'Don't you think? It's going to happen.'

~

I was clocking up hundreds of dollars Ubering all over Los Angeles. In the morning, I sat in the backseat, treated to a bottle of water and offered countless bags of sweets. The Uber drivers in LA worked hard for their tips.

'You look like Jim Carrey,' I told the driver.

'It's the beard,' he laughed. 'Where are you going?'

'I'm off to meet a mermaid.' I told him about my book.

His daughter was now twenty-two, but her favourite film was *The Little Mermaid*. 'She grew up watching Ariel, couldn't get enough of it.'

'Why do you think she liked it so much?' I asked.

'Because Ariel was a princess, and her daddy was a king.'

'I have a three-year-old,' I said.

'It only takes a second,' he said, 'and they are grown up.'

We passed streets flooded with sunlight, everywhere those tall palm trees, like impossible swizzle sticks. Suburbs of bungalows out the window. I saw a homeless man sleeping outside an enormous tarpaulin tent on a traffic island. Another man in a blank T-shirt walked along the road chanting, 'Some things never change.'

The boulevard I arrived at was boho and bougie — Mermaid Abby worked at the Mystic Journey Bookstore there. I stepped in and felt myself relax. It looked like a nineties self-help den. Books on spirituality and karma, crystals and stones in little jars. You could hold these things in your hand and feel the weight of them — grasp and contemplate a simple stone as though it was a feeling. You could hold it fleetingly, imagine that you had touched the depth of something, and then just release the feeling. *Let go let go let go.* Words Mum spoke to me when I was a teenager consumed by my feelings, aching for a boy who didn't love me back, or that teenage artist so frustrated by the limits of her talent that she threw a shoe across a room and broke Mum's favourite ornament, a church from Trade Aid.

Mum, as a bona fide self-help junkie, would have felt at home in this bookshop. No matter what she did, she never seemed to escape from the labyrinth. Our dreams are so catastrophically important to us.

That day in the Mystic Bookshop, my dream was that my mermaid book would hit the big time.

~

Mermaid Abby appeared, a springy blonde sprite, from within the bookstore's esoteric depths.

'How are you?' Abby asked. 'What do you need?'

'Food,' I said. 'I'm hungry.'

Abby took me to a nearby health food café, and we ordered mix-and-match salads from the numerous buckets available.

Abby was deeply chill. She told me she was in the middle of a 143-day Kundalini meditation. She'd become a freediver because it was more of a mind sport than a body sport. Freediving led to mermaiding.

Abby told me it took forty days to change a habit, ninety days to confirm a habit and 120 days to become the new habit. After 120 days, you are the new habit.

I ate my salad, thoughtfully.

Abby was intelligent and mindful, but she was also the only mermaid performer I interviewed who believed mermaids actually exist. She told me she was a direct descendent of Melusine. This is a story out of late medieval France and Luxembourg: many ruling families of the day — the House of Anjou, the Plantagenets, the Lusignans — were said to be descended from the two-tailed fresh-water siren.

'Wouldn't you rather live in a world where mermaids are real?' Abby said. 'In modern society we've lost something you can't buy. Mermaids bring that magic back in. Something's gotta feed your soul.'

After lunch, we stopped at a low-key James Bond style mansion that belonged to an underwater photographer Abby had worked with. He invited us in, and that's when I met his dog, who was also called Megan.

'I've never met a dog called Megan before,' I said, stroking her fur.

Inside the mansion we padded down into a carpeted den. A row of windows peered into the deep-end of the photographer's swimming pool.

We sat on the soft seating and the photographer gave me his business card, in case I wanted to write about him, too.

'I'm not photogenic,' I confessed.

'That's why she's the mermaid and you're the writer,' he said.

I saw myself through his eyes, suddenly. Abby and I journeyed on to Venice Beach alone, and walked the length of the pier. Kites flew, and the half-moon hung in the sky like a communion wafer. I felt something invisible pulling me in two.

Once a little girl saw Abby in her tail on Venice Beach, put her hands on her hips and said, 'You know, I've never seen a mermaid before.'

'I'm honoured to be your first,' Abby replied.

Her blonde curls whipped over her shoulder as we walked around the streets of Santa Monica. She took me back to her flat to show me her tails. I arranged them — a Mertailor and a Merbella — on an outdoor seat, then photographed them for Instagram.

Abby had once done market research into mermaids for her scriptwriting work. What would it mean to your life if mermaids were real? A hundred percent of respondents answered: *Anything would be possible.*

Real life is so boring, so dull and mundane. That day with Abby, I had seen behind the façade. She gifted me a small dainty drawstring bag of stones from the Mystic Bookshop, and said goodbye. Then the Uber arrived and took me away.

~

En route to the airport, I stopped at the tar pits. The black lake, outside a museum, was contained by an iron fence. I held the warm black bars and peered in at the mammoths trapped in tar. The mummy and baby mammoth stood at the side of the lake, but the big daddy mammoth (one assumes) was trapped in the pool. His mouth open, he trumpeted his upset. His head thrown back, his enormous tusks curved towards the sky. The little baby was also open mouthed, as if calling out 'Daddy!'

The mother's tusks were so long they looped together — her dissatisfaction was harder to see. But the baby's anguish was palpable. *Don't die. Stay with me.*

As I got back into an Uber to go to the airport, I noticed a tiny relic on the gravel road. Half pink, no bigger than the tip of my little finger. It was George, from *Peppa Pig*. I felt like crying out in recognition. George is Peppa's little brother, he holds a green dinosaur and his catchphrase is 'Roar!'

We had watched so many episodes of *Peppa Pig* at home together. I never took any of the plotlines in — it was background noise, a distraction for Fearne. Yet Rich would stop and complain:

‘We’ve seen this before.’ I held George in the palm of my hand, found. I would give him to Fearne when I got back home. I was ready to see her and Daddy Pig again.

On the drive out of LA, I finally caught a glimpse of the Hollywood sign through the car windscreen. There it was, lodged up in the hills, half hidden behind a building, surrounded by haze — YWOOD.

11.

Break Free

'Does yours have brown eyes?' I asked.

'No.' She smiled smugly. 'Does yours have earrings?'

'No. Is yours a boy?' I asked. A false question, she only ever chose a girl.

'No!'

Then Fearne bailed. 'Can I be the judge?' she asked.

'But Guess Who? doesn't need a judge,' Rich sighed. It was a fair point, but a meaningless one.

'I want to be the judge!' Fearne insisted.

'Fine, you can be the judge,' I said, to keep the peace.

'Mummy, can we play your cards instead?' Fearne asked.

Rich groaned. 'That's not a real game.'

Fearne sat on the stool in our lounge like a tennis umpire.

'Okay,' I said.

Rich swept aside the remnants of Guess Who? and I opened up my blue pack of Mermaid and Dolphin cards. Since I got back from America I had been drawing cards daily from the pack to guide my day, then looking up their meaning in the accompanying booklet. The cards were compulsive, intuitive, each freighted with meaning or completely meaningless, like horoscopes. Fearne liked to do it with me. Her favourite card featured a golden-haired smiling mermaid with a sunrise behind her: 'A New Dawn'. It seemed fitting for a four-year-old.

First she turned over 'Mother Healing'.

I frowned. 'I don't think you need that card yet,' I said, though it was hard to know.

I often got 'Mother Healing' and it annoyed the shit out of me. Give me a break, Doreen! Mum and I have come a long way. I loved my mother. Especially now she was a nana.

Fearne started turning over one card after another, until she finally found 'A New Dawn'. 'Here's my card,' she said as though pulling an ace out of the pack.

Rich looked over at my bookstack on my writing desk, then frowned. 'I see you've decided the new hard drive is now to be used to stack books and papers on.'

How negative could he be? Couldn't he see I was trying to surround myself with positivity? I hadn't thought about the submerged hard drive. I had stacked up a Jenga tower of folders and blue-spined books. *Mrs Caliban*, a book about a frustrated housewife who falls in love with an aquatic green merman. A local freediver's autobiography. A transcript of my newest interview with Mermaid Julie. The current copy of *Time* magazine — Rich bought that for me. On the cover an icecap peaked above the surface of the sea, down below it was revealed to be a plastic bag.

At first each mermaid card I drew seemed significant. *Yes! The universe is telling me something*. But now I wasn't so sure. I seemed to draw the same cards all the time. Perhaps the pack was jinxed? Or maybe I just wasn't a very good shuffler.

~

In 2005, Julie Atlas Muz cycled to work, only six blocks, but it was a cold-as-fuck seven minutes in wintry New York. Her bags of kit hung over her handlebars, and two thermoses of peppermint tea were ready to go-go. The Coral Room was a hip-hop bar, open six nights a week, with a 10,000-gallon salt-water tank, sporting 200 fish, installed right behind the bar. Just add Julie.

Julie had been the head mermaid at The Coral Room for over four years. She told me over Skype, years later, that it was still the best job she'd ever had. 'Mermaids are the sexuality of your unconscious,' she said. 'We take sailor's dreams and make them die on the rocks. We crash ships. We're destroyers. I love it. Let's go!'

Each shift was four hours, and the mermaids swam at least twice an hour, for eight minutes. 'I swam from two to three times a week. It was my job, and I was possessive of it. Mermaids are not generous people. We are vapid, we like sparkly things, and we will draw you to your death for our entertainment. We don't give a fuck.'

She had hand-sewn her outfits, made with sequins and fringes to flow and swing and grind underwater. She climbed a ladder into the crawl space above the tank and shimmied along a line of precarious wooden planks. The tank was held together by a row of steel bars. She wriggled out of her clothes and into her birthday suit, locked and loaded her toes, aimed her feet like an arrow, then pulled her tail on.

Splash. She could see — blurrily — the bartenders wave at her and she'd wave back. The tank was only six feet deep. She had to be careful not to kick or drag her tail along the gravel bottom and send the fish poo swarming. 'If you do a kick, that's going to cause a cloud of fish poo that is not going to get filtered for six hours,' she said.

The Coral Room had started out with thirty lookdowns, skinny, silver-dollar-looking fish that live in schools. Julie said, 'Fish have memory, they are smart and they have definite and distinctive personalities, for sure.'

She also worked with Chicken, a pufferfish, and Sugar, an emperor snapper with dominance issues. At first, Julie thought Sugar was being friendly. Then she realised he was territorial. For two months she was intimidated by Sugar, until Al, the aquarium's resident fish expert said, 'Punch him, Julie. Grab his tail and give him a shake. Show him who's boss.'

In the 2003 blackout in NYC there was no power for three days. It was summertime and really hot. The Coral Room got generators, but there wasn't enough power to oxygenate the water. The temperature rose past 78 degrees, and the fish boiled. 'Especially the lookdowns. It was horrible,' Julie said. One by one, they died, until finally there was just one left.

Afterwards, the punters often said: 'Why is that sad stupid fish always in the corner of the tank by itself?' So Julie swam down to the corner and do you know what she saw? Her reflection on both sides of the glass. 'That's why the lookdown was always in the corner, so he could see himself. Do you understand what I'm saying?' Julie said. 'He wanted to be with his own kind.' The rest of its school gone.

~

'Can I do a performance for you and Daddy?' Fearne said.

'She's stalling again,' Rich said.

'Yes,' I said. 'But quickly, because it's bedtime.'

Fearne stood in front of the TV shyly in her My Little Pony pyjamas.

'I'm going to do Katy Perry 'Roar'.'

We smiled. A Fearne classic.

Fearne swayed slightly from side to side and serenaded us. 'Roar' is an anthem of independence, as Fearne throws off the shackles of her toddler years and becomes a big kid. She belted out the chorus, 'You're going to hear me roar!'

We'd watched the music video on YouTube together. It had a jungle theme. Katy appears in a grass skirt and leopard-print bikini top and confronts a lion during the epic chorus. But my favourite bit was when she wrestles the fake crocodile in the river.

I sang along to the lyrics, too, until Fearne stopped. 'No, Mummy. I sing it myself. Not you.'

~

In the morning Dad came over. He drew 'Break Free' from the pack. A grey dolphin leapt from the waves on the front of the card.

'I've never drawn that card before!'

Dad had just retired.

'It doesn't seem to require extra explanation,' he said.

I consulted the booklet anyway. 'Try different ventures and experiences as a way to grow and learn.'

'I'm down with that,' Dad said.

'What does the symbol of the mermaid mean?' I asked.

'Maybe it's a symbol of hope,' Dad said.

'Maybe it is,' I echoed.

I turned to the light gushing through the kitchen window and felt pierced by hope, or something close enough.

Dad had lived at his place for over twenty-five years. When the waters rise, they will take Lyall Bay. 'I'm looking for a new house,' Dad said, 'further up the Kāpiti coast. Outside Wellington.'

~

I sat at my writing desk and drew 'Father Healing' from Doreen's pack. A purple-rimmed card, with a benevolent King Neptune proudly touting his massive trident on the rocks. The merman didn't look anything like Dad or Rich. But the card brought to mind another old poem fragment I once wrote called 'Letter to Neptune'. 'I am keeping your teeth on a chain around my neck, they chatter in the dark and keep me company.'

The 'Father Healing' card read: *Your personal power increases as you give any father-related issues to heaven.*

'Mummy,' Fearne ran out of the bedroom nude, her face giddy with excitement. I looked up from my writing desk, startled. I thought Rich was getting her into her pyjamas.

'Will you marry Daddy?' she said, smiling and giggling at the same time. She held something in her hands.

'What?' I said.

Rich stood behind her. Shy, and not given to jibber jabber.

'Will you marry Daddy!' Fearne said again.

She handed a box to me. It was grey and decorated with a slinky silver ribbon, I tugged on the ribbon, opened the box. Inside it was a huge silver ring embossed with the skin of a caiman hornback. The ring! The crocodile my spirit animal. The part of me that always snaps.

The croc ring was an enormous meaty circle that I fit on my wedding finger. It was unmissable. The kind of ring that could take out an eye. A weapon. Nothing says lifelong commitment like a crocodile.

'Rich,' I said. 'How did you get hold of this?'

'I have ways and means,' he said slyly, the seahorse bobbing along with its wiry little tail. He was so thoughtful it killed me.

'Well, will you?' he said, and then I realised I hadn't answered.

'Of course I will.'

I stood up and hugged him. Safe, and secure, his dark hair, and muscular body, the nook of his shoulder. I engulfed him.

'This is a surprise. I thought you didn't believe in marriage.'

Fearne hugged our waists, threw her arms around us.

'Family hug,' I said.

'When do you want to get married?' I asked, pulling out of the circle.

The seahorse shrugged. Its work was done. 'You can decide,' he said.

'And where? Your family are on the other side of the world.'

'I don't know. We'll work it out.'

'We've already been together for fifteen years,' I said.

'Exactly. We don't want to rush into things,' Rich said.

'We can have a long engagement and get to know each other first,' I said.

'Can I be the flower girl?' said Fearne, who knew little about weddings but enough to want to scoop a key part.

'Yes,' I said. 'I better tell Mum.'

It had always been Mum's dream to get married, not mine. 'I'll phone her in the morning,' I said. I had been thrown into another dilemma. Can a selkie opt to give away her sealskin? Doesn't the husband have to steal it from her?

~

In the middle of the night, I opened my laptop — ping — and signed in using the secret password from the Pod Squad. The Finfolk sale is released to the squad an hour ahead of the rest of the world. It was the second release of their fabric printed tails and I didn't want to miss out.

When Finfolk Productions began, in Minnesota in 2012, there were only one or two other tail makers in business. The twin sisters Abby and Bryn Roberts were so successful they dropped out of college and began running Finfolk full-time. Of their bespoke mermaid tails, Abby said, 'It's like a beautiful dress. It's not what it's made of, it's what it is.'

'We buy multiple gallon drums of dragon-skin silicone a week,' said Bryn. Dragon-skin silicone was originally developed for knee and hip replacements and cartilage simulation, made to be safe enough to put inside a person's body. 'We met one of the guys that first invented it back in the late nineties. We had him in our shop, in our studio. He was looking at our mermaid tails and said, "I never thought when I was inventing this that this is what people would do with it".'

The twins had told me the market for mermaid tails was still 'undersaturated'. That is why they'd started supplying swimmable printed tails at a lower price point than their moulded silicone tails. I couldn't afford silicone, but I couldn't resist their new printed 'Madison' tribute tail.

I had my credit card out. Fearne slumbered behind me in our double bed, her short breaths like a whale's spout. I could hear her dreaming.

Rich had measured me earlier — I was medium. I had noticed

some mermaids online complaining that their Gen One fabric tails were too tight, but I was going to risk it.

~

When my Finfolk tail arrived I unboxed it and we all got a load of 'Madison'.

'I want to send Dawson a photo of me in the tail,' Rich said.

The day was sunny and the wooden floorboards gleamed. He easily shimmied into the tail.

'Maybe I should be a purrmaid,' he said.

A little bit of knowledge is a dangerous thing.

'Maybe you should be,' I agreed.

I fetched Fearne's sparkly pink headband with pointed triangular cat ears. In front of our fireplace, Rich stretched out in Madison, with the cat ears on, and pretended to lick his paws. 'That's great,' I said. 'Work it, work it.'

He rolled over on to his tummy. I tried several angles.

'It's hard to get the whole tail in,' I said.

The front door was open. Fearne was pottering around nude in the garden, carrying her yellow bucket and spade. She poured water through the top of her Fisher-Price plastic waterplay thingy, and its Ferris wheel turned. It was also a mosh pit for her dolls to swim in, overloaded with dishwashing detergent for maximum bubbles. She strode back inside, nude, and looked at Daddy. Did a double-take in the doorway. Snap. I got the shot. 'That's brilliant,' I said.

'I want to join in,' Fearne sat on Rich's back. A purrmaid and child.

'That's it,' I said. 'That's the best one.'

Her, laughing and joyful. Him, elfin and slender, a man unafraid to dress as a purrmaid. My little family hooked on my big mermaid tail.

~

When it popped up on Facebook that the famous underwater photographer Brett Stanley was passing through New Zealand, it was another sign. Brett often worked with Hannah Mermaid! I had to get him to photograph me in my Madison tail, even though I still hadn't swum in it.

Arriving at the pool complex for my session, I saw Brett in a scuba mask, camera in front of his face, stationed in the dive pool. Depth: five metres. I held Madison casually over my shoulder, like a coat, but I was worried. I didn't want to feel like a haggis again, like I had in Florida with Charlotte.

The makeup artist was chatty.

'What if I drown?' I said.

She laughed lightly.

'I love your enthusiasm,' she said, as she applied the 'natural' look I had asked for. 'You'll probably be the best person on tonight. No one else has had a tail!'

The woman currently in the pool appeared to be doing something with a hoop. Out of water, she was long and lean and shivering. She made a quick outfit change then plunged back in, performing elastically in a range of serene poses, sitting and swinging in her hoop below the surface as though it was a ring of Saturn.

When it was my turn, I couldn't get Madison over my bum. I had to stand, twisting and turning, contracting my bum and trying to ease the tail over my hips. After some help from Brett and the makeup assistant I managed the first hurdle and got into the pool. Madison quickly filled up, like a sock. The tail inflated and became even more buoyant. I swiped my hand along the surface, trying to iron the air and water out.

I'd brought some props — a copy of Will Self's book *Shark* that I hadn't got around to reading yet, featuring a cover image of grinning little boy with jagged shark teeth. Part of mermaiding is choosing what kind of mer you'll be, and I had chosen to be the 'booky mermaid'.

Brett and I propped ourselves up along the side of the pool. He glanced at my book. 'Cool, a Will Self novel.'

'You know Will Self?' I asked.

'I've read it,' he said.

'Wow, that's impressive.' Brett was even more of an intellectual than me.

'Have you swum in the tail before?' he asked.

'No, I wanted to train more, but I didn't have time.' The water eddied around us.

'It doesn't matter.' Brett put me at ease. He was a gracious dude. And calm, very calm. He didn't ask me to blow kisses underwater, thank God. 'It's not about swimming,' Brett said. 'It's about staying under and being relaxed.' Brett talked me through the requisite breathing techniques — the trick was to expel the air from my lungs before I went down. Under the water, he advised me to keep my mouth sightly open. Jaw relaxed. I nodded.

My gaze swivelled to an orange safety rope that dangled into the pool, a weight attached to the bottom.

'Are you ready?' he asked.

'Let's give it a try,' I said.

I paddled for the rope, then lunged to grab it. I twirled around and around like a ballerina in a music box, and everyone looked concerned for my well-being. The tail lurched into weird positions. It had taken on a life of its own.

Brett waited patiently. 'Shall we try?'

Underwater, I concentrated on keeping my face calm, tried not to spew bubbles into the booming vacuous space. Jaw slightly open, eyes peeled.

When I next surfaced, Brett told me to try keeping my hands by the side of my body. I felt bad. Brett was being paid, but money's not everything. What did I want from this shoot?

We tried a few shots of me loafing around horizontally, as though stretched out on a couch. I'd seen plenty of mermaids photographed in this pose, but it's really hard to do — I couldn't get myself horizontal at all. When I descended, my arms naturally lifted above my head — stick 'em up — as though Brett was pointing a gun at me, not a camera.

'It's hard to get your whole tail into the frame,' he said.

'Maybe we should try the props,' I said.

Once we got the book wet, my mersona finally clicked. I was focused. Determined. Hannah Mermaid had once faced a great white in the wild. She roared at it underwater — made herself larger. 'She's fearless,' Brett told me later.

Afterwards, we propped ourselves on our elbows at the side of the pool and Brett flicked through some of the images in his camera. 'Intense,' said Brett, gesturing towards my steely-eyed gaze as I pretended to read *Shark* underwater. 'These are great,' I chattered. Hypothermia may have been setting in. I'd only been in the water for fifteen minutes but was already a wreck.

Brett's business model was predicated on taking underwater portraits of people: anyone and everyone. 'For me, it's about shooting dreams down there,' he told me. To him, and the best mermaids, the distinction between wet and dry film or photography shoots was obvious and profound. They were junkies for the real thing — not for CGI. Brett and Hannah had filmed in a kelp forest off the coast of Catalina, in Cozumel, Mexico and Florida Springs. They had travelled the world together.

At home, later, I put Will Self on the windowsill to dry out in the sun. The book buckled, but was otherwise fine — we were never going to read it anyway. When the photos came through, I was shocked by how gormless I looked in the pool. I didn't look like a mermaid; I looked like the woman I was, unsure, trying, hoping to somehow slip out of my skin. Why was I surprised? The professional mermaids, like Hannah, made it look so easy, but that was the illusion.

Still, I had it. My underwater portrait. Check.

~

Rich helped me pack Madison into a bag. We folded the tail into three segments — the fluke was the tricky bit. The big fins were like prongs, like an oversized floppy fish fork. A soft sculpture, something Claes Oldenburg might make. I took a photo of the bag zipped open — the orange fabric, the teasing little scale pattern — and posted it to Instagram.

I was off to Auckland for a writer's residency, wearing my jeans and a new Finfolk Pod Squad T-shirt. On the front, a fluke rose out of white-crested waves, while in the background a lighthouse cast out a full beam across the tide. Who doesn't like a lighthouse? Lighthouses now seem like symbols more than working places — storybook illustrations, beacons of hope, aspirational Instagram posts.

I was treating the residency like an Instagram op, too. Why not? I was a brand of one.

Getting into town from the airport, I decided to walk to the hotel, carrying my tail in the bag. I know Auckland well. It's where I went to art school. It's where this crazy mermaid saga began. Decades ago, in that tutorial I never got over. I felt the satisfaction of someone who was about to make a big point, twenty years late.

I walked along K Road, my suitcase rolling along on its little black wheels, letting out a ripple of sound. Down the ridge, The Sky Tower was like a false lighthouse, a shaft in the centre of the city. Verona's gold-sequined sign glittered as I rolled the suitcase past the café, squeaking intermittently.

Auckland is always hotter. I marched along, sweating; crossed the main intersection, past fancy car dealerships and the McDonald's. I should have just got an Uber — I had forgotten how bloody long Great North Road is. Finally, I reached my destination.

The Surrey Hotel is an old mock-Tudor building, with white stucco swirls on the walls outside like an ice-cream cake. The décor was stuck in a time warp: cheesy and embarrassing, which was just how I liked it. The residency was supposed to include free pizza from the local Domino's and lunch on Sunday at the hotel's pub. When I booked my ticket for Auckland, I discovered the free pizza was no longer part of the deal. Just as well. I felt slim, almost svelte, back in a pair of jeans.

My tail was a symbol for my great big mermaid book, but it was also an anchor weighing me down. I stood at reception. The hotel was decked out with an old Axminster carpet, threadbare and ponging of pints and long afternoons watching Sky Sports. No one around. I rang the bell. One of those little silver domes shaped like a tit. Press the nipple and it ring-a-lings.

I got the poor sod at reception to take a photo of me, my tail over my shoulder, hand poised over the bell. I had one week to write my masterpiece and then I could eat my roast on Sunday.

I scoped out the pool. That was another reason I had to bring my tail. It was indoors, just beyond reception, a tiny, angular and relatively shallow pool in an interior courtyard.

My room was in an adjacent wing away from the main building, seemingly abandoned. I had the upstairs apartment on the corner, nearest to the road. It was like the granny flat above the old people's home that I had grown up in with Mum. A small, poky kitchen opened on to the lounge. The apartment was stuffy with curdled time and warm air. I plonked my laptop on a wooden duchess in the lounge. One bedroom and a small bathroom with a bath.

I was there but I didn't feel safe, was restless in the humidity.

I had Annette Kellerman's book *How to Swim* with me and tried to read it. The 'first professional mermaid', MeduSirena's idol and Mermaid Raina's tattoo, Kellerman had started out swimming in a mermaid costume at an aquarium in Melbourne. In American vaudeville, she became as famous as Harry Houdini, performing with live eels, then became a goddess of the silent screen.

Kellerman's legacy was also bound up with physical fitness and beauty. She had monetised her looks and body, and wrote books on beauty. She was a life-long vegetarian, too, and later ran her own health food shop. Kellerman was an entrepreneur, and an adept businesswoman. She married her manager; she'd even swum with alligators.

I'd also brought a pair of dark-green gloves with webbed fingers. Instead of finishing *How to Swim* during the residency, I made a video of my webbed green gloves holding the book and turning the pages, as though I was transforming into the Creature from the Black Lagoon. It was part of my brand work, my in-house marketing campaign.

I woke each morning and spoke to Rich.

'I can't get Fearne to sleep at night. I can't sleep next to her. I am so fucking tired. She doesn't want to go to daycare.'

'Fearne!' he hollered, as she did something untoward in the background. He listed all the complaints of their day-to-day lives without me. I felt like shit.

'It's not easy being a mother,' I said, and hung up. This was one of my refrains. Once I watched Fearne nurse her baby doll and heard her say, 'It's not easy being a mother.' She was picking up all kinds of things from me, whether I felt good about them or not. 'I don't want any jibber jabber tonight,' I often told Fearne.

I didn't tell Rich I had had enough of his jibber jabber. But I had. Increasingly, I felt my book had to solve all the problems of the world, address climate change, honour and celebrate the individual achievements of every mermaid, and merman, track their movements across time and space, like Ubers over an app. I'd told all the mermaids I was writing a book about the history of professional mermaids and I had meant to honour their stories. I had notes, random biro scribbles of mermaids and their individual starting dates. Hannah, 2003, Byron Bay. Linden, 2005, Los Angeles. MeduSirena, 2006, Florida. I had also arranged to interview two New Zealand mermaids while I was at the Surrey. I wasn't anywhere near the end.

I ignored my open laptop. Instead, I ran up Williamson Avenue, in the cool morning sun, anxious about keeping my weight off.

When I got back, I sat at the duchess and wrote the title: *I've heard the mermaids skyping*. It was true, but I still hadn't transcribed all the interviews. I'd listened to so many mermaid stories, I didn't know quite where to start or what to say.

~

I woke up in the morning, disconcerted, blinking in the dim light. My first mermaid wasn't Madison at all. It was Coral, a small stubby plastic doll, a toy for the bath who fit in the palm of my hand like an amulet. She had bright-red hair like me, but unlike me she had a turquoise mermaid tail up to her nipples, embossed with one chaste rose.

A sensory memory — of wrapping Coral in brown paper, tying it closed with string. Snip, snip — I heard the sound of the scissors cutting the string. Then, I slipped the package into my bag or my pocket and set off on my red Raleigh cruiser along our cul-de-sac, past Mr Potts' house with its shaven lawn and closely guarded terracotta pots. Old age is pottering around in the garden, but childhood is pottering, too.

I biked down the walkway at the end of the street, touching my finger to the corrugated iron fence and pulling out a ripple of sound, then popped out on the road to school.

I took the hill in my stride, stood up on the pedals. Past the summit, the cruiser picked up pace. I was just a girl on her cruiser, cruising. Riding is like flying; the bike soared, effortless.

Coral was a cool doll that I didn't play with much any more. Her foam lilypad had been picked to pieces, her pink shell comb was long gone. But the mermaid was still cool enough to give away in my school's Lucky Dip. I wouldn't want whoever pulled my gift out to unwrap something STINK and find out it was from me, that freckled redhead with buck teeth, who lived in a house with her mum and Bruce the truck driver and his son and her half-brother.

That was the house where I read *Charlotte's Web* for the first time, then climbed out of my bunk bed, and stood in the lounge bawling. 'Charlotte died!' 'Who's Charlotte?' Mum said, worried, before realising.

Bath times with bubbles, my fingers turning white and gelatinous and spongy from dipping my mermaid in and out of her lilypad. 'Don't you hurt my mother!' I yelled one night from the bunk bed as a fight in the kitchen brewed. Another tragedy — my Happy Birthday Barbie in her frilly pastel dress had her head broken off. Bruce glued it back on, but her neck was stubby and she looked ugly and weird.

I arrived at school and dropped Coral into the Lucky Dip barrel. When I cycled back uphill on my cruiser, my feet and legs had to push hard on the pedals. I had to make an effort now.

I knew that I had put my mermaid in the Lucky Dip not because I didn't love her, but because I did. And now I'd never get her back.

~

Mum rang me at the Surrey. 'How are you, darling?'

'I can't concentrate,' I said.

The afternoon was sweltering, and another sleepless night fretting in the wing of the Surrey lay ahead of me.

'I'm not sleeping well,' I said. 'I'm afraid on my own.'

'Would you like me to come and stay with you tonight after I finish work?' Mum offered.

'Yes,' I whimpered. I did want my mum with me. I was forty-three and like Fearne I still preferred not to sleep alone. My chances in life and art were running out.

Mum arrived. Her small turquoise car crackled on the gravel driveway of the Surrey, and I smuggled her into the apartment as though it was illegal to have your mum stay overnight.

She was smiling, her face and arms open to receive me and my discontents. Her face so innocent, so lovely to see. She had her silly handbag, rooting around in it for her glasses (purple frames), her pottles of pills. 'Nana's pills,' Fearne always said, when she stayed with us.

'I should have brought ingredients to make you some of my famous chocolate pudding,' Mum glanced around the kitchen. She used to make the self-saucing one from the old Edmonds cookbook that looked volcanic, blistered and cracked like a mud pool but tasted great, especially cold for breakfast with runny cream.

'Never mind,' I said. That was another one of our jokes. A saying handed down from my nana. *Oh well, never mind.* Except we did mind, of course.

That night, Mum and I sat in the double bed, together. She wore the long silky floral nightie I bought for the hospital when I had Fearne. Somehow I found that nightie too depressing — it made me feel like a mother — so I'd passed it on to my mother.

I noticed the itchy scratches and patches on her skin. But we laughed and joked together.

'I could do your whiskers if you like,' I said, feeling generous.

'Thanks,' she said. 'But I've already had them done.'

I held the laptop, warming my thighs, and read her bits from my draft.

'It's good, darling,' Mum smiled at me. Her eyes brimmed with love.

'How's Fearnebot?' she asked.

In bed, we poured over photos of her like groupies. Mum and I, her biggest fans.

'Oh, she just suits every colour, doesn't she?' Mum cooed.

'I didn't talk in my sleep, did I?' Mum asked in the morning.

'No,' I said.

'Goodie. Shall I come back tonight after work?' she asked.

~

Nichelle, a nonbinary merperson, visited next. Nichelle's mother made them a mermaid tail when they were just three, then by the time Nichelle was thirteen they were making their own tails. Nichelle opened a laptop to show me.

'Here we go. There's little thirteen-year-old me,' they said. 'Look at my braces.'

Nichelle was now a trained diver and worked in film. They still designed their own tails — one was based on the hiwihiwi or kelpfish, the other on the leatherjacket fish. Both species swam in the sea at Goat Island. Nichelle was also a photographer.

'One of the things I believe firmly is that you can take a photo of anyone and make them look amazing. And I want to show you how I see you as an incredible human being. That's my goal every time I'm behind the lens.'

Nichelle had brought their camera and we trawled around Surrey Crescent taking shot after shot. I felt surprisingly comfortable, in my element, on land. I posed with the hotel cat, a ratty looking specimen, spread out on the Axminster carpet. I didn't pose in the pool — I wasn't game enough.

But I posed in the bath in my apartment above Surrey, pretending to be Madison, brushing my hair and smiling, looking not bloody bad for forty-three.

~

On the last day, Mermaid Courtney arrived for a swim at 11am. She opened her boot, and took out her own Finfolk tail. She'd applied gold accents to the purple fabric. She also had her own silicone tail at home. 'You can't not have a sense of humour wearing a giant rubber fishtail,' she said, showing me her scale template. She'd been working on her tail privately, at home in her parents' kitchen, but other online mermaids had accused her of scale-design theft. We shook our heads. The whole mermaiding scene could get crazy and competitive.

I had seen this side, but chosen not to focus on it. I didn't want to undermine my subjects. It was too easy to portray mermaids in pretty tails as vapid and vain and cruel.

Courtney was a conservation biologist and worked for a local council. She called herself the Mahurangi Mermaid, after the harbour north of Auckland where she was from. 'I think the Māori worldview works really well from a mermaid's perspective. The inclusiveness, that holistic worldview.'

We talked about the relatively small New Zealand mermaid community — Courtney knew of only a handful of mermaids spread out across the country.

She had also just signed up for Mercon, the upcoming Sydney Mermaid Convention. 'It's great you are going too,' I said.

Neither of us looked like Daryl Hannah, but we donned our tails and swam in the shallow pool at the Surrey anyway. Courtney, decades younger than me, said cautiously, 'I guess I don't say I'm a mermaid, because I don't always look like one.'

In the pool, though, she *was* a mermaid — graceful and fluid, a proficient agile swimmer, turning loops.

12.

Her Dream Realised

Mermaid Karin was a Danish actress with a background in children's theatre, and a self-confessed fish nerd. She had started as a keeper at The Blue Planet in Copenhagen, using her aquarist knowledge to grow underwater plants. Then she turned her skills to running children's theatre shows, telling stories about Hick, their resident shark. But when she wanted to introduce a mermaid show inside the aquarium, which had one huge tank — 4.5 million litres of water — she encountered resistance. 'Do you want people to believe in fairy tales?' the marine biologists asked. 'We're a serious institution. People might think mermaids are real!'

Karin pitched her idea to the board, who were unconvinced. So she offered to do a performance in the tank for the staff Christmas party. The staff gathered back of house and sat down to watch. In a silver tail, Karin dove down inside the tank with the sharks and the rays — with Madonna.

Madonna was a two-and-a-half-metre manta ray, huge and white — so white, 'you can't see if she's on top of you'. Karin had to feel her way around the edge, then push off. 'Fish can be rough like sandpaper, but not the manta rays, they are smooth.'

'I'm not thinking much when I am down there,' Karin said. 'I think: *Just be.* I want to be elegant and playful, I don't want to push myself. It's a meditation moment.'

After her performance, Karin walked into the room and the staff gave her a standing ovation. The divers wanted to know how she could do the performance without a mask, without nose plugs. The aquarium director told her there would be a mermaid performance at The Blue Planet no matter what. One female biologist stalked out of the room, threatening to quit if 'you put a mermaid in my aquarium!'

Karin was now coaching two freedivers to perform as mermaids. 'The challenge is they have to let go,' she said.

It was my challenge too. But I couldn't let it go.

~

A week after skyping Karin, I was in Sydney for Mercon. This was my last designated trip, my final opportunity to understand what the mermaid means.

'What is that?' a man asked as I stood at the lights. 'A kite?'

I shook my head. 'No.'

'At first, I thought it was a pair of wings.' The man carried a bucket and held a bundle of torn down posters in his arms, like an urban nest.

'It's a mermaid tail,' I replied. 'For swimming in.'

He grunted, unimpressed. 'That's sick.' He carried his nest of advertising further up the street.

I crossed the park in central Sydney that Rich and I once crossed when Fearne was still an embryo cocooned in my amniotic waters. I was dressed in a long skirt, my Pod Squad T-shirt and my red Birkenstocks. I had my togs on underneath my outfit. I swapped Madison from shoulder to shoulder every now and then to ease the strain. My wrist ached, the fingers frozen into place from holding the tail, with the monofin already inside the fluke, weighing it down like an anchor.

I passed a statue of a wild boar outside a museum, rubbed his snout for luck. Then the New South Wales State Library, where I had already spent a day researching Annette Kellerman until I could write no more notes. I had held Kellerman's handwritten autobiography in my hands, seen a photo of her aged eighty, her leg raised like a ballerina. Once so famous, she'd lived out her last days in obscurity on the Gold Coast.

I also visited the Sydney Museum Powerhouse Collection and met a curator back of house. I stood in the collection wearing plastic gloves and fingering a yellow fabric tail embroidered with diamantes, the one and only mermaid tail in the Kellerman collection. I had touched the wig of real human hair Kellerman had worn; I browsed all the items in the collection that had once belonged to Annette. But it was a brass plaque that meant the most to me. 'In memory of Annette Kellerman whose ashes were cast on the Great Barrier Reef near Linderman Island 13th November, 1975. Her dream realised.'

~

I made it to the ticket booth at the ferry. The lady who took my ticket said, 'Is that a costume?'

I arranged Madison like an ikebana, twisting the tail round a pole and hanging her on the edge of the jetty against the glass wall. I took a photograph of her with the Sydney Harbour Bridge in the background. *Hello Sydney.*

In Manly, I waited for my lift, checking the Mercon Facebook page for weather updates. The day looked a little dismal and I had the aimless feel of a prostitute caught soliciting in broad daylight. I felt over-exposed. A bit grim. Rain was forecast.

Then someone tapped my shoulder. 'You must be here for Mercon.' I turned round. A lovely young woman with black hair and a bridge of freckles across her nose had seen me loitering with my tail. Michelle had her own fabric Finfolk tail in her backpack.

We waited together to hitch a lift over to Collins Bay, chatting about her mermaid adventures. She worked with Mermaid Tempest, who ran her own company and was the organiser of this year's Australian Mercon.

Mermaid Courtney arrived to fetch us — she had full mermaid glam going on, her face decorated with sequins in a scale formation. Her friend — the driver — was not a mermaid and had come prepared with a book to wait out the day. We shoved into the car and zipped off towards Collins Bay.

In the car park there, two other mermaids were unpacking their tails from the boot of a four-wheel-drive. Bree was a squire and horse-rider who worked in a castle; she seemed to be into the jousting scene. Her friend Lou worked in palliative care, had red hair and a green Ariel tail.

We were all normal women, un-Photoshopped, our best and worst angles on display in broad daylight. The view of Collins Bay was beautiful.

In *Ways of Seeing*, the art critic John Berger wrote, 'Women watch themselves being looked at. This determines not only most relations between men and women but also the relation of women to themselves. The surveyor of woman in herself is male: the surveyed female. Thus, she turns herself into an object — and most particularly an object of vision: a sight.'

I thought John Berger was basically right. But I wasn't sure if the surveyor within myself was male.

Our monofins and tails overflowing from our shoulders and bags, we trekked together down the dirt path that led to the bay. It was steep. Our tails gave us something to talk about — it was like My Little Ponies all over again.

A fit, rangy older lady in leggings who'd been walking her dog stopped to ask what was going on. 'There's a mermaid meet up on the beach.' 'How wonderful!' She looked full of endorphins.

Builders worked on an expensive mansion above us. 'I'm a merman,' one shouted. 'Mer-MAN.'

We made it on to the beach and crossed the sand. Mermaid tails lined up instead of towels. The tails were multi-coloured, each represented someone's inner mermaid, the secret way they saw themselves. I lay Madison down on the beach.

Hannah Moy aka Mermaid Tempest bounded over and gave me a big hug. She had strawberry ringlets and eyes of the greenest green and looked no more than twenty. She'd started performing as a professional — her mermaid name Tempest was inspired by Shakespeare's play — at fourteen, , and now ran a team, including three mermen.

She turned to the gathering. 'This is Megan and she's a writer and has probably met more mermaids than any of us.'

Andrew wore a pair of glossy blue tights with a scale pattern and a T-shirt that read: 'I am — literally — a merman'. He seemed relaxed. I told him about the builders calling out MER-MAN.

Andrew told me he had never personally experienced much prejudice. For him, mer-swimming was a recreational outlet. He'd been looking for a different water sport to get into and discovered mermaiding.

On a small table at the back of the beach three drones sat on a small table. The number-one thing drones find out in the ocean: other drones.

Vanessa was another Kiwi now living in Oz. 'I'm an expert at blowing bubbles,' she said.

I looked in her blue eyes. 'Are you serious?'

'Yes. I'm doing a workshop on it tomorrow.'

Mermaid Tempest rounded us up for a quick group talk on safety.

We were to swim with a buddy. If an accident happened, we were to hold up an arm, stay calm and call for help. With a buddy beside you it would all be okay.

A mermaid has to be sighted to exist. We moved into formation, tails held over our right shoulders, side by side. A line of would-be selkies, suburban sirens. Dressed up to make-believe. We placed our left hand on the shoulder of our nearest sea sister and stared out to the sea. Our mother, welcoming us home. The sea was contested, crossed and colonised, divided and ruled, fished, outfished and Instagrammed. And the horizon, the place where sea meets sky, was the site of the story.

For another photo, we all raised one arm to the sky in salute. Perhaps we were there at Mercon to surprise ourselves. To feel, like Mermaid Abby did, something more than the possible or plausible or even probable. To be a mermaid is to embrace the necessity of everything unknown and unnecessary. Or just to be a bit coy.

After the photoshoot I began my transformation on the sand. Photography was banned from this part of the event — the professionals had their fans to consider.

Andrew watched my graceless metamorphosis and said, 'I've never seen someone struggle to get into a fabric tail before.'

We lined up at the water's edge. The little teasing hem of the sea was frightfully cold. But the drone was on its way and it was time to shine.

We waved as it flew overhead. I lay in the shallows, next to a little blue-haired mermaid with a matching Fin Fun tail and a starfish ornament in her dark hair. Her name was Cheeky.

'Daryl Hannah is a skank,' Cheeky said. 'She came on land to find a boy she'd kissed.'

I laughed. 'You're the first person who has said that.'

'I'm interested in hot men and cold water,' Cheeky said.

'Me too,' I replied. I instantly fucking loved her. Cheekiness is one of my favourite vices. I found out later Cheeky had previously worked in the sex industry, which made sense.

It was her first swim in the sea in a mermaid tail, too. The Fin Fun brand was all she could afford. It's an entry-level tail.

After the photos, a group of mermaids passed the pain barrier and headed further out into Collins Bay. They frolicked, taking turns on the world's smallest water scooter. Mermaid Tempest's partner, Joel, controlled the drone that swooped above the pod. Eventually the sirens returned to shore, and a long photoshoot commenced beneath the terracotta cliffs.

Annette

~

The last event of the day took place in a small wooden hall back near the ferry terminal. The tables around the edges of the hall were arranged with various merchandise, from Ariel trinkets and bracelets to the first silicone skins of the Selkie Sisters, a new Australian tail supplier. The drone table was empty apart from the drones and a guy who sat behind it, looking at his phone.

The retailers cleared out and the workshops began. A woman around my age sat next to me and we chatted about our projects. 'I'm a life coach,' she said. Then she stood up to run the first workshop, 'Creating Your Preferred Reality.'

The modest little hall didn't feel like much of a place to create any kind of reality, let alone your preferred one. After introducing herself to the assembled mermaids, the life coach said, 'When I grew up there were three career choices for women.' She wrote them on the whiteboard: Secretary. Nurse. Teacher.

The life coach didn't seem any older than me. My mother trained as a teacher, then became a nurse aide in an old people's home. When I was in high school, I wanted to be a lawyer for a while, then an artist. My parents were liberal, they never stopped me, never overwhelmed me with their own visions for my future. Mum always believed in me; Dad was more pragmatic. When I got into art school, he said, 'It's a risk.'

I didn't understand then what he was trying to say. We stood that day in the hallway of his dark house by the sea. 'Life is a wave, and you want to be out there surfing, on the crest of it.' I frowned. I didn't want to be surfing! I didn't understand his analogy — I didn't know what the word 'career' even meant. I was still playing make-believe. I thought a job added plumage, like Finfolk's branded mermaid tails. Later, I learned how bound up we are in the economy; how, for some, choices were defined more by wallets than dreams. My own dream was still fatter than a mermaid's purse. I was banking on the idea that I could create my preferred reality as a writer.

I'd never felt that limited by my gender, but in some ways I had been by my dreams. What is the true cost of creating your best self and your ideal job?

The life coach told us she had become an award-winning film producer. 'I literally lived my dream,' she said, in an echo of the most famous mermaid on the planet.

The room of mermaids burst into spontaneous applause.

I wondered about the continent of sadness that lurked behind the upbeat line. The role of the life coach has arisen only recently. It's an aspirational job in the West, because so often we are not living our dreams. The professional mermaid is an aspirational job, too. But every self-help book contains its opposite, its shadowy underside — helplessness, brow-beaten dreams, hurts and resentments and what-ifs and if-onlys.

'Life is created twice,' the life coach told us. 'First in the mind and then in actions.' She told us we had to send our mind a message — we had to put the exact address into our GPS.

We sat down, ready to nut out the plan.

The first line read: 'Describe yourself audaciously.' We were given a minute to write something down.

The life coach — wisely — picked me to read out my response first.

'Mer expert of the universe, swimming through your mind!' I said.

The mermaids laughed. The ice was broken. We worked our way through the rest of the questions.

What do you want? 'To be an internationally recognised writer,' I wrote.

Why do you want it? 'To earn financial and intellectual freedom. To make the world more delightful!'

How does it benefit other people? 'It will edutain,' I replied. 'Surprise and delight people, and deepen our reality.' I felt less sure of things with every answer.

When do you want it? 'By 11 December, my birthday.' Very clear for the GPS.

What will you give? 'I've given a lot of cash and time already,' I replied, starting to feel peeved. How much more did I have to give?

How will you celebrate? 'Buy a house,' I wrote, my deepest shame, that I am middle aged and have no home.

I remembered a story Mermaid Tempest had told me. At one child's birthday party, the little girl went back into her house and came out with a present for Tempest. The child opened her palm; in it was a crushed goldfish.

The life coach asked a young mermaid to read out her sheet. 'What do you want?' she asked.

'To go to Disneyland in Florida,' she replied.

Time to go. Vanessa — the bubble blower — hugged me. Tonight, the mermaids were going to a ball. Tomorrow there were games on the beach including the Merwrangler race. Mermaiding is about community. Floating online, crossing borders, hating fiercely but loving fiercely, too.

On my way back through town, a man in a posh black suit waiting at the lights looked twice at me. 'Is that a fish?'

'Yes, it is.' I smiled. Office workers flitting about, the city in wind-down. 'It's a mermaid tail.'

'Are you going to wear it?' he asked.

'I've worn it already. I've been at a mermaid convention.'

'Can I ask a stupid question?' he said. 'What do you do at a mermaid convention?'

'A mermaid convention is a meet-up of recreational and professional mermaids,' I replied. 'What do you do?'

'I'm a barrister,' he said.

'I thought so,' I replied.

'Well, we're by the courts.'

The lights changed, and he left. So did I.

13.

Christ of the Abyss

I sat at my desk and waited for the call. Rich and Fearne had gone out to a local street festival and I was alone, my stomach turning. Something was wrong. But what?

I dealt three mermaid cards from the pack. 'Music for Manifesting'. The golden-haired mermaid on the card held a giant golden harp. I felt irritated. No. Waterhouse's Mermaid looked down at me, her comb rushed through her hair, then snagged on a knot.

I sighed. She sighed. We had waited a long time — I had been waiting to hear back from the publisher for three months. 'It can't be good,' she said.

'Shut up,' I replied.

My iPhone rang and I seized on it, lying on the rocks of that foreshore, next to the pāua shell. I shivered, because I had no top on and my tail was blue and silver. I had it curled around me for protection.

The sea blew in froth, cold and salt-ridden. Just me, alone on the rocks.

'It doesn't work,' the publisher said. Her voice was the brisk voice of reason.

'There's no book here,' she said. 'We can't publish this.'

I felt my tail tense and contract. I rushed my hand over it, trying to stay warm. My hair straggled around my torso, shivering, goosebumps puckering my skin. My whole body cold and wet. My nipples still bore the scars from our Tramadol days and nights. I had nothing to protect me from the brutal logic of that phone call.

Sentences, a handful of sentences. The pebbles on the shore, water eddying around them, jostling them slightly as it moved in and out. I clung to that phone, clamped it to my ear, trying to understand what I was hearing: the sea's long breath withdrawing, with no mermaids in it.

My tail shrank. The sea crept out. I sat at my desk in our rented flat, in a city of houses I could not afford, a pack of Doreen Virtue's Mermaid and Dolphin cards on my desk. I struggled to keep my publisher on the line, she had to go to her own family, her own daughters, the remnants of her weekend. 'Are you going to be okay?' she said.

'Well, I'm not going to kill myself,' I replied.

My tail had been lopped off at the waist. My tongue hadn't been cut out, but my voice was hoarse.

Next I had to phone Rich and let him know. That was the worst thing.

'What?' He was shocked. His voice hollowed out. 'I'm gutted,' he said. 'Gutted.'

Then my tail went silent. I put the mermaids back on the hook.

~

Mum arrived at our door with a deep gash in her forehead, tugging her floral suitcase into the lounge. The blood oozing from the wound. Night dark and aghast outside, the steps to our flat in deepest shadow.

'Mum! What happened?' I said.

'Nana,' Fearne cried, more with excitement than fear.

'I fell over on the steps,' she said. 'I couldn't see. Silly Nana.'

'You should have called us. We could have come down to get you,' I scolded. Out of shock, that meanness deep inside me, always triggered by her vulnerability.

'Are you okay?' I asked. Trying again. 'Yes, I'm okay.' Rich making her a cup of tea. 'Ahhh. That's a lovely cup of tea.'

That lounge, the little stage for our family.

She plonked down on the couch — and smiled, an expression of relief, wiped the sweat on her brow. Her glasses were broken. She held out the frames, 'Blast!' she said. 'I will have to take them in to an optometrist.' But in her eyes was gratitude, just to be here, with us, with Fearne and me.

I brought her a cloth and she wiped her face.

'Nana, read me a story?' Fearne said.

'I'll do it,' I said. 'Nana is hurt.'

'No, it's okay, darling. I want to.' Mum rallied her energy and put Fearne to bed and read her a story.

I looked at Mum in the grainy atmosphere of mid-morning, both of us seated side by side on the Egyptian sofa. 'What's wrong?' I asked.

'Nothing,' she turned to me, her face pale and still. 'I guess I'm just a bit tired,' she said. A new mood had overtaken her, she was quieter, more interior, less interested in playing with Fearne.

'You're not yourself,' I said.

'Aren't I?'

She was dressed in the long silvery-blue nightgown.

In our lounge, above my computer, Waterhouse's *A Mermaid* was still my example of what a mermaid should be. The mermaid scowled at me. 'You're not paying enough attention to your mother.'

'Children don't mind what you look like. They don't care that you're old,' Mum mused.

I didn't reply but I clocked the statement. It lodged inside my gut.

Mum scratched at her shoulders, covered in faded freckles and a few age spots. Things she couldn't stop picking at. I glanced at the thick white whiskers above her upper lip.

Mum looked at me, and said, 'Do you have to tweeze every day now?'

The silver tweezers were attached to my fingers — I could pince my own chin hairs without a mirror, just by feel. I had got into the habit of constantly plucking as I sat on the couch, as though my chin whiskers were something I could get to the bottom of.

Her look was one of concern, perhaps even guilt.

'You must have got them from me.'

'Oh well, never mind,' I replied.

Mum managed a smile. 'Have a banana?' she joked.

'When are your next blood tests?'

'In a couple of weeks. Once a month,' she said.

'And the count was up in your last tests, is that right?'

I had never understood the process, just knew that her cancer had been in remission for years, but they still monitored her bloods.

'Yes,' Mum said. 'The doctor says I will have to start being treated again at some stage but we don't know when. It's been seventeen years. I've been so lucky. Most people don't usually live this long with multiple myeloma.'

~

'I'm not coping, I'm not coping,' said her voice down the phone, crying. Real. So real and I had to save her. I had to keep us both afloat. 'Mummy has to go and help Nana.' 'No!' Fearne said. Rich helped me pack a quick bag for the flight. I was dressed in jeans and a sweatshirt, ready to roll up my sleeves and do some work.

'I want to come,' Fearne grumped.

'Not this time, darling. Next time. Nana is sick and she needs me.'

This time when the cavalry arrived, it was me. But I can't drive, so Mum picked me up from the airport, then drove us both to her chemotherapy at the hospital. The cavalry isn't always what it's cracked up to be.

'I'm worried Fearne will be scared of me with no hair,' Mum said.

'She'll be fine, Mum,' I said. 'Fearne loves you.'

A weak smile. Mum showed me the little fuchsia-pink hat she had bought to cover her baldness.

'It's nice,' I said.

'I've just got no energy. It's so much worse than last time,' Mum said.

'But the prognosis is good,' I tried to keep her focused on the future. We still had the future. 'Have you had a banana?'

We navigated the long hallways of the outpatient ward. Just a woman in a pair of Rolla bell-bottom jeans and her mother in a little pink hat. I sat down in the waiting room, next to a coffee machine that also did hot chocolates. It's the little things. Mum weighed herself on a big white pair of scales. 'I've lost a bit of weight,' she said, coming back holding her purple paisley bag. I thought of the poem 'Warning' again, except Mum's hat was pink instead of red, and it did suit her. She had chosen it well. Mum looked washed out, steeling herself to go through with it. 'I don't think I can do this again,' she said.

'You can do it,' I replied.

Mum nodded. She had to take more than ten fat pills each day now. The pills as big as pearls, hard to swallow without gagging, without retching. She no longer wanted to eat. After chemo, she couldn't keep anything down.

'Thanks for being here,' Mum said. Her hazel eyes on mine.

I put my hand over hers. 'We'll get through this,' I said, because she needed me to be strong and she named me Megan because of that. I am strong.

One doctor had suggested she might still live another eight years. In another eight years Fearne would be twelve years old. Eight years yet to be Fearne's biggest fans.

'It will all be worth it,' I said. Reassurance isn't one of my top skills.

I flicked through women's magazines, but I couldn't pay one iota of attention. The TV on the wall mindlessly chattered. The waiting room was a place of suspense. In every person seated around us, I sensed the same story. Is this it? Will I get better or worse? Is this the beginning or the end? I watched a family — a dad, a young mum in a turban and a little girl. My heart ached, in a low-grade way. The watercooler took a gulp, refilled. How much time left?

'Lee Dunn?' A nurse called.

The treatment was low-key for an observer like me. Mum sat on a large La-Z-Boy-like contraption. The nurse wore a mauve plastic gown. The chemicals they pumped into Mum's veins through the needle came in a toxic plastic container. Mum made chitchat with the nurses, keeping herself jolly, as though optimistic banter could hold her aloft. Maybe. But I've never been one for positive self-talk. For affirmations. I looked off to the side, as though she was having blood taken, rather than chemicals poured into her body. As though treatment should be discreet.

After she had her quota, we walked stoically through the big industrial carpark. We waited at the machine, as she queued to pay and for the machine to print out the ticket.

'Maybe I shouldn't go through with the treatment and the stem cell operation this time,' Mum said. Her lower lip wobbled. She wasn't looking at me. Her whole demeanour was turned away from me to some interior place only she could see.

'What do you mean?' I said. 'Why?

She confessed, her face pale and bewildered. One of my uncles had suggested it might not be worth it. He was down in the South Island, dying slowly of a degenerative disease. My aunt had suggested the treatment might be worse than the cancer itself, that it was better to let nature take its course. 'It's God's will.'

'I felt so terrible after the first round of chemo,' Mum said. 'I don't know if it is worth it. I might not live much longer anyway.'

'Easy for them to say,' I barked. 'What about me and Fearne? You could be there for her to grow up. Don't you want to see that?'

'Yes,' Mum said tentatively. 'I just feel so awful. I have no energy.' Her expression teetered beneath the pink hat with its silly little rim. I couldn't believe the irresponsibility of my aunt and uncle. Lucky for them with their religion and their belief in a Catholic god and an afterlife. I had no faith in anything beyond the here and now. Once mermaids and mermen were gods, symbols of a pagan afterlife.

But I also remembered my Skype with Ali Luminescent — a sparkle-haired, stilt-walking faerie-mermaid-unicorn. I interviewed her ages ago, as she sat on her tiny outdoor balcony in New York. She worked two days a week as a speech language pathologist. 'I'm a swallow specialist,' Ali had told me. She took X-rays of patients swallowing, helped rehabilitate the muscles in their mouths and throats. On their deathbeds, many of her cancer patients confessed that if they had known what the treatment was going to be like they would have just lived with the tumour.

I couldn't agree, couldn't let Mum say that.

'But we can't just give up,' I said. 'You only get one life.'

'Yes, all right,' Mum said. We crossed the carpark past some god-awful brick chimney to nowhere, and climbed into her little turquoise car. She paused a moment, her key in the ignition. 'Are you okay?' I asked. 'Yes.' Then we got going.

But she wasn't okay. And I wasn't okay either. We arrived back at her flat, and the sadness settled around me. Mum lay on her bed. 'Just resting,' she said.

~

In the living room, while Mum slept, I found her copy of *Playing Big* again. I had returned it long ago, but now I needed Tara again. I leafed through and found a chapter, 'Hiding', that I hadn't paid attention to before. 'One of the ways women often hide is behind other people's stories,' Tara wrote. 'Women hide by collecting and collating other people's opinions and omitting their own personal story and opinions.' It was another stingray barb to the heart.

Mum came in, her face was groggy with sleep.

'Mum, do you think I have been hiding behind the voices of the mermaids?' I asked.

'No, I don't think so darling.'

She apologised for not having done any transcriptions lately.

'Don't worry about it,' I said. 'You've just had chemo. You can get back on the transcribes after dinner.'

~

I was stewing on the mermaids. Was I hiding? Was there something in this process I had missed? I also made a couple of stews with Mum. We used pre-made Maggi sauce packs, because neither of us could be bothered to make a stew from scratch. I wouldn't even know where to start. Afterwards, we sealed the stews in plastic containers. I got out the Sharpie, wrote the days of the week on the containers, pressed each seal down, then pushed them one by one into her freezer. When I left for Wellington, Mum could just pull out a meal and heat it up in the microwave. I called her two best friends, Kathy and Maata. They agreed to help out.

Preparation is everything. As a former project manager, I knew this well. Kathy and Maata sat with me around the table in Mum's dank damp flat. I hadn't printed out an agenda, but I told them what to do. I outlined the necessary action points. 'Mum needs more help,' I explained. Kathy had an extra room and we agreed Mum would move into it soon. Mum couldn't stay living with my half-brother, who needed so much help himself. She needed someone to help *her*.

'Mum needs people checking in on her daily,' I said. Sage nodding all around. Everyone was on board. It was complicated that Mum was sick in a city I didn't live in. It was complicated that I lived in a little rented flat with no spare bedroom for her. It was complicated that Mum had left Mike as a little kid, and that he had so many problems and had been living with her off and on for the past decade. I felt terrible, but supressed it, like pressing down the plastic lid on a stew. Mum showed her friends out as I waited inside.

When she returned, Mum said proudly, 'Maata says you are a powerful leader.'

I stood up tall, because I am tall. Mum is short, but I take after Dad. When I changed out of my jeans, I looked glamorous in my woollen charcoal pencil dress and shoes. I meant business. I was there to kick cancer's butt and one of the things I had going for me was that I didn't have it. I was back in my role from childhood: *Don't you hurt my mother!*

I remembered the Powerful Leaders Creed. Mum wrote it ages ago with a friend at work — their private joke about their toxic workplace. *Powerful leaders support other powerful leaders!* Mum had the list laminated.

The next day Mum's real boss and someone from HR came round to the flat and I sat at the table again in the quiet turmoil of the afternoon and told them she wouldn't be coming back to work. I spoke to her boss as one powerful leader to another. I was forceful and assertive, there to stop anyone taking advantage. I was also there to see if I could shake something extra out of her employment contract for long service.

Mum had some idea that she might get a payout on the grounds of ill health. But as we sat at the table it became apparent that Mum was only owed four weeks' leave and her leftover holiday pay. Of course she had no income protection insurance — she'd have to survive on the sickness benefit and her paltry retirement fund. Cups of tea were finished. Biscuits had. Her boss and the woman from HR left.

The two of us together again.

Mum and I went out in her car to The Warehouse and bought her a motivational diary and a wall planner in mauve colours. She chose an adult colouring-in book too, and back home she half-heartedly coloured in an outline of a glamorous flapper with a black bob wearing a jaunty beret.

A cancer counsellor visited next and we sat on the grey sofa drinking more cups of tea. 'How do you feel?' the counsellor asked. 'Better because Megan is here,' Mum said. But the chemotherapy hadn't completely kicked in yet. Once it did, Mum explained, she would be unable to sleep or eat or do anything but lie on her bed. 'Get out for a walk,' the counsellor advised. 'Just one walk, once a day.'

Get out for a walk. Get an adult colouring-in book. Colour it all in. Keep positive. Say an affirmation. Say ten affirmations. Swallow them like pills. Ask a friend to send a text. Join a cancer group. Meet others. Hang in there. Microwave a stew.

~

Every day for the rest of my visit, we went out for a walk. We'd wander along the side of the road together for a few minutes. The days were bright, so much brighter than the flat. Mum strode along determinedly, in her faded jeans, but I could see how much will she was putting into every step. To keep going. To not let go. In her little pink hat.

Most of the time, she lay on the single bed in her room next to the soft cushions and floral furnishings, everything feminine in the way of a cheap interior design store.

She got up and dashed to the bathroom. 'Sorry, darling,' she said. Holding her hands over her behind, as though she could keep a secret.

'Don't worry, Mum.'

'I get terrible diarrhoea,' she confessed.

No need. A brown patch on her nightgown. 'Can I do anything?'

'No, darling.' A long sojourn in the bathroom, then the flush of the toilet.

She limped back to her bedroom, her hand over her chest. 'I need to lie down again. It's so much worse than last time.' A half belch. Her skin pale.

I found her knickers shucked off on the floor, a pool of brown drizzle. I put them in the wash basket.

'Oh blast,' she said, running out of her bedroom again.

Everything coming out of her, a rag doll spewing through the seams.

Mike got home from work and trudged inside, wearing his boots and overalls from landscaping. 'How is she? How was the hospital?'

'Mum needs us to help her,' the powerful leader explained, condescendingly. 'She can't just have hotdogs for dinner. She needs to eat something good for her.'

A powerful leader can be hypocritical, too, especially when under pressure. I can't stand cooking, and I like hot dogs. But I had to lead.

'Okay, sis,' my brother said. His eyes looked pink but not from crying. His body seemed twitchy, a manic energy.

'I need to go to the shop and get her some pads or something,' I said. 'Everything is going straight through her.'

'Do you want me to drive you?'

'No, I'll walk, it's just up the road. I'll go now — Mum needs it now.'

I blasted the news in his face, then left the house, striding towards the shops with my wallet in my hand. Did no one understand that this was fucking urgent?

~

I once asked a merman where the best place was that he had swum.

'The Christ of the Abyss,' he replied.

The statue is an eight-foot-high monument made from bronze and copper and scraps from ships sunk during World War II. The statue sits on a concrete base off the coast of Genoa in the Mediterranean Sea and commemorates the first Italian diver to use scuba gear, Dario Gonzatti, who died during a dive in 1947. On a calm day sailors can see the arms of Christ reaching out to them from below the sea, offering a benediction of peace.

Christ of the Abyss now has replicas in Grenada and in Key Largo, Florida, where a merman once swam around it on one breath hold. The original statue is one of the most-visited diving spots on earth.

I showed Dad a photograph of the Christ of the Abyss. His arms stretched deep underwater, the statue covered in corals and barnacles.

'This does something to me,' Dad said.

'Same,' I replied.

When he was young Dad used to skindive and had once nearly drowned. His life played before him in the water like a movie — it was peaceful, he told me. Dad had escaped that time from the embrace of the abyss. An underwater photographer once told me that, contrary to popular opinion, most people drown on the surface, in just a few centimetres of water. We don't sink, we float, but take on more and more salt water until we can't breathe.

When I was a little girl, I loved to swim, like I loved to ride my bike. I remember being in a public swimming pool — that echoing chamber, the chlorine lapping into the vents of the pool, the bottom white and deep, but not fathomless, falling without fear, submerging without death, swimming, then rising. I felt the coolness all around me. Is this how the myth of the mermaid began? This embryonic holding, this flow into pure being?

~

My mobile buzzed on my desk and my hands flew over my heart. 'What is it, Mum? Is everything all right?'

'Yes, I'm okay, darling.' A pale little voice. 'I've got a spot for the stem cell transplant, but it's in December. I have to be there for three weeks. I'll miss Christmas with Fearne!'

'That's not important, Mum.'

'I haven't missed a Christmas with her yet.'

'I know. Not much of a place to spend your birthday either,' I said.

'Or yours,' she replied.

'Oh well, never mind.'

'Never mind about the cancer,' Mum said. She managed a giggle, then in a warble of pure dismay: 'Flip! I haven't even got you a birthday card yet.'

'Mum, truly. It doesn't matter. I don't need a birthday card.' I paced around the flat while I spoke to her. Stared out at the harbour through Fearne's bedroom window. A miscellany of books along one wall. Bloody books. I paced back into the lounge, looked up at Waterhouse's mermaid still brushing her hair on the bloody wall.

'I did get Fearne a Christmas card to explain why I can't be with her this year. It's in the post,' Mum said. She sighed down the line, all the wind taken out of her sails.

'That's good, Mum,' I said. 'Fearne understands. She loves getting post from you.'

Half lies. Fearne only understood dolls and more dolls, Christmas presents and treats. Love and attention. Chocolate. Ice cream melting on a cone.

Out the window, the ferry in the harbour didn't seem to be moving. Our lives were drifting towards Christmas. Then what?

'I haven't got the baby doll for her yet,' she confessed.

'I sent you a picture of the one she wants. It's another Baby Alive doll. You should just be able to get it from The Warehouse.'

'Okay, darling. I'll pick it up before I come for the weekend. I just have no energy,' she said.

'Are you sure you'll be okay to visit?' I asked.

'Yes.'

The first stem cell operation, years ago, had worked well. Her prognosis was good.

~

No running up the stairs. Rich walked slowly behind her, carrying her floral suitcase.

'Nana!' Fearne ran to the door. Her face lit up.

'Hello, darling,' Mum bent down to give her a hug. Her face was wan, she looked far away beneath her little pink hat.

'You've lost a bit of weight,' I said.

'Yes,' she replied. A line of sweat on her brow. Her skin had a vague yellow tinge.

'I'll take your suitcase. Come and sit down, Mum.' My funny little mother needed some taking care of. I ushered her to the sofa. 'Would you like a cup of tea?'

'Yes, please.'

Rich made the ceremonial tea.

'Nana, can I see your pills?' Fearne got her little hands into the paisley bag, now falling apart.

'I've got an empty packet you can play with.' Mum handed her the silver packaging. Fearne took it, gleefully, seizing on it like treasure. 'I can make Play-Doh pills,' she said. 'Then I can take my pills like you, Nana. Just pretend though.'

Nana looked winded.

'Can we play dolls, Nana?'

'Remember I told you Nana is sick, Fearne. We need to just take it easy.'

Easy, easy, let's make it easy.

'Nana needs a rest first,' Mum explained to Fearne.

'I want to try on your hat,' Fearne said.

'Are you sure? Well, I suppose you can,' Mum said. A shrug in her fuchsia-pink cardigan.

'Nana, where's your hair?' Fearne said.

Mum had a bald head like a newborn. She looked like Mrs Potato Head.

'I've lost my hair from the chemotherapy,' she said. 'That's why I bought the hat. It will grow back though.'

Fearne tried on the hat and giggled. Mum giggled, too.

'Let me get a photo,' I took out my iPhone, as though I might later be required to sketch this scene on a vase for posterity, like the siren painter from Greek antiquity. On Instagram, I posted the photo of Nana smiling, her eyes gentle and brimming with love. I wrote 'Fuck cancer' in the caption, to let my few followers on social media know I wasn't sentimental about Nana and Fearne. Not one wee bit.

~

In the hospital bookshop, I found Mum a birthday card with a purple cartoon armadillo on it. The Armadillo of Resilience. The Armadillo of Courage. It looked cheerful and jaunty, like it didn't have cancer.

Mum was upstairs in her ward, recovering from her stem cell operation. It was her birthday, and I was not organised.

My hand had dithered over the many floral birthday cards; the polite, feminine flowers, *Happy Birthday Mother* in cursive scrawl, the letters embossed in gold. I couldn't abide those cards. They looked funereal . . . And Mum wasn't dying. I had left her upstairs in her pale-blue hospital gown, sitting vacantly on the chair beside her hospital bed. She had not been handling her treatment well, but her prognosis was good.

My birthday is in December, too, a week before hers. For my forty-fifth birthday she had given me a card that read on the cover: 'Make a wish'. A stock photo of a cupcake with candles in it. I opened the card and read: 'Not that one.'

It took me a while to get the joke. But then I understood. Not that one.

A hospital bookstore is not a glad place. I browsed the self-help books out of habit. I saw a cover that appealed: *The Truth Will Set You Free, But First It Will Piss You Off!* The font was turquoise, Mum's colour. The author, Gloria Steinem. I flicked it open. I had always thought 'a woman needs a man like a fish needs a bicycle' was a Gloria Steinem line, but it isn't. The quote actually belongs to Irina Dunn. No relation, ha. I stood in the bookstore for a long time, reading. I wanted to buy it, but I had no money — I was out of work — and put it back in the pile.

I took the elevator back up to Mum.

'There wasn't a great selection,' I explained, as I handed over the card. A purple helium balloon sat beside Mum. And a teddy bear. Gifts from someone else.

I had written inside the card: 'It will all be worth it this time next year.'

'Yes,' Mum smiled.

I sat on her hospital bed filling out a job application. The mermaid project had dried up; so had my contract as an archivist. And Fearne would soon start school. I had no excuse to be working part-time any more. I felt guilty and said, 'Do you want the bed back?' Mum said, 'No, it's fine, darling, I'm sick of being in bed. I'm happy here in the chair.' She turned to me, a smile. Her eyes soft.

Mum had zero immunity after the operation and couldn't risk seeing many people in case she got an infection — there was a two percent risk she would die. Two percent wasn't that high. But she couldn't be exposed to children and their litany of daycare infections. She had to stay in hospital for the rest of December, and wouldn't be allowed out of the ward until the new year.

'I'm so sad I won't be there for Christmas with Fearne,' she said.

'We understand. We'll miss you. But we just want you to get well.'

My own resilience was thin. My sense of humour nil by mouth. Apparently, armadillos are dedicated mothers. They also have a thick, plated skin. I guess that was my psychic attraction to the birthday card — I was trying to give Mum the thick skin she'd never had. In her original colour — purple.

'Will you be okay?' I said. The end of the day, night falling behind the venetian blinds. I had to fly back to Wellington. I stuffed my backpack with my job application and my laptop, held the strap over my shoulder, felt the weight of it.

Mum looked up at me from her hospital bed, her face still white, and drawn. 'Yes, I'll be okay.'

I lingered in the doorway. 'I don't want to leave you alone,' I said.

'Don't worry, darling. Trish will be here soon.'

My aunt was arriving from the South Island in the morning to take over.

'But it's your birthday,' I said.

'Oh well, never mind,' she said. Our joke.

~

She wasn't okay. On my return to Auckland, I called in the hospital priest, a tall Samoan man, to read her last rites. He must have met her weeks earlier, when she arrived in hospital for the operation that in the end she couldn't recover from. She became one of the two percent.

'Last time I saw this woman she was well,' he said, looking at me across her hospital bed. I nodded. 'Yes.' I knew exactly what he meant. On the bed in intensive care, Mum lay bald and white, beyond our reach or comprehension. He noticed the framed photo of Fearne on the table next to the bed. 'Her granddaughter?' he asked. 'Yes,' I said. 'Her only one.' 'Life passes to the next generation,' he said. What else was there to say?

In the intensive care ward, in the small room where she was going to die, Mum whispered to her brother Jim, 'Tell Megan the story.' Jim had just flown in from Australia, an uncle I hardly knew, a lean religious man. Jim and I kept vigil around her bed. The two family members tasked with sending her over to the other side where God or the abyss was waiting to claim her. Jim had his Bible and his beliefs. I had the framed photograph of Fearne.

Jim told me how my granddad used to work on the railways in Lawrence, the small town in the South Island where Mum grew up. He took the kids walking by the tracks on the weekends. There were five siblings; Mum was the youngest. The walks were long. 'How much further?' the kids asked. 'How much further?' My granddad would always reply, 'Just around the corner.' 'How much further?' 'Just around the corner', until it became family lore.

As we waited that night for her oxygen to be turned off, for her breaths to get shorter and then longer apart, Mum turned on her side, in the foetal position, white and interior, so pale, slowly going colder and whiter, as she did this last work, this last critical job, in the business of being alive, to let go.

Jim passed me his Bible and I read, thankful for words, for something I could cling to. He said, 'God, we're letting her go' and he meant it. 'She's precious to us,' he said. And I finally burst into tears. 'Yes, she is precious to us, she is precious,' I said. That bit I truly meant. 'I'm beaming her up,' I said. It was as biblical as I could manage. I kissed her white cold hand, held it to my cheek. Mum.

I didn't know what god she was going to or if that god was a he, but I knew I was letting go of the life that had sustained me. I felt myself clinging to the edge of her hospital bed, or to her hand, holding it, the shape of her fingers, her nails, everything particular about her. She was going, the deepest part of me going with her, my childhood, my child self, my mother, my matriarch, just around the corner.

In the hospital bathroom I splashed my face with water and looked into the mirror and saw someone else staring back.

14.

Motherless Mermaids

They were the saddest words I had ever had to write: *My wonderful mother has died.* On Facebook I posted a photograph of Mum and Fearne — the one of Fearne smiling up at her. Mum said, 'That's the moment I knew she loved me.' In the photo, Mum was wearing her old mesh top, purple and maroon, swirling colours. A classic Nana op-shop find. I posted the news of her death to her Facebook page to pick up any friends I had not found in her phone. But it was the replies from my own Facebook friends that touched and surprised me. The comments stacked up. I read every one. I didn't know how much I needed to be seen in my grief.

Then into my inbox, a direct message from inside The Wreck. 'I lost my mother exactly a week ago today,' MeduSirena wrote. 'Now we are both motherless mermaids. I like to think the torch has been passed to us and they are now seeing the world through our eyes and experiences.'

Amen.

~

I descended to the wreck. On New Year's Day I called a funeral parlour. The undertaker arrived, a young brunette dressed in black. She sat outside with me at a garden table at my cousin's house. The day was foggy, suitably vague, like me. We sketched out the details of what needed to happen next. Death has a business end and I was the powerful leader at the table. My voice was faint, washed out from lack of sleep. I was the person in charge of making sure Mum's death was logged and chartered, that she was cremated in a suitable timeframe to let family say goodbye and return to their respective homes.

Jim needed to get back to Australia. My aunt Trish from down south took up the task of finding a Catholic church for the service. Organising a funeral in early January turned out to be difficult. Everything was closed for the holidays. Or booked. Hymns needed to be chosen. I needed to order a casket, an urn, establish an order of service, sort out a venue for the wake. Write her obituary, put it in the paper. These were not tasks that could be left to my half-brother.

I did the things Mum would have wanted me to do.

~

She had left a will and notes about her funeral in her neat upbeat handwriting. Sprigs of lavender for the casket. I hadn't been able to get through to her funeral insurance company, didn't yet know what they would pay for.

I had barely a cent to my name. The foolishness of my life's choices were laid bare. I had been eking out an existence with part-time work and trying to write my book. I didn't have Doreen Virtue's mermaid card pack with me, but it was just as well — I had no more cards to draw. Rich and Fearne arrived on a flight, and we were reunited. The relief to see them, my family. 'Mummy.' I kissed her sweet golden-syrup hair, her face. Breathed in the smell of her and him. We were already a small family but so much smaller now.

That evening, in the darkness of the kitchen, we scrolled the funeral parlour's website. 'I like the white coffin,' I said, on instinct. It wasn't the cheapest option but I knew it was right. Rich and Fearne and I agreed that Nana would prefer the turquoise-coloured urn. We needed the coffin for the funeral, the urn for the ashes. I fancied bringing her home in the urn, keeping her close on the mantelpiece, looking over me and Fearne. I didn't want her to be left alone. Her loneliness still so real to me.

'Don't worry about the money. We can put it on the credit card, we'll be fine,' Rich said.

Money. A terrible thing to think about after the death of your mother. The one question I didn't often ask the professional mermaids — how much money do you earn? As far as I knew, the mermaids didn't perform solely for the money, but because it brought greater meaning and joy into their lives. They'd brought greater meaning and joy into my life too. A sense of purpose. On her last day of work Mum had called me, bawling her eyes out. In between ragged sobs, she said, 'I love my work, it gives me so much purpose. I love helping people.'

I put Fearne to bed in the spare room, all of us sleeping in a line together on mattresses on the floor, and then I read Rich my speech for the funeral. In my tribute to Mum, I said, 'You came late to the role of Nana, but it was a role in which you had no peers. You knocked it out of the park.'

~

I googled 'how to tell children about death?' and the answer was to be direct. 'Fearne, do you want to come and see Nana's body?' I asked. I didn't know if it would be good for her to see the body, to know what death looked like. Fearne paused over the bucket of Lego in the lounge, where she was sticking different heads on to little bodies. She shook her head. I felt relieved, for her and for me.

Mum's turquoise car was in our possession now, and Rich drove it across the harbour bridge, to the funeral parlour on the other side of Auckland, near where Mum had lived before she died.

The air was tinted sepia, swirling around us, casting the world in an unearthly shade of orange and umber.

'God, look at the sky,' I said.

'It's the Australian bushfires,' Rich said.

'Really?'

I'd missed the bushfires on the news — racing through towns, leaving the burnt-out carcasses of trees and cars and homes, a black summer.

Rich and I walked through the ash-ridden air to the funeral parlour. A staff member ushered us through to a small, dimly lit room. Mum lay inside the white coffin, dressed in an outfit her best friends had chosen for her. A nice maroon dress, purple beads, the little pink hat on her head, so she wouldn't have to go into the afterlife bald.

She was wearing a scarf I'd never seen her wear in real life. But it was nice. I swirled my fingers through it, told her how much we loved her, how I had organised the funeral, found her notes and everything. 'You left everything in good order, Mum,' I said. 'I'm sorting it all out. But we will miss you forever.' I placed the photograph of Fearne she took into the hospital under her hand.

Her skin had a slight tinge of yellow, and I could see the light stitches keeping her eyes shut. She had shrunk slightly. This is the process of death, of embalmment. I toyed with her scarf, then finally stopped talking, remembering Hannah Mermaid telling me about the Ted Talk she gave just after her father died. 'I just have to surrender.'

I let go.

Rich was so choked up he couldn't speak, but stood beside me until we left, then turned and said, 'Goodbye.' As though we might come back. As though she might come running back up the steps to our flat one day, yelling 'Fearne!' And Fearne yelling, 'Nana!'

~

The next day, Fearne found a dead sparrow on our walk around the neighbourhood. She hovered over it and I let her take a good look. Ants crawled over and out from under its feathery body. I took a photo of the sparrow so she could look at it later too. Its tiny beak.

On the news the bushfires were still burning. A photo went viral of a firefighter feeding a bottle of water to a koala, its feet singed.

'Did the baby koalas die? Fearne asked.

'Some of them. Not all of them. Some were saved,' I replied.

Children had died, families, a grandmother and her two grandkids in their bathtub, wet towels wedged under the doors and windowsills.

~

The funeral was held at a small brick church across the road from the Surrey Hotel, where not so long ago I swam in my Madison tail and Mum slept in the double bed with me every night, the two of us side by side, plucking whiskers and sharing random jokes and photos of Fearne. I liked the coincidence, drew strength from it. I also liked the modernist stained-glass windows at the church, designed by Milan Mrkusich. They were abstract, just slants of colour and shape, triangles of light. Water, fire, baptism, grief, sorrow. Above the entrance doors, a geometric Jesus stretched his arms above his head as though in welcome. Light poured through him. The church flooded with people. Nana was popular. I didn't know who half the people were. Friends, workmates, blasts from the past. I didn't care, so long as everything went smoothly. I was doing my duty, ticking things off the list. I didn't want to let Mum down.

Dad arrived from the airport. 'Hello,' I said. 'Give me a hug,' he said. I was distracted. On show. Desperate to greet the right people, to not exclude any of the guests who were here because they knew and cared about my mother. I could see her white coffin at the front of the aisle. Flowers on top. It looked nice. Tasteful. Fearne had a Creme Egg in her hand because I couldn't find a Kinder egg to bribe her with. I was performing the role of host. I approached a woman next to an old man with a beard and watery blue eyes. 'How did you know Mum?' I asked, looking at her.

'Megan, you probably don't remember me,' he said. It was Dave, an ancient boyfriend of Mum's from my childhood. A vague memory of walking along a beach. Mum and Dave holding hands; me lurking behind them, seething with hatred for him. That day, I had found a plastic dolphin on the edge of the surf. Squeezed it, salt water dribbled out. We were near some hot pools. Must have been swimming.

'I read about her death in the newspaper,' Dave said.

I had written the death notice.

'She was a very anxious person,' he said. I could see he wanted to get his two cents in, some pearl of wisdom, but I didn't want to hear it.

A group of matronly women with short haircuts approached. 'Megan?'

'Yes,' I said.

They were old friends of Mum's from her counselling days. 'She was so proud of you when you went to London and were publishing poems,' one said. 'Yes,' the others agreed. My long-forgotten poems.

I nodded and smiled. Fearne yanked my arm. 'I don't like Creme Eggs. I want a Kinder egg.'

'I couldn't find a Kinder egg,' I said.

Another old friend from her university days in Dunedin told me how Mum was always so unique. 'She stood up one night on a post in the Octagon and gave a tribute to her feet.' It was a sweet diatribe about how useful feet can be. 'Have you ever really stopped to think about your feet?' Mum apparently said. I clocked it — how wonderful, how ironic.

The priest who took the service was the nice one from the hospital; another coincidence I drew strength from. Later, there

were complaints that the sound was bad. No one could hear what he said. The microphone was echoey. I could barely make out what he was saying either, but I wasn't listening properly. I was just getting through it.

The priest stopped and looked at me and said, 'Your mother suffered.'

The only words I heard. I nodded. It was true and we had both seen it.

Fearne held my hand as I walked at the front of the coffin, Rich on the other side. The pallbearers included Dad and my half-brother, and my uncle in the lines behind us. Walking her out. The coffin was so heavy I was surprised. Yet we steered it into the hearse and threw sprigs of lavender on it, as Mum had asked. Her friends from her last job gathered outside the church and sang a waiata as the hearse drove away. Their voices so beautiful. 'Thank you,' I said. 'Thank you.'

~

The next day, I opened the door to Mum's last bedroom. I was there to clear out the contents, to pack her belongings into boxes, close her bank account, cancel her rent and bills, send her clothes to the op shop.

Mum was a great op shopper. Mounds of clothes had accumulated on her single bed, the place she slept alone, in a dingy rented room. All her life she had wanted to get married, have her own house and a husband, but it never happened. Her bedroom was decorated in soft colours, blues and mauves, the bedspread had a print of flowers.

My cousin was there to help. She held up clothes, This? This? I shook my head or nodded as a signal to keep.

Maroon clothes, old lady colours, misshapen shoes, purple beads, the silly fussy scarves . . . Things that she thought were classy and I thought were gaudy.

Trish, my aunt, was also reckoning with Mum's closet. 'Megan, what about this? May I have it?' 'Yes, take it.' I was touched by anything people wanted to keep, as though keeping something meant her life hadn't gone to waste.

'Can I have this, Mummy?' Fearne held up a necklace.

'Yes. Yes.'

Fearne also took the vintage doll with strawberry blonde hair that used to sit beside the dollhouse. She slipped the little gauzy socks off her plastic feet. Knick-knacks, bric-a-brac. A pair of ceramic ballet shoes on a pink ribbon was plucked from the dresser and dangled in front of me. I shook my head.

'Your mother loved those shoes,' my aunt said, scolding.

I couldn't give a fig about the ballet shoes, but I wanted the statue of the Virgin Mary in her pale-blue robe. I saw it across the blue room, as though across the seabed. Mary held her palms open at her sides. 'That belongs with me,' I said.

I rejected a little stone church ornament, lovely as it was. Instead, I took a wee sculpture of Noah's Ark I gave to Mum years ago.

My cousin appeared before me, her crenellated fans swaying. I had become the mermaid in 'Diving into the Wreck'; I was turning my body in the deep element. Rich was the merman circling the hull with me, removing the cargo. Box by box. I combed Mum's bookshelf for treasure. The tiny little gift books of my childhood. Charlie Brown — *I Need All the Friends I Can Get*, its black and yellow cover tattered. *My God* by Mel Calman, a Jewish cartoonist. God depicted as a chubby cherub sitting on a cloud, fretting: 'I think I've left a volcano on somewhere.'

I had found my mother's humour, her voice, she was my God. Before I flew anywhere on my mermaid adventures, I'd say, 'Pray for me', and she'd say, 'Yes darling, I'll pray for you.' Mum made me feel safe.

I found the photograph album of Fearne's first year too. The photo of Fearne turning to look at her nana, the day when Mum first thought: *She loves me.* That love was reflected back. Love flows into children, moves around them like water, like air.

I cried out. My cousin put her hand on my arm. I was now the only mother left. I would no longer be able to send photographs of Fearne to Mum every day. She was no longer there to be Fearne's biggest fan.

I took all Mum's paperwork. A laminated affirmation thanking the world for her chemotherapy, a duplicate pack of her Pearls of Wisdom affirmations in their delicate mesh bag. I inherited my grandmother's string of pearls, too. Heavy, obviously the real thing, with a grey-creamy gleam, once plucked from their oysters in chambers of the ocean, then looped on to this silver clasp. I didn't intend to wear them, yet I took them, more loot from the wreck. I also collected my grandmother's rosary beads, putting them like pebbles in my pocket.

I opened a small hessian sack and pulled out slips of paper, handwritten wishes for me and my brother. For my brother to be happy. For me to be fulfilled. For my financial freedom. I added her paperwork to mine.

I took my mother's heavy brass twenty-first key and her wooden wonky fortieth key, the shape bent, as though by time. An old joke present from my aunt.

A box called Life's Memories, tied shut with a blue ribbon. An old Bible that I recognised; Mum's obsolete mobile phone; her mauve gleaming laptop.

Then I found a sliver of a book from the early seventies. I flicked the book open. Mum's voice! Mum published only three poems in her life. They were written when she was a twenty-one-year-old trainee nurse and collected here in this slim book, barely more than a pamphlet.

I opened a floral notebook and found a letter to her past. *Dear past*, she wrote, *I'm writing to you in the hope that by doing so I'll let you go peacefully. God, I've barely started to write yet! I wanted to have my own set of cards, a book or two, and I've barely gathered enough wisdom yet to share and yet time is shortening in front of me.*

All this time I thought my desire to write was my own, and that my longing to publish books was about my dad and his stacked bookshelves. But here were the origins in Mum's paperwork. Mum was the silent woman denied a voice, and I was the articulate woman with the strength to do her work.

Outside Mum's bedroom, I encountered her friend and flatmate — her face like a lantern fish, her eyes gleaming but not with grief. 'How much do you want for the fridge?'

I looked at the two-storey fridge-freezer Mum had once owned. 'Keep it,' I said, and cut the anchor loose.

15.

Lessons from the Terrible Fish

I signed out of Skype. For good. Relegated the mermaids to my rugged orange hard drive. Their voices stored inside it, like the sound of the sea.

Rose the New York mermaid. Hannah, Linden, MeduSirena, Aysun, Cookie, Raina, Jax, Pearl, Callie. Triton Mahtlinnie, who lived on a boat in Puget Sound. The image of the frilled fins along their arms, their black and purple tail, their webbed gloves thrilled me. 'Everything is more fun in a costume,' Triton had said. Until it wasn't.

Then there were all the other mermaids I hadn't spoken to yet. Their data stored in my Mermaid Log in Excel. Snippets of their lives and motivations. The log contained every species of mer available, every gender and colour. I had wanted to acquire their data, to make sure I had covered every base. *In the sea, the mermaids come and go, talking of Waterhouse and toxic masculinity, you know?*

I had wanted to readdress David Foster Wallace's famous essay 'Consider the Lobster', from the point of view of Salvador Dali's

Dream of Venus pavilion and his lobster telephones. Those surrealist phones reminded me of my time treading water in the gallery basement, but with a private hotline to the lives of mermaids. Motherhood had snatched me out of my old life and turned me into a shell of myself. But the mermaids had brought me back.

Some had got away though. The South African, who sent me a PDF of her book on Atlantis. Mermaid Crystal, who was busy and couldn't help yet. Mermaid Melissa, too — the first woman to officially add 'Mermaid' to her name.

I had been a big game hunter and a bottom feeder rolled into one. The mermaids had helped me with my quest. They recognised one another, the way Sylvia Earle could distinguish between fish. Same species, different tale.

I analysed their selfies, as they mined the sublime on Instagram. The mermaids supplied images of escape. They swam the deep blue, the pale blue, the mid-blue, and sometimes, often, they just sat on the rocks. It was surprisingly difficult to hold space by just basking, one mermaid said.

I was finished, but I was also on the hunt for the END. Where was the full stop for this project? I couldn't keep writing, but I didn't want to quit my job as a woman writing a book about mermaids, either. It was the best job I'd ever had. The pay was terrible, but the sense of purpose was immense.

~

'Tell me again how Nana died,' Fearne asked. A year had ticked by with no mermaids in it, and I was putting Fearne to bed.

'What do you mean?'

'Tell me the name of her cancer.'

'Multiple myeloma.' I had not yet told her it is a cancer of the blood. 'Nana got very sick and she went to hospital and they were trying to make her better but she was too sick and so she died in hospital. She was old,' I told her. A white lie as we lay in bed together.

'Nana died when I was four,' Fearne said, and began to cry. Her mouth turned into an upside-down U. She had a look of total misery, hot-pink eyes. 'Tell me about when Nana died. I like to hear this story,' she said.

I had told her the story many times.

Fearne's chubby fingers twirled in my hair. She still liked to grab my fringe — this is how she self-soothed, except she was not self-soothing, because I still slept with her and she still needed my hair. She scrunched my fringe; far more streaks of grey were coming through since Mum had gone. I was an older mother, I had Fearne at forty — what silly reckless behaviour. Now that Mum was dead, I worried about the future, about whether my life would be long enough to see Fearne grow up and thrive. Mum was not here to say, 'It will be all right, darling.'

'I had more toys I wanted to show Nana,' Fearne cried. 'Nana was the best at playing dolls. She was the number-one doll player.'

This got me. This really got me.

'Are you crying, Mummy?' she asked.

My mouth must have been in that upside-down U of pure misery. I was ugly crying. I had not cried in a while.

'Nana should not have died when I was four. That was not a good time for her to die,' Fearne said.

I reminded her that one of her other little friends had a nana who died.

But Fearne said, 'I only have two nanas and they both died.'

'Most people only have two nanas,' I said.

'Can babies die?' Fearne asked. A friend at her school had said babies can die.

'Yes, babies can die but it is very rare. All living things can die,' I said. I turned out the main light, switched Fearne's glow-in-the-dark narwhal night light on. It was one of many toys Mum had not lived to see.

I was changing, my hair turning grey, my hands, my skin losing their youthful zeal. I grew more whiskers on my chin that Fearne watched me endlessly pluck, as though the life of a forty-six-year-old woman consisted mainly of two pairs of tweezers, aimed like chopsticks in my hand.

'What if you die when I am a teenager?' Fearne asked.

'I am not planning on dying,' I said to her and myself in the dark.

'But what if you do?' Fearne said. 'I will be sad forever.'

Then she said, 'What if you die and my daughter never meets you?'

~

In one notebook I found in her papers, Mum had written down all her passwords. Nineteen were simply the word: Lawrence.

After Christmas, we passed flooded farmland out the car windows. We drove deeper into the South Island, finally arriving in Lawrence, the town where Mum had grown up. An old mining town, barely more than two intersecting streets. We parked the hire car by a little playground and got out. Playgrounds were always the first port of call. Fearne ran over. One fixture was very old, a little white set of rusted monkey bars. It could have been around in the fifties when Mum was born. I touched it. Fearne swung on it, landed on tough gritty chips of bark, dusted herself off.

Next we wandered up the main street, the old theatre where Mum had once watched movies with her granddad on Friday nights. The old stone buildings all had plaques outside that described their former relevance and majesty. Otherwise, the town looked like something that had collapsed in on itself long ago. We found the old church she once attended. In the grass over the fence was a big, ragged sheep chewing grass. It looked at me across the fence, earnest and inquisitive. Not the Lamb of God. Just a sheep.

I got Rich to take photos of us in Lawrence, even though I always looked dire outside, in strong sunlight. I felt like a has-been, on a sentimental pilgrimage. The best kind of pilgrimage.

I didn't even know the name of the street she grew up on, yet we found her old house. The garden was completely overgrown and overrun. I thought of that eight-year-old girl in the sepia photo, smiling and holding her doll, her whole life still to play for.

We'd visited the house several times during my early childhood and had photos of us kids perched in the tree by the roadside, a gesture for Mum, an act to meet her needs, her feelings. Later, when she first trained as a counsellor and was straining for a new identity, she came back here and climbed again into the tree. Mum's feelings were all around me, like water I moved through and breathed. I couldn't tell any more what was her and what was me.

The tree was still there. Thick and dead, barely more than a stubborn stump, its branches reaching out. We took more photos next to it, me and Fearne and Rich. I was ugly in the photos, overweight, weighed down by life and grief. Squinting in the outdoor glare. I wore a large lime-green jumper from a hip store but I didn't feel hip. I felt an exhaustion with myself and my limits. My own defiled dreams. The property was inaccessible, abandoned. We'd never be able to cut our way through the overgrowth and get into it, to walk along the wide deck or enter the old bedroom, where she once lay in bed and watched car lights stripe the wall. Where she wrote her first poems by moonlight.

I thought of that old love of hers. He didn't come to the funeral, and I didn't send him the little tasteful booklet I'd produced for her service, because I didn't want him to be able to archive her away neatly. I could withhold what she never could. And yet he must have loved her. Or he loved her enough to come to Lawrence. I had found a book of photos of a trip they once took as a couple, Mum still in mid-life and happy. He posed in his jeans, inside the local church.

We visited the cemetery on the hill. I felt choked with tears, though not one member of my family rested there. Sheep walked away from us behind nearby fences. The graves old and lavish, crumbling and falling apart, then down a hill, in the shade, the Chinese cemetery, a handful of wooden graves, for the Chinese community that had come to Lawrence for the gold rush and wound up buried in this green farming land.

We ate tepid chips at a bad café — 'I want tomato ketchup,' Fearne said — and visited the local opshop. It was filled to the brim, one of those shops that you can't turn around in without worrying that something from the past will fall over. So much of life resists story.

Then we stopped in Dunedin, and got a photo of me and Fearne sitting in the bottom of the St Kilda whale, swallowed whole.

One night, back at home, I walked into the kitchen and said in a small, stunned voice, 'My mum died.'

'Where did that come from?' Rich asked.

The wreck.

~

Every morning I looked in the rectangular bathroom mirror bolted to the wall of our rented flat and the terrible fish looked back.

Sylvia Plath wrote the poem 'Mirror' aged twenty-seven, after the birth of her daughter, Frieda, and committed suicide two years later by crawling into that oven, aged thirty. When it came to growing old, she didn't know much. But for generations of Western women, her art became our mirror.

Four decades after her death, in London, after several bottles of wine, my artist friend Yvonne stood up in the lounge and recited 'Mirror', with reverb. She put an echo on the end of every line, so that the mirror was reflected back on itself, each word twinned. The poem ended on the image of a young girl drowned in the mirror, and an old woman rising towards her like 'a terrible fish'. Yvonne and I laughed. We were only in our mid-twenties and she had just won a big art prize and come to visit me in London. I was wounded, secretly seething with jealousy.

For years I wrote brief dispatches in the voice of the terrible fish. What are we talking about here, Sylvia? A piranha? A blobfish?

An anglerfish? One of those spiky ministers of the deep with jaws that bite and eyes like streetlights lit up on stalks?

The terrible fish had been after me for years, but now it really was on my tail.

Yvonne's too. Lately her self-portraits had focused on her crêpey skin and emerging jowls. Yvonne always went for the psychic jugular, especially when she aimed the camera at herself. I looked at her latest photographs online and then messaged her, 'Remember the terrible fish?'

'Reciting "Mirror" used to be my party trick!' she wrote back. Yvonne was working on an upcoming talk about her art called 'Rogue Wave'. Rogue waves come out of nowhere and engulf everything. Yvonne said art is like that, too — ideas that are so insistent they can't be ignored.

And so, the terrible fish rose from the mirror every day to pluck and put on mascara and get ready for work and school. I now knew this from experience. There are few things the terrible fish does not know from experience.

Terrible is a matter of perspective, though. The blobfish isn't ugly in its natural habitat, four thousand feet under water, it's only when it gets dragged to the surface that it collapses into a gelatinous hacky sack. Sylvia Plath probably didn't mean to shame the terrible fish for its appearance, but she could have done a bit more research.

'I'm turning into an old woman,' I complained one morning to Rich.

'Whereas I'm turning into a dashing middle-aged man.'

Reconsider the lobster — as a partner. Lobsters mate for life, a little-known fact. Rich was wearing yellow-and-white striped socks with lobsters embroidered on the ankles, which I had bought him for Christmas. Except not on his feet. No, he had rolled the socks on to his arms as though they were shoulder-length mittens and was dancing along to a Dua Lipa track.

'Do Zoidberg!' I said, referring to the hapless, lobster-like alien from *Futurama*.

Rich scuttled back and forth across the lounge, snapping his hands like pincers, saying, 'Woop! Woop! Woop!'

Topless, he caressed his slinky, wiry torso with the lobster socks.

'It's just as Dua Lipa imagined it,' I said, in my pyjamas, wobbling from side to side. Depression skipped a beat.

Fearne joined in, a terrible mimic, given to pouting and odd, unrhythmic hip thrusts and choreography stolen from Lady Gaga, Ariana Grande and Little Mix. I watched her strut and thought, I really shouldn't be letting her watch YouTube this young.

The music video is such a rich elixir! I don't know how it feels to be Dua Lipa but I do know how it feels to listen to her. It feels like happiness, like bubbles rising up and up and up.

Before we left the flat, Rich said, 'You don't look after yourself. You don't drink enough water.'

'You're right,' I replied, and I drank two glasses, straight up.

'What's that?' He pointed his finger at my cheekbone.

'It's an age spot,' I snapped.

'Will it come off?' he asked.

'No!'

~

I stopped at the chemist because a friend had recommended vitamin B6. ('We're going through all sorts of depletion, try it.') Mum used to tell me to get women's multi. Or evening primrose oil. Or iron tablets. Or her cure-all: a banana. At the chemist, the terrible fish couldn't see any B6. Found a B-vitamin mix. Is that the same? Had not brought glasses. Squinted to read label. Hoped that the zealous shop assistant, an older woman with salty shoulder-length spirals, would spot the fish and show mercy.

'Do you need some help there?' A sing-song tone, her question mark rising.

I'd encountered the assistant at Unichem before. We once had a terse moment over a parcel I needed to send.

Now I needed her.

'Do you have any vitamin B6?' I asked.

She found one small pottle, good for water retention and energy. Or maybe it was good for something else. 'This has the strongest dose.' I sensed I finally had her on the right topic. She started to run off sentence after sentence about the benefits of vitamin B.

'I'm perimenopausal,' I said. The terrible fish likes to cut to the chase.

She led me further along the aisle. 'I've given this to some other ladies.'

Natural hormone balance support. The rectangular box was fuchsia-pink and sported a white flower. She advised the possible benefits, whilst not overselling them, all through her white surgical mask.

'I am forty-seven,' I told her. I said it to remind myself. She could see quite clearly that I was a middle-aged customer. It's me who thinks I am somehow still a seven-year-old trying to tell her mother that she feels sad and hasn't eaten a banana.

'I'm a bit further along than you. I'm fifty-three,' the shop assistant said. 'I'm an old bag.'

I touched her arm because I loved her a little bit then. She was on HRT but not sure if the level was right yet. She got dithery, found it hard to make decisions. Once she was the kind of person who could select a gift easily. Now she might find herself leaving the shop with nothing. 'You're fine on big things but a towel gets left in the wrong place at home and it sets you off,' she said.

I didn't have the balls to tell her I wasn't fine with anything right now and lived in anxious terror. I couldn't care less about a towel anywhere, even if it was damp and reeked of onions.

I looked at the list of symptoms on the box.

'This is me,' I said. 'All this.'

I followed her to the till and paid. 'I eat sweets sometimes, for energy,' I admitted.

She recommended getting some good-quality chocolate

instead and chopping it up, just a couple of pieces with some nuts and seeds.

'Almonds are the women's nut. Brazil nuts are good for men.'

Bloody almonds again.

'Come back and tell me how you get on with the pills.'

'Thank you,' I said.

~

I needed cheering up, I wanted to feel happy. I picked up my phone and watched MeduSirena's latest dance on Facebook. She had dressed up as Liza Minnelli — she seemed so up! Liza Minnelli also reminded me of my mother. I think it's the short, blunt haircut. Mum had one of those for a while.

I blinked back tears, sadness always rushing in like the tide sizzling into a rock pool. I couldn't get that crabby feeling out from underneath me.

'It's the perimenopause,' I told Rich.

I scratched at my shin under the covers.

'Why are you always scratching?' he asked.

'Because my shin is so demonically itchy.'

I pulled back the duvet. My red shin blazing with irritation.

'Doctor?' He suggested.

'Maybe the B vitamins will help.'

Fearne came out of her room, looking surly. The irritation switched tracks. 'Can I have the iPad?'

'Yes,' I said, because it was easier.

'We should send her to iPads Anonymous,' Rich grumbled. 'I wish I'd never got her that iPad.'

In the kitchen, he held up a plastic bottle accusingly.

'This isn't recyclable.'

'Sorry,' I said, because I could never remember what did and didn't go into the recycling bin. Turned out recycling was just another capitalist ruse.

~

Fearne came to me and asked me to draw a mermaid with crayons.

I put the paper on the carpet.

I drew a solitary mermaid with a green tail, seated on the rocks, her back to the viewer. She looked towards a distant lighthouse. The lighthouse is meant to protect ships from sailing on to rocks.

I liked to read Fearne a book called *Hello Lighthouse*. The sea is so stylised; its waves rise in lovely, peaked prisms, then crest and curl into foam. I can almost hear the trill of the surf. And the refrain that repeats inside: 'Hello Lighthouse, hello, hello, hello', each repetition an echo of the wind or the sea.

Fearne snuggled in close to me, our attention focused together, as we lay in her single bed and read, before we turned the lights off and narwhal nightlight on. I like the way the book carefully and attentively depicts the seasons. The water turns to ice and seals lie fatly on its surface; whales arch their backs and pass; the Northern Lights are a fluorescent green.

Bad things happen — a storm breaks a ship on the rocks, giant waves thrash the lighthouse, later it is blanketed in fog and the keeper must ring a bell in warning — but the lighthouse stands tall and sentient throughout.

At the end, the keeper, his wife and daughter must leave. On the final page, they stand in the doorway of their new home, on a clifftop, and look out towards the old lighthouse's steady yellow beam.

What was the relationship of the mermaid to the lighthouse? Where did my relentless desire to be seen come from?

The desire rolled in and out.

I had stopped skyping, but I still cast the net, fishing for compliments, hauling in fresh spates of likes, though I no longer added mermaid and puffer fish emojis to my Instagram posts. I watched the mermaids from a distance, examined one on her Facebook page. Every angle of her jaw presented fetchingly. Her swoop of long hair cascading over her shoulder. She thought it was her good side. I felt her need.

Beneath every buoyant post on the state of her life: *Like me, like me.*

~

I'd heard the mermaids skyping and I had over 800,000 words of their interviews stored on my hard drive to prove it. The voices seemed muted, underwater, far away, like the sound of the sea in a shell. *There is no rule book to follow,* said Hannah Mermaid. *This is a self-made career.* Quotes inched out like hermit crabs, the sea's white noise.

Yes, the world is burning but there's still beauty in it. I literally lived my dream. Something's gotta feed your soul. Exhale the human, inhale the mermaid. The ocean needs our attention. You can't just do birthday parties. You can't just do corporate appearances. You have to be able to diversify. I would say the two hardest things are the hours and being cold.

I thought of Mermaid Linden back at the start of her career, when she slept above her parent's garage, having nightmares about building her first silicone tail. It had cost her so much time and money. I thought of the bravery of Mermaid Karin, who'd swum with manta rays, piranhas, and even a small crocodile. I thought of Ali Luminescent, the sparkle-haired speech pathologist who'd inspired the multi-coloured mermaid emoji. A friend at Apple had designed it in her honour. For Ali, mermaiding gave her and others the permission to be joyful.

And Mermaid Lila from Hawai'i. She'd once worked as a federal fisheries observer — 'a fancy way of saying I counted fish'. Once she was in an Alaskan bar waiting out a storm with 100-mile-an-hour winds and texted her mum to let her know she was safe, she was not at sea. A guy in the bar said to her, 'Hey there is such a thing as real life. Get off your phone.' Mermaid Lila snapped back at him, 'Mind your own fucking business. I'm texting my mother.'

I could hear the mer-message the sirens were trying to send me. So I applied for a writer's residency to start work on my mermaid book again, and I bloody got it. My office was in a wooden building perched at the top of the hill, overlooking the city and the sea. I took Madison — of course — hung her over the spinning chair in my office. Posted a photo of my name on the door to Instagram. Waited for the likes. Hung Waterhouse's *A Mermaid* above my Dell computer. I decanted my books on to the shelves and hung my new mermaid-themed calendar on the wall. Outside the window, the sea glinted like a knife, a boat on its surface trailing white lines from the hull. I turned back to my Skypes.

I sorted through pages with a highlighter, striping yellow through notable quotes. I read through my notebooks from my mermaid journeys. I was the archivist again, trying to dredge the past back up into the light.

~

In the doctor's surgery, a line of plants had been placed on a grey fold-out table at reception. I assumed the plants absorbed germs — they were in a line next to the sanitiser and the cardboard box of blue surgical facemasks. I sat opposite, waiting in my corner, glancing at my phone and suddenly I heard 'The Sound of Bread' on the radio. I couldn't instantly place the song. Though I could see the album cover, that simple beige cover, from Mum's own collection.

The plaintive voice, 'You sheltered me from harm . . .' A catch in my throat. Tears blinked into my eyes again. I'd never thought about the song before, but now it was obvious it was written to a caregiver, not a lover, to someone who represents the heart of the family.

'Can you look at my shin?' I asked the GP, rolling up the brown leg of my overalls.

'That does look sore,' the doctor said.

'It is,' I said. 'It's so itchy. Perhaps I have leg cancer? I can't die before Fearne!' She listened sympathetically to my monologue of middle-aged anxieties, her brow creasing. She must have been my age, more or less, yet she seemed a font of wisdom.

'I can't stop crying some days.'

'Has there been a change in your circumstances?'

'Yes.' I told her about the residency, about how last week I got off my spinning chair and lay on the office floor staring at the ceiling. Felled by some invisible force.

'Maybe I've got too much time alone. It's not good for my anxiety. I can dwell on anything,' I said. 'And I do.'

'You have venous eczema — I'll prescribe you a cream for that. I'm also going to refer you to the Vein Clinic.

'For this anxiety . . .' She paused, looking at me gently. She knew my feelings about depression. 'Do you think anti-depressants could help again? 'Cause they can be good for anxiety. Start with half a tablet, then build up to one a day.'

I nodded, in no position to refuse.

What lies at the bottom of the sea and shakes?

A nervous wreck.

16.

Oceanic Feeling

The train clicked past the countryside. A fifty-minute trip out to Dad's new place up the coast. 'Let's see who can hold their breath longest,' Fearne said, as we shot into the longest tunnel. She puffed out her cheeks like a blowfish. I glanced at our reflections in the window, her long hair and mine. I leaned over and kissed her head. My favourite thing to do. 'You breathed,' she said. 'I win!' I had forgotten I was meant to be playing a game. During the last phase of the journey, the train passed a cliff close to the sea, and I steeled myself to look out at the mawing tide, always afraid the train would somehow fall into it, our lives lost.

The sea was wild out here at the coast, pooling in white rushes and foam. It was not a stretch where I ever saw a swimmer. 'How long now?' Fearne asked.

I glanced up at the map. 'Two more stops.'

'We need to do something special for Daddy when we get home,' Fearne said.

'Like what?'

'Daddy works so hard for us. To pay the rent so we don't get chucked out of our house,' Fearne said.

'What are you thinking?' I asked.

Outside the window, jagged raindrops ran diagonally over the glass.

'He would like a toolbox,' Fearne said.

Yes, that was a good point. He would like a toolbox.

'But he has his orange toolbox,' I reminded her.

And his two bicycles. The orange Surly and the grey Ritchey. The wheels spinning around, and me and her a spoke in between them. I sighed. The clock ticking, the sand falling through the hourglass of our lives, and Rich doing nothing that he likes, except for riding his bicycles.

'Daddy works on weekends. He works so hard,' she said.

'I work hard, too,' I said, keen to assert my status as a provider and a feminist. Even though I was on a year-long residency still wrestling with a book about mermaids.

'Daddy is the only one who works on weekends,' Fearne continued.

Not entirely true, but I let her have it.

'He would like to eat dinner at a table,' Fearne said.

True. Rich rides to work on his bike, and rides home at night in the dark, his bike lights on, feeling the traction as he climbs the steep hill to our street, to come and sit down on The Worst Sofa in the World and eat his dinner off a plate on his lap.

The way we live is the way I lived growing up in that rented flat with my mum. More treasure might be able to save us — there is a Doreen Virtue mermaid card called 'Treasure Chest', in which a mermaid opens a chest glowing with gold. But I hadn't pulled that one out in a long while. I'd stopped using the cards all together, in fact.

'We could get the fold-out table out and eat off it. On those things,' she said. 'What do you call them?'

'Placemats?' I suggested.

'Yes. Daddy would like that. But that's not enough. It needs to be extra,' Fearne said, thinking. 'We will eat dinner at the table and I will eat vegetables,' she concluded. 'That will make Daddy happy.'

'Yes,' I agreed, 'that will make him happy.'

~

As we pulled into the station, Granddad stood at the platform in his big winter coat and black beanie, waving. We followed him through the underpass and crossed the carpark, avoiding puddles as the tart winter air lashed at our skin. 'Where shall we go first?' He asked. I had already briefed him that we wanted to go op shopping, because Fearne enjoys op shopping. She must get it from Nana, I told him.

Dad nodded, his hands plunged in pockets. A lighthouse is not easily tempted into idle chitchat. His gaze was always fixed ahead in these moments, at a horizon line I couldn't see. Father healing. I focused on the spiritual truth of Dad. My likeness to him, how I felt more at home in myself when things were right between us. I looked at his profile, as though his nose, his face, was a piece of coastline I was skirting around.

We checked out the big Salvation Army first. The smell — that odour of must and getting by, the breadline of poverty, the scent of other lives still clinging and needing airing out. Drawers of broken Barbie dolls, the squeak of coat hangers on aluminium racks. I stared at a cluster of Strawberry Shortcake dolls in a glass cabinet. 'Thirty dollars,' I said. 'Not cheap.'

'Yes,' Dad replied. 'They've gotten wise out here to the retro trend. I'll take you to my favourite op shop next,' he said.

As we pulled up, I saw a wedding dress on a mannequin in the front window.

The dress was traditional, shoulderless, with a scalloped fitted bodice, brocaded flowers and a long flowing mermaid train. 'Wow,' I said. 'Look at that. A wedding dress!'

'Are you going to try it on, Mummy?' Fearne asked.

'Maybe,' I said.

Dad looked stunned. 'Well, this is unexpected.'

Two elderly ladies staffed the till, like a pair of owls.

Fearne went searching for dolls and toys at the back.

I zoomed in on the dress in the window and examined the price tag. It looked unworn. 'It's only fifty dollars,' I said.

The dress looked my size. I googled the name on the tag. It was a label from Barcelona. Rich and I went to Barcelona once, years ago, before Fearne. Another sign?

One of the ladies approached, like a seagull swooping in on a chip. 'Do you want to try it on?'

'No, I shouldn't. It's probably a hassle to get it off the mannequin,' I said.

'It's no trouble.' She jimmied her hands under the skirt of the dress, detached the mannequin from its stand and got the dress out for me.

I carted it off towards the changing room, reams of thick bustling silk, the swishing of the train — a real wedding dress. I didn't have a wedding dress the first time round, when I got married to the Irishman who called me a beautiful amoeba. I wore an electric-blue kimono. I had always said to myself that if I got married again, I'd have a white wedding dress.

'I don't really suit white,' I said.

'Give it a try,' she said, ushering me into the changing room and closing the curtain behind me. 'It's gorgeous.'

It was a lot of material to fit into the booth. I popped the dress on over my jeans, keeping my red bra on, then tried to zip the back of the bodice up.

I poked my head out of the changing room.

'Dad, can you help me?'

'Yep.' Dad stepped forward and I came out and turned around so he could fumble with the zip. The sales assistants watched him, and one said, 'It's been a while since you've done that, hasn't it?'

Dad blushed, but took their joking good-naturedly.

I looked at myself in the mirror. 'Not bad,' I said.

'It suits you,' the assistant said.

'Get it, Mummy,' Fearne said.

I took a selfie in the mirror and sent it to Rich with the word, 'Thoughts?'

'Should I get a photo of the back?' Dad asked.

He took one. The mermaid train gushed out at the sides, theatrical and splendid. It was beautiful.

'Crickey dicks,' Rich replied. 'Looks good.'

'I'll think about it,' I told the owls behind the till. The person most interested in attending my wedding was gone now.

We ushered Fearne back into the car and drove up to the playground by the beach, but it was too cold and drizzly to stay there for long. The three of us walked up a hill and watched the sea swirling, its own white mermaid train pooling in then drawing out again. We walked under a cluster of pine trees, smelt the thick, green, crisp scent of the needles under our feet and above our heads. I looked back at the frothing tide.

'Let's go back and get the dress,' I said, suddenly decided. 'I mean, it's only fifty dollars, what have I got to lose?'

But when we pulled into the carpark, the shop was closed; the dress back in the window, worn by its headless mannequin bride.

'I could pick it up for you on Monday when it opens again?' Dad said.

'Yes,' I said.

~

'I've been asked to interview Lorde,' I gushed to Rich on the phone.

'What?' he said.

'I have to do it, don't I? I have to fly to Auckland and you know how I feel about flying. What about Covid?'

The first waves of the pandemic had been and gone, but cases were on the rise again. The sun outside was scorching. The air filled with the shrill persistent chirping of cicadas.

'Yes, you have to do it,' he agreed.

I had previously thought little about Lorde and her musical iconography. I knew who she was of course, everyone in New Zealand has seen that photograph of Lorde and Eleanor Catton reading in a bed in a New York hotel together, the two of them representing what life can be — Catton had just won the Booker Prize and Lorde had won two Grammys and met David Bowie!

'You realise I'm forty-seven and uncool,' I'd told the magazine editor over the phone as I paced around my office. The editor had sent me a DM on Instagram. 'Why me?'

The editor explained that Lorde was given a list of writers' names and she chose me. She wanted me to write the feature article about her for a local fashion magazine that she was guest editing, as part of the promotion for her latest album.

'I don't know anything about fashion,' I said.

'We have that covered,' the editor assured me.

I knew, vaguely, that Lorde had just released an album called *Solar Power*. On the cover Lorde leapt over the camera, bare-legged in a thong, the sun streaming through her oatmeal bumcheeks. It was a little racy, but also sunny and fun. A slice of youth and young womanhood. I remembered how triumphant I felt in my twenties when I looked good in a pair of hotpants. It was something worth celebrating. I looked out the window at the familiar stretch of harbour. Waterhouse's mermaid was still on the wall above my desk and Doreen Virtue's cards tucked away in a drawer, just in case. The editor explained that they would pay my airfare to Auckland, and for a hotel, and gave me the deadline.

'Okay,' I said. I felt sweaty and giddy, but also buoyant and light. As light as a woman in her late forties, bogged down by mermaids, can be.

I strutted around for the next few days, feeling pleased with myself. I walked into my favourite clothing shop and chose a light-blue dress. 'I need something new because I'm interviewing

Lorde!' I said. Next, I ran into the curator and his girlfriend down the street.

'I'm interviewing Lorde!' I said.

'God, what are you going to ask her?' The curator's girlfriend was relentlessly chic and also fiercely witty.

'I don't know,' I confessed. 'I need to listen to more of her back catalogue.'

'Lorde has been around longer than the Beatles,' the curator pointed out.

That intimidated me. I was no longer just a mum on the run from her hard drive of mermaids, but a disciple of Lorde.

~

At home, I watched loads of music videos on YouTube. Fearne joined me at the desk to stare into the Apple Mac. Her favourite Lorde song was 'Green Light'.

'But honey I'll be seeing you wherever I go . . .' The music built to a crescendo.

On screen, Lorde in her tight, fuchsia mini-dress poked her head out of the backseat car window and let the night stream past her face. Later, she pounded the roof of the car in a pair of white sneakers.

'I want that green light, I want it,' Fearne sang along in the lounge, throwing her arms around.

Then, suddenly: 'Mummy, why does she want the green light?'

'Good question,' I said.

'Can I ask her some questions?' Fearne said.

'Yes,'

'Can I come?' Fearne asked.

'No.'

A pout.

'What questions would you want to ask?'

'What's her favourite snack?'

~

Listening to Lorde, I was struck by the almost unbearable sweetness of her voice. She homed in on what it meant to be alive, and I heard her femininity rising.

The final song on the album, though, 'Oceanic Feeling', was not what I was expecting. The whole song pulled me under.

'It's a blue day,' Lorde sang. The song opened like a church hymn, holding one long deep note, and the sound of cicadas. It was not a hit, not a banger, but long and meditative and dreamy, a prose poem. On the surface, the song was about swimming and the height of summer, but when I listened to it, I felt a sense of time enveloping and swallowing and engulfing me. The verses changed like seasons. Lorde sang in a high falsetto about her cherry-black lipstick gathering dust in a drawer, but also wondered what her future daughter would look like, who she would be. 'Will she have my dreamer's disposition or my wicked streak?'

The final verse changed tempo and tack entirely — 'Oh can you hear the sound shimmering higher?' — and the last lines filled me with tears. 'I'll know when it's time to take off my robes and step into the choir.'

Arriving in Auckland, I first bought a bouquet of flowers and took an Uber to the cemetery where Mum's ashes were buried. I had not been able to get back since we put her ashes in the ground, one sodden day. Mike had shovelled water out of the hole, then wiped her plaque down with his bare hands. I met him at the grave again. This time it wasn't raining, thank God. We hugged. I put the flowers down for her. 'I still can't believe it, eh sis. It still seems like yesterday.' Four years had come and gone. Four birthdays that Mum didn't live to see. 'Fearne is eight now,' I told Mike. 'She still misses Nana.'

I felt a dissolution of self — grief, sharp and fragrant, the fleetingness of everything, a cicada shell on the grounds of the cemetery while the cicadas hummed and chirped their highwire noise from the trees.

The term 'oceanic feeling' was first coined in a letter to Freud and describes a oneness with the world, a sense of eternity, the limitlessness of a small child who cannot yet tell where they end and the world begins. The mermaids were swept up in swells of Oceanic Feeling, and so was I. All the stories we tell ourselves about who we are and who we might be, but also the stories of the world, sinking and rising from the sea. Stories of waves and cicadas, of Ariel and Atlantis, of Coral the doll I threw into the Lucky Dip, and of the coral reefs out there, bleaching, utopias and dystopias crumbling. Mum believed in God, but I didn't.

On the headstones, no one listed their occupations or CVs.

~

The house of our Lorde was a white glossy villa. I arrived on a too-hot day, with the Mermaid Oracle cards in my handbag. In the hallway I passed a dresser with shells arranged on it and a cupboard that contained a washing machine — Lorde's washing machine! — then we sat down at the long wooden table in her kitchen. I glanced around, noting her brown three-tiered spice rack as though it was a symbol of her soul. Lorde's spice rack, I thought. It was hardly the starting point for a scintillating magazine article. Yet the spice rack reminded me of the flat I grew up in with Mum. I hadn't seen a spice rack in an eternity.

Lorde had read my first book and that was why I was there. She sat and talked, wearing a clingy nutmeg dress and bare feet, at once down to earth and radiating an extraordinary aura, her blue eyes alert and present.

On *Solar Power* she sang 'I'm kinda like a prettier Jesus'. True, but she also reminded me of a prettier Gollum. I'd read Lorde describe herself as Gollum in earlier articles and hoped she might tolerate the appropriation. She had a physicality in her arms and movements, a gestural intensity that intrigued me.

I asked her who her voice came from.

Her father, she said. The whole family could sing. Her siblings, too. Her father liked fishing, had taught her to tie knots. She liked to sit with him and just talk about the tides, that kind of stuff. 'He's very calm. He's very patient. His vibe is very sort of . . . he's in tune with the natural rhythms. You know?'

I did know. I felt my vibe was in tune with my father too.

At one moment she answered the door. Some lights needed fixing on the roof. Lorde's electrician, I thought. Summer breeze and the sound of cicadas sluicing through the open doors. In her backyard, I spotted a narrow rectangular pool, a festive shade of turquoise. Later, a beautiful, tanned friend of Lorde's arrived and went for a swim in it.

'Do you think everything happens for a reason?' I asked.

'No, sometimes I think you just get fucked,' she said.

We took a break and drove to a tiny beach, an inlet in nearby Herne Bay, a rich suburb. Lorde was at the steering wheel, her friend beside her; I was happy to be in the back seat, a passenger. It was a blue day like the one she described in 'Oceanic Feeling'. We stared out at the birds on the harbour. Their silhouettes like shadow puppets from a children's play. Or perhaps the birds were thoughts about to lift, and I had to try and catch them. Then Lorde did a u-turn and we headed back to complete the interview.

At the big wooden dining-room table, I got my Doreen Virtue mermaid cards out.

'What's this, Megan?'

'These cards were given to me by Mermaid Linden who lives in Los Angeles.'

'Oh my goodness,' Lorde said.

'I noticed on *Solar Power* there's a lot of critique of wellness culture, but I wondered if you would shuffle the deck. You ask the pack three questions and then pull out three cards in answer.'

Lorde pulled out her three cards. She got 'Contemplation Time'. 'I often get that card,' I said. But she also got 'Play Time'. The card features two leaping dolphins, symbolising the importance of play to manifest joy. A lot of *Solar Power* was about playfulness, Lorde said. Her third card was 'Empowerment': 'You're more powerful than you realise. This card confirms that your inner power wants to surface.'

'I felt called to bring the cards to you,' I said. 'I'm deeply sceptical of them, but I use them all the time, trying to jumpstart my intuition.'

I told Lorde how much I liked 'Oceanic Feeling'. 'It chimes with my mermaid obsession,' I said. 'Especially the last lines about stepping into the choir.'

'Well, that is a mermaid thing,' she said. 'T. S. Eliot's mermaids, right? From "The Love Song of J. Alfred Prufrock".'

'I've heard the mermaids singing, each to each,' I said. 'I do not think they will sing to me.'

'"Till human voices wake us, and we drown",' Lorde said.

'And we drown,' I replied.

I was treating Lorde like a prettier Jesus, as though she could divine life's answers. But she was also nice to me, and I liked her for herself. That simple word: *like*. A button to press and press again.

When I got home, I put the mermaid cards away and didn't draw them again. Some spell was broken. I showed Fearne a photo and little video on my phone. 'That's Mummy and Lorde,' I said.

'I want to meet Lorde!' Fearne said. 'Why did she blow me a kiss?'

~

I sat in front of the Dell computer in my residency office and contemplated my Pearls of Wisdom, Mum's final gift to me, in their little mesh bag. The cards contained a picture of an oyster shell, half open, a pearl gleaming whitely inside its womb-like interior. The font she chose was feminine, as though only women take care of their interior lives, their fragile self-esteems, their dreams. I combed through the aqua-blue cards, feeling like I was shuffling her feelings of sadness, loneliness and loss.

I do things the way I see best
I am forgiving towards myself
I am doing the best I can

The affirmations were shadowy, tentative. I imagined a mermaid flashing her tender underbelly, her scales that glinted with vulnerability, her hopeful song that was discordant. The mantras whiffed of things that didn't work out, dreams that pancaked instantly.

I spend time outdoors doing things I enjoy isn't an affirmation at all, but a sentence written by a woman who didn't really like the outdoors or spend much time doing anything other than driving to work or the shops in her little turquoise car. *I am feeling more confident now* only made me think of all the times when she wasn't.

But then I noticed other pearls.

I give myself time to heal
I let go of any need to blame the past
I'm my own best friend and I treat myself accordingly

I had scoffed at the notion of self-love for years, but maybe it *was* time to start looking after myself better. Maybe it was time to actually commit? I put the cards back into their dainty bag.

~

'Welcome to the happiest day of your life,' Anna said.

'Thanks,' I said, smiling.

Anna wore a stylish white robe like a minister. But with purple bits, a bit Prince. She was a brunette and marketing guru whose marriage had ended, but she'd gotten over it and decided to marry herself instead.

At the art gallery she was offering the same opportunity to others, staging the same ritual for them. People arrived in the white gallery foyer dressed in their own special outfits. Numerous people wore white dresses and even veils. One chick held a basket of freshly picked flowers.

I was an innocent bystander — I wasn't serious about marrying myself. I had not brought my op-shop wedding dress, but wore my brown Lee jumpsuit with deep pockets down the front. It was an outfit I felt good in, and I wasn't itching either. 'I'm not a participant,' I said to someone who asked.

After the congregation formed, Anna told us to form a circle around the outside of the room.

In the middle of the gallery was a makeshift aisle, leading to a pulpit up the front where a long vertical mirror had been placed. Each person needed to see what they were getting into when marrying themselves. It was a joyous, tongue-in-cheek occasion. We clapped as individuals marched alone up to the mirror. Once each person reached the mirror, they pledged their own vows to their reflection.

One bride pashed the mirror. The woman carrying the basket threw petals down the aisle, doing some seriously dodgy rhythmic hip thrusts along the way. A man in a suit hugged the mirror. Each time, the audience cheered. Goodwill and good vibes clogged the atmosphere like confetti. As the candidates kept rolling up to the mirror, one by one, I suddenly joined the line. Who was I not to marry myself?

As I walked down the aisle alone, I threw my hands up into the air and shouted, 'This is for my mother!' The crowd roared.

~

The Specialist Vein Clinic was white and soothing, on the top floor of a villa that looked out over four lanes of traffic. No one could see in through the net curtains.

'Can you take off your jeans?' Dr Lupe asked. She had a calm presence. Calmness is a quality I appreciate. Especially in a vascular surgeon.

'I'm just going to feel the veins. Is that okay?'

'Yes.'

I stood still, while she pressed gently but firmly along my tree roots. That's what the veins looked like — big gnarly tree roots. Thick and bobbly, erupting up, nudging the surface of the skin.

'They're pretty bad,' I said.

'Mmm,' she said. Neutral.

'I mean, they've always been ugly, but the eczema's the kicker. I've never experienced anything like it. It's so itchy,' I said.

'Well, the surgery should help with that,' Dr Lupe started working her fingertips along the other leg. Her touch felt pleasant, kindly, good-natured. We were going to get to the nub of it together.

'It's a lot of money,' I said. Eight thousand dollars.

'Yes.' She was empathetic. I didn't go on about it, but we were putting the money on our credit card.

When the operation rolled round, I would be put under local anaesthetic and they would pump some kind of Polyfilla into my veins to collapse them, then singe the little veins closed with a heat wand. Or something like that.

We discussed the risks of the surgery. The risk of a blood clot was heightened for ten days after the procedure. I would need to wear compression stockings day and night and in the shower. Compression stockings, fine; blood clot, no.

'Veins seem important.' I looked at her meaningfully, trying to impress upon her the importance of my life.

'Veins are important, yes, but these ones are no longer working properly,' she explained. 'The blood is going down to the feet, but then pooling there. The veins are not pumping the blood back up. Over time you will likely get more symptoms like the venous eczema, and that can lead to ulcers.'

'Right,' I said.

'Do you have any questions?' she said.

'Has anyone ever died from this operation?' I asked. 'I can't die. Is the risk two percent?'

'Much less. It's less than one percent.'

I nodded. I would have preferred no risk at all.

~

I carried Fearne's school bag over one shoulder and my own bag over the other. Sweating vaguely in the afternoon sunshine, on my next mission. My armpits reeking of onion. I bent down, the bags swinging, and fossicked under my skirt, itching my shin. 'For God's sake.' The more I itched, the worse it got.

Fearne and I trawled through the children's department on another emergency present-buying mission. We whirled around, going in two different directions.

'We could get Scarlett a book?' I said hopefully.

'No, books are boring,' Fearne said, migrating on autopilot to the doll section.

'We're not buying you anything today,' I cautioned.

'I know!'

I managed to steer her towards a shelving unit filled with stuffed animals. Seahorses. Large, gormlessly cuddly whales. Even starfish with padded little suckers.

'Look, Fearne! A stingray!'

I picked it up and started stroking it.

The stingray had soft smooth fur. It was blue with white dots on top, and pure white underneath. Luxurious, and soothing to smooth your hand over. I stroked its tail and didn't get stung.

'Ohhh!' She gasped with pleasure and grabbed it from me. 'Let's get this.'

'For Scarlett? Are you sure she'll like it? I thought she was into tigers.'

'She'll love it,' Fearne said.

I didn't need any more convincing. It was love at first sight. Then I passed a box of eco water balloons, backtracked and picked them up, too.

'Maybe we should give these to Scarlett instead?'

At bedtime, I read to Fearne, with the narwhal on the table beside us and the stingray placed over my stomach.

She scrunched my hair.

I stroked the stingray.

'My emotional support stingray,' I said.

'You're very unique, Megan,' Fearne said.

'How so?' I asked.

'Well, you have an emotional support stingray.'

~

In the clinic waiting room, a large photograph of aqua-blue water adorned the wall, as though beaches are naturally soothing places. I didn't think it was appropriate. Beaches are traumatic if you have white legs and varicose veins. I sat on the sofa shaking my crossed leg, uncontrollably. I was wearing a lobster T-shirt and matching yellow trainers. Rich, my resident seahorse, sat next to me.

'I'm worried,' I said.

'Don't be worried.'

I had drunk no water, let alone necked back a flat white or a wine. And I'd worn my skirt for easy on-off action.

'Megan?' the nurse entered the waiting room. An older woman in scrubs. Short ringlets of hair like a cherub. She looked like she meant business.

We followed her into the hallway.

'Can Rich come too? He's my support person,' I bleated. My skirt rustled around my chunky legs and bubbly blue veins.

'He can wait at reception. He can't come into the operating room,' she said, as though that was obvious.

My support seahorse blushed and bobbed off along the hallway, looking relieved.

In the operating room, another pair of post-menopausal nurses awaited me. They could have been salty sea hags, tending the waves by Marooners' Rock. If they were real mermaids they would have had silver tails. Dignified. And very clean. Sterile even. They wore surgical caps over their hair.

The brisk nurse ushered me to a side room and said, 'Sit over here. You can put your clothes in here, then put this gown on. When you're ready, come back in and we'll be waiting for you.'

I looked at her blankly from my rock, hoping for some more jibber jabber.

'Are you all right?'

'No. I'm worried I will die.'

The sirens looked amused. 'No one has died yet,' said one with a white bun and twinkling eyes. She was instantly my favourite.

'You let us do the worrying,' said the lead nurse.

I got changed next door, shedding my chequered skirt and lobster T-shirt, socks and bright yellow trainers, and re-entered the operating theatre. Private healthcare: you pay for it, but it is so much nicer.

Dr Lupe entered smiling with her clipboard. She went over the risks again, but I didn't want to go there.

'You look like you know what you're doing,' I told Dr Lupe. Then I signed the clipboard. Far away, the mermaids were singing.

'I can't die. I haven't finished my book yet and I'm the only mother left,' I explained. I turned to the other nurses. 'I had my daughter at forty. I should never have had her so late, because now my mother is dead. This is why you are meant to have them young! So everyone is still alive.'

They nodded and laughed.

I suddenly said, 'Do we have to do this now?'

Dr Lupe's brown eyes swung around to hold my gaze.

'Would you like me to come and hold your hand?' the nice siren said.

'Yes,' I whimpered. 'You can be my mother today.'

She came over to my head and stared down at me, very blue eyed. The kind of woman who makes you believe in sea hags and vascular surgeons.

'Say "goodbye veins!"' she said.

'Goodbye veins.' I lay back on the bed. The anaesthetic went in and I went under.

~

In the 1987 film *I've Heard the Mermaids Singing*, main character Polly, played by pixie-like actress Sheila McCarthy, is an inept secretary working at a small but chic art gallery. Polly has her art rejected. She has to face the question — do I continue even if everyone thinks I am a joke?

Director Patricia Rozema was only twenty-nine years old and had just been fired from her job when she made the film. It was produced on a small arts budget in Canada and filmed in Toronto. Rozema titled the movie after the T. S. Eliot line, she told me, because 'Polly was kind of a Prufrock' — 'someone who doesn't consider themselves worthy of society's conception of cool, worthy of the enterprise of even making art.'

Rozema wanted the mermaids to be Polly's peak vision, the most sublime moment in the film.

'People loved the film,' she said, 'because the idea of the unanswered artist is never addressed in most people's lives. Nurses, accountants, bus drivers, that part of them that feels like they could do something expansive if they just tried hard enough.

'I didn't make any connections to siren calls. I just thought of it as something unbearably beautiful. You can hear it, but you can't reflect it back.'

~

'Can we play Marauding Mermaid before bed?' Fearne begged.

'Fine.' I looked up from my mermaid manuscript and down at the fawn-coloured compression tights: some dried blood and big purple bruises blooming under the surface, just as I'd been told. But the ten-day risk had passed without a blood clot, so I was winning.

On the floor in the lounge I lay underneath a blanket, as though I was a purple villainous wench like Ursula, waiting under the waves.

'I'm surfing along here,' Fearne said, voice filled with zeal. She was seated on her new skateboard, an optimistic purchase from Daddy Pig. She pushed the wheels back and forth, going nowhere.

'Arrgh!' I rose up out of a blanket and attacked Fearne, the young gurfer, dragging her off her surfboard and pretending to chomp her bare legs. 'Nothing like a tasty young gurfer,' I said.

Fearne squirmed and laughed, kicking her legs. 'Again! Again.'

'Okay, one more time.' I retreated back under the blanket. 'The Marauding Mermaid is looking for something tasty for her dinner,' I cackled.

When Fearne thinks of mermaids she thinks of me: her mother.

We went through two more rounds, but finally when Fearne said, 'Again?', the Marauding Mermaid turned back into the Marauding Mother. I hustled her into the bathroom and squeezed blue toothpaste — did you know toothpaste contains algin from seaweed? — on to her brush. 'Hold still. I can't get in there properly.' I scrubbed her teeth as best I could, Fearne fidgeting the whole time. 'It's very hard being a mother,' I sighed, in my dressing gown.

I examined my chin in the bathroom mirror.

'I don't know how I will ever finish this book. I don't know where the myth of the mermaid begins or ends. I've got too many to represent. Maybe I should just give up?'

'Megan, write from the heart.'

Fearne was seated on the loo, but she stood up on the blue stool in front of it and put her hands on my shoulders.

I looked into her mischievous brown eyes.

'Write what you think about mermaids and write what you think about fish.'

Father Healing
"Your personal power increases as you give any father-related issues to Heaven."

17.

Pearls of Wisdom

It's funny you should get in touch with me just now because I've lost my voice, said the message. I took out my phone and glanced at the screen.

Daryl Hannah just messaged me.

We sat in a narrow café in Islington, crouched into a little corner at a wooden table, drinking our coffees. 'Daryl Hannah just messaged me!' I said.

'What?' said my friend Jenny. She and I were getting older together. Her bobbed hair and lovely blue-grey eyes. She had put up with my mermaid obsession for too long.

'I wrote to her. Just before we left, I sent her the link to my *Guardian* article on mermaids and she read it,' I gushed. 'She said "good article"!' It was like Daryl Hannah had picked up a seashell and heard my dream inside it. The article in the *Guardian Australia* was titled: 'I've heard the mermaids calling but I still haven't found my voice.'

Rich, Fearne and I were in the UK for Christmas visiting family. The article was like a message in a bottle, which I'd lobbed into the online ocean. A mermaid had tweeted the article to Daryl, copying me in, then Daryl started following me on Twitter. That was exciting enough! I sent her a direct message weeks ago — it was the last thing I wrote on my residency, the Madison neoprene tail from Finfolk draped over the spinny chair in my office. Dear Daryl. No, was that too self-conscious? Did I even mean it? Was I writing to her as a person or to an imagined audience looking over my shoulder? I sent her a long 'Megan pours out her soul' message that I wasn't sure I had any right to send. I asked Daryl if I could interview her for my book.

My heart raced, my blood was pumping. 'I'm open to connecting,' Daryl said. 'When my voice comes back.'

I was happy to wait. Usually, waiting is not my strong suit, though God knows I've been forced to wait — for mermaids, for a baby, for a real job, for a house of my own, for trying to change the world.

In the early hours a few days later, Rich, Fearne and I flew to Copenhagen. We were going to Malmö, a short train ride away, to spend the weekend with Rich's friends. Rich was excited, a keen traveller, with a reluctant woman and daughter in tow. 'It's a shame we can't go back to Copenhagen,' I said wistfully. 'I would have liked to see the Little Mermaid again.' If I saw the statue again maybe I'd be struck by a sudden and brilliant epiphany.

On the Ryanair flight, I sank two wines — she who flies into Copenhagen prefers to arrive mildly drunk. But they made me edgy and I needed a wee.

As the customs queue moved slowly forward, I saw her — a life-size replica of the Little Mermaid, behind cordons, as though she too might need to have her passport verified. 'Oh my God. We have to get a photo,' I said. It was a sign!

'Fearne, you have to pose,' I said.

I jumped us out of the queue. Fearne sat on the floor, splaying her legs out behind her as though she had a tail, and twisted her body into the same pose that the sculptor's wife must have once held patiently. I took several shots. Fearne in her pale-mauve jumper on the floor before the Little Mermaid in the airport passageway. Then I sent one to Daryl Hannah.

'How cute,' she said. 'Your daughter is in the same pose.'

~

'What are you going to ask her?' Rich said the night before the Zoom.

'I don't know,' I said.

The question top of my mind was: 'Do you know the oceanographer, Sylvia Earle?' Earle had been a *National Geographic* explorer-in-residence since 1998 and established Mission Blue, a non-profit foundation to protect the ocean. Her nicknames now? 'Her Deepness' and 'The Sturgeon General'.

I had started my hunt for mermaids because I had wanted to be as beautiful as Daryl Hannah. Now I couldn't help but wonder if I hadn't been selling the concept of beauty cheap.

Beauty was a smokescreen for the soulfulness of the mermaid, the connection to spirituality and the sublime. Daryl was now an environmental activist, a woman who would call out racists complaining about a black Ariel. Like many mermaids, she was living her convictions, prepared to make a stand for what she believed in, to be a force of good for this planet. (I was somewhat more imperfect, still an eater of burgers, though I had cut back, and I hardly ever got a takeaway coffee either. I didn't drive or smoke, never had. Did that count?)

I had watched a video of Daryl speaking about the environment. On it she said, 'We need a different vision of what success looks like.' Less consumption, fewer things, less churn. I agreed. I too needed a different idea of success, one that was less about being seen and more about just being me, in all my mundanity. Less internet, too, I thought, alluring though it was to look into that bottomless screen.

Before our Zoom, I looked around the lounge. Outwardly, not much had changed. We still lived in the same little rented flat.

We still sat every night on the Egyptian couch that was The Worst Sofa in the World. The MacBook was the same one I had skyped the mermaids on. The material rewards I had programmed into the GPS in Sydney had not manifested. Still no house.

I opened Google — it was International Women's Day.

I connected on Zoom to a black screen that read FRANK. Eventually the screen disappeared, and a man sat in a large spacious room. 'You must be Frank,' I said. 'Yes, I am. How'd you know?' he asked.

'A wild guess.'

'Daryl will be here soon.'

'Thank you.'

Then she arrived, long limbed, her blonde hair spilling over her shoulders.

'Megan, it's so great to see your face.' Daryl came in close to the screen. It was like I'd always known her, and I guess in a way I have. I've watched her in *Splash*, as Priss doing backflips in *Bladerunner*, as Elle Driver with that eyepatch in *Kill Bill*, and as the art dealer on *Wall Street* who dicks over Charlie Sheen. Hell. I've seen her as a giantess in *Attack of the Fifty Foot Woman*. Don't forget her performance in *Steel Magnolias* either. Or *Clan of the Cave Bear*!

She was amazing, intimidating. I knew so much about her. She drove an eco-friendly car, rescued animals, had her own kiln. She and her husband had recently travelled by train to Canada to lend their support to an old-growth logging protest.

'You know,' I said. 'I don't even know what to ask at this point. I've come so far on this journey to meet the mermaids.'

'Well, don't worry about it. You can ask me anything, and eventually, you'll hone it down into whatever you need,' she said.

Daryl's earliest memory was of falling into a swimming pool at her parents' country club and looking up to the surface, mesmerised by the reflections and refractions of the undulating water, the muffled sounds of the world's noises. She was not concerned about air. Daryl grew up in and around the Great Lakes. When she was seven her father taught her to scuba dive. She used a pony tank, strapped to her bathing suit. Sometimes they would scuba dive to neighbours' houses because it was easier than walking. 'We were always on a boat or being encouraged to put a worm on a hook or gut a fish — that, I struggled with emotionally.' She became a vegetarian aged eleven.

Like all the top mermaids I'd interviewed, Daryl was as comfortable in water as she was on land. She had also trained as a ballerina with Maria Tallchief, the first Native American prima ballerina, who was one of her mom's friends — a great outlet because she was so painfully introverted and shy. As a kid, Daryl told me, she tied her feet together and fantasised and played out different mer storylines. She spent hours in the water until her feet and lips turned blue and her mom forced her to come in for dinner.

It was strange to hear this woman talk about her childhood, having a mom, to realise that she, too, was just human. She had been shy and awkward and teased in school! How was that possible when she was clearly so extraordinary?

Daryl had loved spending time in the library at school because she wasn't picked on there. She read Oscar Wilde's *The Fisherman and his Soul* — her favourite mermaid story — and Hans Christian Andersen's *The Little Mermaid*. The stories resonated with her because the mermaid was only part-human.

'I have always been cognisant of the fact we are animals, however much we deny it to ourselves. I was also drawn to the unrequited love aspect. I was always crushing on someone that I was too shy to even look at, so I understood her inability to communicate her love or to be recognised.'

Daryl also marvelled at the fact that the Little Mermaid gave up almost everything to try and find love. She gave up her tongue, her voice. She had to accept an excruciating amount of pain whenever she walked. And she nearly lost her immortal soul.

I had nearly lost my immortal soul getting to this point. I was finally in conversation with her! I knew I was being a bit of a drama queen, but when I thought of the freckled little buck-toothed redhead who ran a bath after watching *Splash*, I felt my whole life unspooling.

After a fortune teller told Daryl, aged thirteen, she would grow up to be a prima ballerina, she promptly quit. She hated the competitiveness of ballet. I loved her felicity, her strange determination. She was enthralled by late-night TV, used to watch old movies from the thirties and forties, Fred Astaire, Gene Kelly. That was when she fell in love with the movies. 'So really, it was way back then that I started thinking about making *The Little Mermaid* into a movie, but not the musical Disneyfied one.'

Later, she moved out to California and started acting. It was the process of immersion that she loved, not the fame. 'I enjoyed living in the fairy tale, living in the fantasy, believing the fantasy, and then having the sets and the costumes there so you can really live in it.'

By the time *Splash* rolled around, 'I'd had my feet wet already, so to speak,' she told me. She'd done *Bladerunner*, *Summer Lovers*, *Reckless* — in her words a crappy horror, an urban Western. At the same time she had the chance at *Splash*, Daryl was offered a role in a movie playing a musician — she loved to sing — performing songs written by Bruce Springsteen and Stevie Nicks. It was a hard choice to make.

'I entertained tossing a coin, but then I realised that I would be devastated if *Splash* really got off the ground and someone else played the mermaid. I knew the part inside out already. I knew I had to do it. I had practised for it for years.'

The rest was history. Daryl had a strong feeling that the mermaid should be played as an innocent, rather than a cheesy seductress, which is what people wanted back then. It was a stroke of genius; it made Madison more sympathetic to children like me. She was experiencing the world for the first time. 'My allegiance was to the Hans Christian Andersen fairy tale. That tale told me the mermaid was pure of heart,' Daryl said.

The first time she was recognised in public was just after *Splash* came out. A group of schoolgirls saw her at The Louvre. I imagined being one of those students, seeing her wandering through the museum, like Botticelli's Venus, a goddess stepped out of a painting and come to life. The students were so intense, and Daryl was so shy, that she panicked. She ran away, then fainted. The staff brought her an orange juice.

I started grilling her about *Splash*.

'Tell me what it was like filming the scene in the science museum.'

Madison is held captive in a rectangular tank, her orange tail flaking, distressed, covered in tail rot.

'That was filmed on a sound stage,' Daryl told me. She was surrounded there by other aquatic species in their own tanks. One fish was almost a foot long and confined to a tank it could barely turn around in. Daryl knew how that fish felt: 'Not only did I understand it intellectually, but I had also experienced it physically,' she said. 'I was freaking out and telling them they had to get him out of there. He didn't have enough room to move.'

When they shot in the Bahamas, Daryl said that the barracuda loved to hang out in the shade of the boat and watch everything that was going on. They were very curious. She often made friends with sea life while diving. One time a Napoleon wrasse followed her around for a week and a half, hanging over her shoulder all day wherever she went. She told me fish were like people — some are sweet and goofy, some are jerks.

Lately, whenever she returned to dive in any of the places she visited in her youth, she found shockingly drastic, undeniable changes. Then she amazed me by saying she had swum with the oceanographer Sylvia Earle.

'She's a real mermaid. She's the real deal,' Daryl said.

'I love her nickname, Her Deepness,' I said.

Daryl first interviewed Earle for her blog, it was the second ever video blog series on the internet. They were good friends. Daryl had served on the board of the Sylvia Earle Alliance. They had dived around the world together, in Galapagos and Palau.

Sylvia Earle had got a pair of ruby-red flippers made for her — like Dorothy's ruby-red slippers, but fins for diving. 'I'll send you a photo,' Daryl said. 'They have sparkles and everything.'

Then I asked her the one real question I had for mermaids. 'How do we save the world? What's the one thing we can all do?'

'Oh gosh, that's a hard question. Go into nature. Love nature, understand that the world beneath that watery blanket of the ocean and the water bodies is as lush and full of world as the one that you see up above.

'Push for solutions and change. One of the easiest things to do, especially for the oceans, is to not buy things. Not to think of yourself as a consumer.

'Do whatever is within your means to protect things.'

'You've given me so much,' I said. 'This desperate perimenopausal writer from New Zealand, trying to write something about mermaids! Thank you from the bottom of my heart.'

~

On Mum's birthday I took Fearne op shopping. The weather was glum, the city covered in a low-hanging fog. No flights. The last few days had been wind-lashed, my mind driven mad by large racing gusts of wind, getting up in my face. It was nearly Christmas again. Presents ticked off the list. Fearne told me she did not believe in Santa, but she did believe in Mrs Claus.

'We're op shoppers, like Nana,' Fearne said. 'Put this in your book: "The world's my oyster and I'm the pearl".'

'Where'd you get that?' I said, stunned.

'Cleo said it on *Mako Mermaids*.' She had been bingeing it lately but still refused to watch *Splash* with me. '*Mako Mermaids* is better,' she said.

'How do you know?'

No answer.

'Daddy will go mad,' I said, after bagging a cockatoo soft toy at the op shop. I mean — a toy cockatoo! I couldn't just leave it there.

I was wearing the bright-fuchsia cardigan (overly hot) that Mum used to wear. Fearne carried Nana's bag with the purple and paisley patchwork pattern, garish. It was a conspicuously old-woman item.

'If Daddy was here, he'd be embarrassed,' I said, as we danced to Miley Cyrus's 'Flowers' in the shop. Fearne knocked a sign off a shelf and I simply picked it up and put it back. 'Daddy would have been embarrassed about that,' she said.

'Yeah, well, I'm more chill than Daddy about some things.'

We collected a range of tat that pleased us — none of it sea themed. Fearne had to have an old seventies-style musical doll, in a big white frilly dress, like a harlot, with a face made out of a stocking and ringlets of blonde hair. I said yes because Nana herself once had one of these dolls, in a black dress with white trim, although I think Nana might have actually hated it. I bought Dad an old Disney game called Goofy Finds His Marbles. It had a drawing of Goofy on the cover. Dad liked Goofy. Or was it Donald Duck?

'I think I will be an underwater photographer when I grow up,' Fearne said.

'Really? Why?' I asked.

'So I can photograph shipwrecks,' she said. 'That's where all the fishes are.'

I didn't take her too seriously as she also wanted to be a vet, a gymnast, a teacher and a pop star.

We had just exited a shop when I said to Fearne, 'Let's pop across the road.' We stepped inside a dark shop on the corner, the wooden interior pleasingly decked out with perfumes. The windows on the outside were glazed with grey frosting. I'd walked past the shop for years — it had an illustration of a mermaid on the front. She was carrying a suitcase. But I had never seen the shop open before.

Two older ladies were inside — partners, I guessed. One looked like Popeye's girlfriend, Olive, if she had made it to her sixties. The pair were selling artisanal solid perfumes in small cream ceramic pots. The women hovered; diligent small business owners, surrounded by their ethical, scrupulous choices.

I browsed, not intending to buy,

'We have had our top scents made into roll-on perfumes,' said the one who looked like Olive Oyl. Her dainty little eyes were filled with kindness.

'Do people like a roll-on perfume?' I asked.

'Yes, they do.' Her voice was neat and expansive. She was gently waiting for me to become snared.

'Ooohhh. Fearne, smell this!' I tried on the perfume with a cockatoo on the label.

'The scent is stronger than the solid perfume range.'

'That's our most popular scent,' Olive said.

'We're straight into the good stuff,' I said. 'God, it's so lovely. What's in it?'

'It has a base note of vanilla,' she said. She told me about the origins of their business in Greece, back when she was a teenager.

Then I spied the mermaid stamp in the background, on reams of brown butcher's paper. The stamp was rectangular, with an outline of a mermaid, her arms wrapped around her tail. The mermaid lay her head on her knees, and her long hair draped down. Behind her ear, a frangipani.

I'd have to buy something so I could get that stamp on the packaging.

'Mummy, I like this one.' Frangipani.

'What about Aloha?' I said. 'Smell this?' We tried one on each wrist.

I got Pacific Goddess, and Aloha for Fearne.

'Would you like them wrapped?'

'Yes,' I said. 'Where did you get the mermaid stamp?'

'Hawai'i.'

'I've always wondered about the illustration of the mermaid on the shop window,' I said, looking at the glass.

'Oh, I used to run a guesthouse here called The Mermaid,' she said.

'You own this place?'

She nodded.

Now I leaned in seriously and asked what I always ask, 'What do you think the mermaid means?'

Olive Oyl blinked. My question was the fin of a great white shark closing in.

'The mermaid is global,' she offered. 'There are mermaids in every culture. Everyone recognises them.'

'Yes,' I said. 'The mermaid *is* global.' The whole shop was now under a spell, as though I was holding my hands around a singing bowl, catching spirals and spirals of sound.

'Mermaids are extraordinary,' Olive said quietly.

I agreed. I found them all extraordinary, even the ones that were completely ordinary. Their voices, their simple stories of rising.

'Why do you think mermaids are extraordinary?' I asked.

They stared at me, alarmed, but I had just bought two of their top-selling roll-on perfumes, and I had a child with me, so they kept going.

Olive said, 'The mermaid represents a woman with freedom in every sphere.'

It was the final pearl of wisdom for my set. A clear, vibrating note from the singing bowl moved through me.

'Thank you.'

I took the brown paper bag, and we wished each other merry Christmases. Full of zeal, I strode back on the street, my daughter beside me. A huge inexplicable bubble floated past us, but we couldn't see where it had come from.

~

'Okay. I'll watch *Splash* with you, but don't think you're going to get a good opinion out of me. I'm a bit over mermaids,' Fearne said at home.

I laughed. I mean, who wasn't over mermaids at that point?

I had a pen and picked up a nearby notebook.

'Hey, that's my diary, you dingus,' Fearne said.

'I need to take notes,' I said.

'Okay, you can use it.'

Rich poured two glasses of red and joined us on the sofa. The Egyptian hieroglyphs had seen a lot over the years.

'It's not on Netflix,' he said. 'Should I subscribe to Disney+?'

'Subscribe to Disney+!' Fearne said.

'And cancel Netflix?'

'We're driving your father over the edge,' I said.

'Yes, you are,' he said, taking a long sip.

The credits came on and the word *Splash* flickered on the ocean, starbursts twinkled. The song 'Wooly Bully' started up and Fearne leapt off the sofa, holding a cat wand that had three stripes of fun fur attached to the end of it. Ziggy, our new cat, was nowhere to be seen. But Fearne danced and frolicked to 'Wooly Bully', twirling the wand like a baton, its red, orange and yellow stripes flicking. She was open mouthed, her big front teeth poking out; her adult teeth were coming through. 'I am comedy gold,' Fearne said, twerking. 'It's hard being this talented.'

Splash opens on a boat cruising Cape Cod when the characters Allan and Freddie Bauer are children. Freddie spills coins on to the floorboards then crouches down to collect them, an excuse to peek up ladies' skirts.

'Is he trying to look up their skirts?' Fearne asked.

'He totally is,' Rich said.

The script was old-school but the sexual innuendos didn't bother me too much. The interest young Freddie displays in the opposite sex seemed on point. Vaginas do smell quite fishy. Apparently. And sex was consuming for most of my youth. Before I met Rich I was always chasing after it, in love with some dude who couldn't care less about me. Life is at least partly about that hot pursuit.

I elbowed Fearne. 'See that, the little Madison did a tail flip?'

'Yeah,' Fearne said, drolly. 'It was ugly.'

'Concentrate,' I said.

'Is that Daryl Hannah?' Fearne asked.

Daryl crouched behind some bushes by the beach, watching Tom Hanks, washed up in his suit on the white sand. Could this really be Cape Cod? Never been there. Looked quite tropical. Daryl's hair was obviously a wig. I don't think I got that as a child though. I believed everything, hook, line and sinker.

Tom woke up and called out to her. 'Hey!'

'Is she acting Madison?' Fearne asked.

'Yes,' I said.

Madison ran down to the beach, her long blonde wig sashaying, like Venus, the goddess of love.

'I saw her buttcheeks!' Fearne yelled.

'He's a bit plump,' she said of John Candy.

'Thoughts on the movie so far?' Rich asked.

'I don't mind it,' Fearne said.

'They used to shout a lot in eighties movies,' Rich said.

'We shout a lot here sometimes too,' I said.

Then the story swept everyone under.

'This is way better than *Mako Mermaids*,' Fearne said. 'There's more kissing.'

God, I had virtually forgotten that *Splash* was primarily a love story. That was never what had excited me — or at least that's not what I remembered exciting me as a child. Madison was constantly kissing Allan, Tom Hanks. They kissed easily, without shame or delay. 'Are they really kissing?' Fearne said.

'Well, yes, but in the story,' I said. 'They are actors.'

At the ice-skating rink, Allan asked Madison to marry him. I had forgotten about the wedding proposal, too. My own wedding dress from the op shop was stashed in our wardrobe. I hadn't married Rich yet, but it didn't mean I was never going to.

In *Splash*, Madison said, 'No', but not because she didn't love him. Tom Hanks was crestfallen. Not really. His character Allan was crestfallen. He didn't realise yet that Madison said no because she was a mermaid. Growing up, getting cool clothes, going to Bloomingdales, seeing the world, falling in love, kissing — these were things that all happened to Madison in her six days in New York City, and most of these things had happened to me, too. Give or take the turquoise leg warmers. But they had not happened to Fearne. Not yet.

'The bath scene is my favourite scene,' I said.

Daryl grabbed a container of bath salts. Closed the door. Dimmed the lights. Ran the bath and poured the salts into the water, picked up a hairbrush and started brushing her long hair just like Waterhouse's mermaid.

When her tail unfurled, the camera cut to that aerial view of her lying in the bath.

Fearne said, 'I wish I had one like that! Her tail looks like yours. She obviously copied yours. Or maybe you copied hers.'

'When I was little I wanted to grow up to be just like Daryl Hannah,' I said.

'If I keep going to my swimming lessons, I could be like Daryl Hannah,' Fearne said. 'I could borrow your tail.'

'Yes, you could.'

'How do mermaids wee and poo?' Fearne called out from the bathroom.

'Beneath their anal fin,' I replied.

Rich looked at me.

'What?' I said. 'Too much information?'

~

When the package arrived, it was delivered to Rich's work just in case it needed to be signed for. He brought it home and we unwrapped the box. 'Take photos,' I said. 'We have to capture this for posterity.' Inside the bubble wrap was a small ceramic vase in the shape of a mermaid tail. In the vase she'd placed a bouquet of matches with green heads, the bundle tied together in a green ribbon. 'I hope this brings some more light into your world,' Daryl wrote on the note.

'Daryl Hannah's vase will be our family heirloom,' Rich said.

The vase was stippled with dots and glazed a dark chocolate brown. The end of the mermaid's tail curved around to her waist, and culminated in a fluke, like the pose of Waterhouse's siren, but without the body or the head. The fluke got chipped en route, but Rich glued the pieces back on and I didn't tell Daryl. I turned the mermaid around and admired her bum. She even had buttocks — and a bumcrack — just like a real woman. She was perfect.

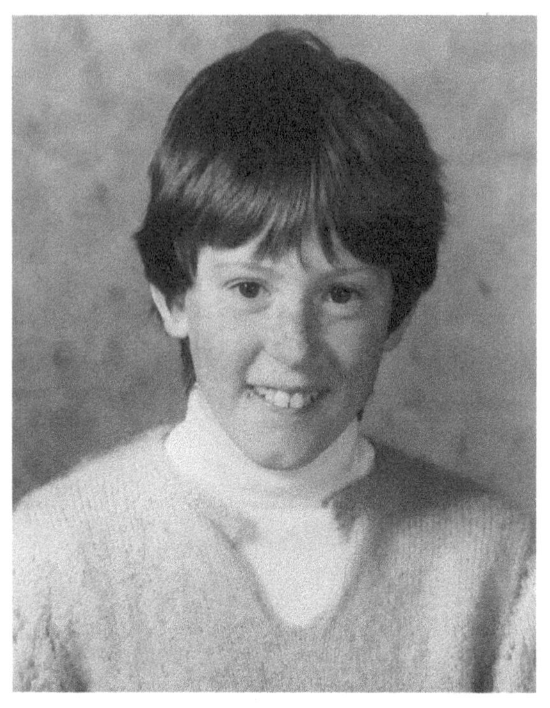

Megan, 1984, the year Splash was released.

Image credits

Hannah Mermaid, The Bahamas. Photographer: Stuart Cove. Page 11.
'Pearl of Wisdom' card, Lee Dunn. Page 37.
Film still of Glynis Johns (1923-) from *Miranda*. Courtesy of Alamy. Page 57.
'A Devil Considering a Dying City (Camden Town Series)', 1991 (oil on canvas), Alexis Hunter. Courtesy of Bridgeman Images. Page 66.
A Mermaid, John William Waterhouse, 1900. Public domain, via Wikimedia Commons. Page 85.
Fearne and The Little Mermaid statue, Copenhagen, 2017. Photographer: Richard Crane. Page 105.
Whale in the Marlow Park Playground, Dunedin. Courtesy of Allied Press Ltd. Page 126.
Weeki Wachee performer on seahorse. Page 149.
Salvador Dali, *Dream of Venus* pavilion, The World's Fair, 1939. Eric Schaal ©Fundació Gala-Salvador Dalí, Figueres, 2024. Page 171.
MeduSirena, The Wreck Bar, Florida. Photographer: Roy Anderson. Page 188.
Hannah Mermaid. Photograph: Brett Stanley, 2024. Page 204.
Mermaid Linden, Dean's Blue Hole, The Bahamas. Photographer: Greg Browning. Page 217.
Julie Atlas Muz, *The Coral Room*. Photographer: Andrew Brusso. Page 228.
'Madison' in Sydney, 2018. Page 238.
2000/66/110 Wall sculpture depicting Annette Kellerman. Collection: Powerhouse Museum. Gift of the Dennis Wolanski Library, Sydney Opera House, 2000. Photo: Richard Weinstein. Page 245.
Christ of the Deep 9 bronze statue with mermaid Pennecamp State Park Key Largo Florida. Courtesy of Alamy. Page 267.
A Mermaid Being Mobbed by Seagulls, Giovanni Segantini, 19th Century. Public domain, via Wikimedia Commons. Page 274.
Salvador Dali Sculpture, *The Lobster Telephone*, 1936-38, One of Six Commisioned. On display at the Salvador Dali Museum, St. Petersburg, Fla. Courtesy of Alamy. Page 293.
Father Healing card from Doreen Virtue's *Magical Mermaids and Dolphin Cards* set. Page 313.
Daryl Hannah's tail and fishy, 2023. Photographer: Richard Crane. Page 326.
Megan, 1984, the year *Splash* was released. Page 330.

Text credits

'Oceanic Feeling'. Words and Music by Ella Marija Lani Yelich O'Connor © Copyright Kobalt Music Publishing Australia Pty Ltd. Print rights for Kobalt Music Publishing Australia Pty Ltd granted by Hal Leonard Australia Pty Ltd ABN 13 085 333 713 www.halleonard.com.au All Rights Reserved. Unauthorised Reproduction is Illegal. Pages 6, 301.

The Love Song of J. Alfred Prufrock, *Collected Poems 1909–1962*, T. S. Eliot, Faber and Faber Ltd. Pages 68, 69, 304.

Words and Music by Olivia Newton-John © Copyright Zargon Music administered by Hebbes Music Group Pty Ltd. Print rights administered in Australia and New Zealand by Hal Leonard Australia Pty Ltd. ABN 13 085 333 713 www.halleonard.com.au Used By Permission. All Rights Reserved. Unauthorised Reproduction is Illegal. Page 128.

Meg at Sea, Helen Nicoll and Jan Pienkowski, Puffin, 2012. Page 159.

From *Diving into the Wreck: Poems 1971–1972* by Adrienne Rich. Copyright © 1973 by W. W. Norton & Company, Inc. Reprinted by permission of the author and W. W. Norton & Company, Inc. Copyright 1973 by Adrienne Rich. Pages 176, 180-183, 190, 193, 194, 196, 197.

'Green Light'. Words and Music by Ella Marija Lani Yelich O'Connor, Joel Little and Jack Antonoff © Copyright Kobalt Music Publishing Australia Pty Ltd, Sony Music Publishing Australia Pty Ltd and EMI Music Publishing Australia Pty Ltd. Print rights for Kobalt Music Publishing Australia Pty Ltd granted by Hal Leonard Australia Pty Ltd ABN 13 085 333 713 www.halleonard.com.au All Rights Reserved. Unauthorised Reproduction is Illegal. Page 300.

'Solar Power'. Words and Music by Ella Marija Lani Yelich O'Connor and Jack Antonoff © Copyright Kobalt Music Publishing Australia Pty Ltd and Sony Music Publishing Australia Pty Ltd. Print rights for Kobalt Music Publishing Australia Pty Ltd granted by Hal Leonard Australia Pty Ltd ABN 13 085 333 713 www.halleonard.com.au All Rights Reserved. Unauthorised Reproduction is Illegal. Page 302.

Acknowledgements

I hope you are sitting comfortably, because she who writes a mermaid book in her forties, after having a baby, does not do it alone. Or fast.

Thank you to Mermaid Linden for the gem, 'mer-moir'. I am proud to write a mer-moir. A MER-MOIR!

Thank you to 'the Mermaid Trifecta': Mermaid Linden, MeduSirena and Hannah Mermaid. You have let me fold your stories into my own. Thank you for this honour. You each inspire me in different ways, and it has been my pleasure to learn and write about your careers. Mermaids make their own luck.

Thank you to Raina the Halifax Mermaid for her generosity with her knowledge of the community and her contacts. Raina first introduced me to Annette Kellerman; she has 'The Diving Venus' tattooed on her arm. Raina also inadvertently enabled me to contact Daryl Hannah by copying us into the same tweet!

Most of my Skypes and mermaid interviews took place in 2017 and 2018 when I was still in my early forties. (*The Little Mermaid* reboot with Halle Bailey hadn't yet happened, nor the Netflix series *MerPeople*.) When I travelled to the United States in 2018, I encountered so much kindness from the mers I interviewed — not to be sniffed at in a world that is so unequal, unjust and inhumane. Thanks to Robert Short for his time, and to Merman Jax for being such a cool down-to-earth person.

Please be aware that some timelines, events, scenes and characters in this book are composites. But the mermaids are real. I am indebted to *all* the merfolk I interviewed. One of the hardest things about the process was accepting that I could not profile and highlight every performer. Each person had their own fascinating story, I collected so many pearls of mer-wisdom. (If the world wants a new pack of mermaid playing cards or a collection of mermaid quotes, DM me.)

I still have my Madison tail from Finfolk Productions, who now supply their swimmable mermaid tails in scuba knit fabric. Please note, my mer-moir is in the past tense—but the mermaids are still swimming! Their performing careers are ongoing, though Mermaid Rachel from Dive Bar, Sacramento, told me Barbosa the batfish died, aged 17 years old. He was her longest running co-worker. Rachel buried him in her backyard. RIP Barbosa.

Alas, due to an untimely decision by management, MeduSirena and her aquaticats are no longer swimming at The Wreck Bar. This makes me very sad for all the people who will never get to see her show. There is only one MeduSirena! The lives of mermaids, like all performing artists, remain capricious.

I am also indebted to Professor Sarah Peverley and Dr Jennifer Kokai. Jenny, it was great to meet you in Copenhagen all those years ago, and to read your book *Swim Pretty*. This was formative in my consideration of mermaid performances. You also introduced me to Dalí's *Dream of Venus*, which I have not been able to let go of.

Sarah, you sustained and informed this book with your immense foundation of mermaid research. Thank you for answering my emails and my countless questions. But more than that, it has been wonderful to know you are on the other side of the world writing not one, but two books about mermaids. And it was another moment of mer-synergy when we realised that both our first mermaids were 'Sea Wees' dolls. You are the Shelley to my Coral.

Many other authors and thinkers have contributed, sometimes knowingly, sometimes unwittingly. Thank you to Philip Hayward and the conference delegates at the Island Dynamics 'Mermaids, Maritime Folklore and Modernity' conference in Copenhagen. Thanks to Paul, our awesome tour guide.

Huge gratitude to the underwater photographer Brett Stanley. I hate having my photo taken, but Brett, you made it easy, even though it was underwater. Thanks also to you and Hannah Mermaid for consenting to the *Splash* tribute 'fishhook' photoshoot. (See back cover.) Even though, irony of ironies, it was a 'dry' photoshoot!

Now, it is time to get personal. Thanks to my mum and dad. I love you both, even when it does not seem like it. Mum is gone now, but not from this book. Fearne and I think of her often. Dad, we are glad you are still here. You have always believed I had something to say about mermaids.

To Rich and Fearne: we have sailed through the stormy seas together. I couldn't have done it without you. Once Rich and Fearne came home from a weekend away together (so I could write) and she said, 'Haven't you finished your book yet?' Rich and Fearne know too much about mermaids and about me.

Long-suffering friends and writing allies: Jenny Downham, Helen Curran, Kushana Bush, Yvonne Todd, Kirsty Baker, Anna Knox. You all know what an egotistical arsehole I am. Thanks for listening and being my friends anyway. Esther and Ruth from Space! Thanks to Anne Burgess for her support and encouragement across the years, especially after Mum died. Special thanks to Pip Adam for her integrity and grit and compassion. Thanks also to Noelle McCarthy for truly understanding the strange highs and lows of publishing a memoir about a woman and her mother. Thanks to Harry Ricketts, for being a steady guide and mentor, even when I am capsizing. Thanks to Lorde, for being an unlikely mermaid muse at the end of one long, hard year and the beginning of another.

I am also grateful for being appointed the Writer in Residence at the International Institute of Modern Letters in 2022. I wrote the guts of this book on that residency, even though I was having a massive meltdown at the same time. Thanks to writer and filmmaker Tim Worrall, who had to step down from taking up the residency that year. I was the runner-up. (Love you, Tim.)

That same year I was invited by Christina Barton to curate an exhibition, also titled *The Mermaid Chronicles*, for Te Pātaka Toi Adam Art Gallery. This was a career highlight and helped bring my mermaid project back to life.

To my publisher: Claire, we have been through the mermaid wringer together, but I couldn't have done this without you. Thanks for understanding that my true subject is myself. But also mermaids. Your Spidey skills as an editor are formidable. And to Anna Hodge, you are my Gordon Lish. I'm grateful for your care. You were handed a blobfish manuscript traumatised by the pressure of the earth's atmosphere, and you coaxed it into shape. This terrible fish owes you.

I also owe Tara Mohr, an author I have never met. But I have cleaved to her book *Playing Big* across my forties, and it was her question, 'What's the gasp level action?' that finally propelled me to America to meet the real mermaids.

Last but not least, Daryl Hannah. What can I say, Daryl, that isn't in this book? You are my OG mermaid and you are a kick-ass person. Thanks for all you have done as an actress, but also as an activist for the health of the planet. You continue to inspire me.

Now everyone, shall we save the world?

Megan Dunn is the author of two irreverent works of non-fiction, *Tinderbox* (Galley Beggar Press, 2017) and her memoir in essays *Things I Learned at Art School* (Penguin Random House New Zealand, 2021). Megan works as a curator, art critic and essayist. She has a master's in creative writing from the University of East Anglia. In 2022 she was the annual Writer in Residence at the International Institute of Modern Letters, based at Victoria University of Wellington, Te Herenga Waka.

Megan currently lives in Wellington. She is also interested in crocodiles.